American Christians and Islam

Evangelical Culture and Muslims from the Colonial Period to the Age of Terrorism

Thomas S. Kidd

Princeton University Press
Princeton and Oxford

Published by Princeton University Press, 41 William Street, Princeton, New Jersey 08540

In the United Kingdom: Princeton University Press, 6 Oxford Street, Woodstock, Oxfordshire OX20 1TW

Library of Congress Cataloging-in-Publication Data
Kidd, Thomas S.
American Christians and Islam : evangelical culture and Muslims from the colonial period to the age of terrorism / by Thomas S. Kidd.
    p. cm.
    Includes bibliographical references (p.) and index.
    ISBN 978-0-691-13349-2 (hardcover : alk. paper) 1. Missions to Muslims—History.
2. Missions, American—History.   3. Islam—Public opinion—History.   4. Public opinion—United States—History.   5. Protestants—United States—Attitudes—History.   I. Title.
    BV2625.K53 2009
    261.2′70973—dc22   2008026661

British Library Cataloging-in-Publication Data is available

This book has been composed in Minion

press.princeton.edu

Printed in the United States of America

10   9   8   7   6   5   4   3   2   1

AMERICAN CHRISTIANS AND ISLAM

To Jonathan and Joshua

CONTENTS

LIST OF ILLUSTRATIONS

Preface

SINCE THE TERRORIST ATTACKS on New York and Washington, D.C., on September 11, 2001, many pundits have asserted that the world is witnessing a global conflict between Islam and Christianity. A number of conservative American Christian leaders, following this trend, have generated news and controversy by casting severe aspersions on Islam and the Prophet Muhammad. Some have gone so far as to suggest that Islam had demonic origins, eliciting public indignation from both religious and secular critics. There was a time in America, however, when such ideas about Islam would not have generated any outrage, for they reflected commonly held interpretations. The great eighteenth-century American theologian Jonathan Edwards, for instance, expressed a standard view when he identified Islam, along with Roman Catholicism, as one of the "two great kingdoms which the devil. . . erected in opposition to the kingdom of Christ." Muhammad, "being a crafty man," promised his ignorant followers "a sensual paradise" that they would enter through martyrdom in *jihad*, Edwards explained. The Prophet established his religion by violence, and fulfilled a prophecy of Revelation 9 that spoke of swarms of locusts emerging from a smoky abyss. Edwards anticipated that Christ would destroy Islam, along with all the other forces of the devil, at the battle of Armageddon.[1]

From Edwards's example, and many others in this book, we can see that much of the recent American Christian hostility toward Islam derives from a long historical tradition. Americans' interest in Islam has, of course, intensified since 2001, but we should not imagine that their interpretations of Islam are substantially new. Americans, and conservative American Christians in particular, have returned repeatedly over the centuries to several key themes regarding Islam. This book will illustrate how American Christians have dreamed of seeing Muslims convert to Christianity, and have celebrated anecdotal cases of Muslims becoming Christians. Evangelical Christians have similarly desired to send missionaries among Muslims to preach the gospel to them, and eagerly consumed stories of the missionaries' successes. Finally, Christians like Edwards have often included Muslims in their scenarios of the last days, and blended geopolitical news and opinion with eschatological speculation (views about what would happen before the second coming of Christ).

Why have these themes persistently appeared in American Christian writing about Islam? Traditional Christians' exclusive system of faith has held that people could only find forgiveness from God in one manner: through Jesus and his atoning death on the cross. Therefore, all other world religions present challenges to the Christian faith. Devotees of other religions seemingly fail to answer correctly the most important question in life: What must one to do to be saved? To Christians, Islam poses a unique threat out of all the world's religions. As the only other monotheistic faith that was also aggressively evangelistic, Christians have long seen Islam as one of their major competitors—sometimes their primary competitor—for souls on the global stage. If history was moving inexorably toward Christ's ultimate triumph, then Muslims would either have to be converted or defeated in the last days. Islam appears to many conservative Christians as a worrisome but tantalizing religious and cultural opponent. Accounts of Muslim converts, missionary triumphs, and last days victories have often served to comfort Christians regarding the outcome of the perceived contest between the two faiths, even if the facts on the ground did not always merit optimism.

This book falls within a literature on Western views of Islam that had become very well developed even before 2001. Edward Said's classic but flawed 1978 book *Orientalism* has shaped much of the discussion about Western views of the Orient. Said argued that Western study of the East, and particularly the Middle East, has always served political purposes, and that "Orientalism" represented a Western tool "for dominating. . .and having authority over the Orient." Moreover, Said insisted that Western knowledge of the Orient was "discursive," in the sense that its rhetoric masked deeper cultural agendas and ultimately revealed more about the West than the East. Some readers will want to know where I stand on the sometimes fierce debate about Said and Orientalism. Although his argument seems to have been overstated and compromised by factual errors, I am relatively sympathetic to Said's Orientalist thesis regarding much of the West's knowledge of Islam and the Middle East. Applying the implications of the Orientalist thesis to American Christians' beliefs about Islam, readers should note (strange as it may sound) that I do not consider this book to be about Islam itself. It is about American Christians and the views they produced about Islam, which normally catered to constituencies within American Christian communities. I believe that American Christians' views about Islam usually divulge more about American Christians than about any actual Muslims.[2]

Some readers may also wish that I would assess the fairness or accuracy of American Christians' views about Islam, but I fear that such a task is largely beyond my competence. My training is in American religious history, not the global history of Islam. Because many of the views about Islam described here are outrageously negative, and put their exponents in a very poor light, some may wonder whether this book is actually intended to vilify Christian writers and paint an overly rosy picture of Muslims. This is not my intention. My own view is that with more than a billion Muslims living in the world, it is very difficult to say what "Muslims" in general are like. I am painfully aware of the horrific violence committed by Muslim extremists in the name of Islam. But when it comes to the question of what Islam is, or what it causes its followers to do, the answer is best left up to experts' studies of particular groups. It matters whether we are talking about Hui Muslims in China, Hausa Muslims in Niger, Sufi mystics in Pakistan, Taliban fighters in Afghanistan, or Iranian immigrants in America. Obviously, this list of individual Muslim groups could go on and on across the globe. Muslims traditionally embrace certain core doctrines about Allah, the Prophet Muhammad, and the Qur'an, but the faith's implications in the lives of believers surely are not unidirectional. The same can be said for Christianity.

Readers will also note that, despite the expansive title of this book, its subject is more limited than "American Christians" generally, especially as it moves into the twentieth century. The main focus here is conservative American Protestantism, or what we now commonly call evangelicalism. I do note some liberal Protestant, as well as Catholic, views, but mostly for comparative purposes. My primary justification for this selectivity, beyond maintaining a reasonable length, lies within the topics and sources I am considering: memoirs of missionary work, popular eschatology, and conversion narratives. Most of these literary genres have been dominated by conservative Protestants in America. Since the 1920s, American evangelicalism has developed into a more distinct subculture within American Christianity, but one that has enjoyed ever-increasing influence in politics, publishing, and pop culture. I trust that readers will understand that the narrative I have presented here is thematic rather than comprehensive. Other authors might well tell the story in a very different way.

Readers not familiar with my work may also find it helpful to know that I am a practicing Christian, which surely accounts for part of my concern with what American Christians have thought and written about Islam. Too much American Christian writing on Islam has cultivated sensationalized ideas about Islam and the Prophet Muhammad, at the expense of charitable understanding. American Christians—and Christians elsewhere—have often essentialized and stereotyped Muslims out of pain, anger, and fear. They have not just reacted this way since 2001, but since America's colonial era. Some readers might protest that the sin of stereotyping does not compare to the atrocities committed by some Muslims in the name of their religion. I would only remind such readers that this book is about Christians, rather than Muslims. Verbal and literary violence is violence nonetheless, and often sets the stage for the physical violence of war and domestic persecution. Admitting one's own failings, in any case, does not necessarily imply a "moral equivalence" with others' failings.

Most of my own previous writing has been on eighteenth-century Anglo-America, and as I researched that era I kept noticing (with eyes newly sensitized by the attacks of September 2001) references to Islam and its Prophet appearing in colonial and Revolutionary-era literature. Frankly, I was surprised to find it there. The more I investigated, the more I realized that American, British, and other Western Christians have produced long-standing conventions of thought about Islam, much of which stands in continuity with contemporary themes. The first chapter, then, considers the uses early Anglo-Americans made of Islam. Often, they employed Islam in intra-Protestant theological debates, and associated opponents' religious views with Muhammad's. Early Americans also had to face the threat of the Barbary pirates, who routinely captured European Christians and held them for ransom in North Africa. The threat of Barbary piracy, and the theological challenge of Islam, helped generate popular stories of Muslim conversions to Protestant Christianity, and also led Christian theologians to consider Islam's place in the last days.

The American fear of, and theological engagement with, Islam grew more prominent in the early republic, a trend that the second chapter of this book investigates. Barbary piracy had waned in the middle of the eighteenth century, but after American independence pirates attacked American ships with the (correct) assumption that the fledgling nation would struggle to defend its seafaring interests. Barbary captivity narratives reached new heights of popularity, and eschatological writing concerning Islam became even more common. Following earlier patterns, the eschatology of the early republic followed historicist models, which interpreted prophetic passages like Revelation 9 as referring to the rise of Islam. Historicist interpretation waned following the overzealous forecasts of William Miller and his followers, who predicted that Jesus would return in 1843. A whole new school of prophetic interpretation, dispensationalism, surged in popularity in the late nineteenth century. Dispensationalists offered a less certain accounting for Islam in prophecy than historicists had. Dispensationalists saw most of the prophecies in Daniel, Revelation, and other Biblical texts as yet to be fulfilled, so that Jonathan Edwards's sort of reading of Revelation 9's smoke locusts became passé.

The perception of a growing clash between Islam and Christianity aided the effort to send American missionaries to Muslim lands, which is the subject of the third chapter. Missions to Muslims proceeded in the broader context of the first large-scale British and American missionary movement, which began in the early nineteenth century. Although it proved very difficult legally and practically to evangelize Muslims overseas, Americans soon produced hosts of missionary tracts and memoirs related to Muslims. Muslim conversion narratives became more popular and abundant, too, along with "Bible lands" travel narratives describing the life and religion of Middle Easterners. This literature conveyed an impression that Muslims were spiritually hungry and ready to convert en masse, even though the actual numbers of converts were very small.

Some American Christians became frustrated about the lack of actual missionary success among Muslims, and set out in the late nineteenth and early twentieth centuries to accomplish the "evangelization of the Muslim world in this generation." This ideal served as a subsidiary goal of the missionary movement's desire to reach the whole world for Christ. The effort to organize Muslim missions, and the growing dispensational focus on the Jewish homeland, are the main topics of chapter 4. The key leader in coordinating American missions to Muslims in this period was the prominent missionary and Orientalist Samuel Zwemer. While missions advocates like Zwemer anticipated a gradual conversion of the world's population before the return of Christ, the dispensationalist camp saw in the collapse of the Ottoman Empire, and the new impetus to create a Jewish nation, signs that the end might occur more suddenly. While dispensationalists did not initially give a prominent place to political Islam, the controversy over Israel in the mid-twentieth century did begin to establish Arab Muslims as Israel's great eschatological enemies, along with the Soviet Russians.

Chapter 5 will show that in the 1920s and '30s, the American missionary consensus fell apart over issues related to the fundamentalist-modernist crisis in the American churches, which had significant implications for missions to Muslims. Because of the fallout from the theological wars of the 1920s, conservative missionaries slowly came to dominate most mission fields. New non-denominational evangelical missionary agencies like the Sudan Interior Mission focused primarily on proselytism and conversion, not on social aid or education. As evangelicals began to control most mid-twentieth-century missionary efforts among Muslims and other non-

Christians, other conservatives developed a more elaborate eschatology focused on the nation of Israel and her enemies. Increasingly, conservative American Protestants pointed to the inevitable eschatological hostility between "Isaac and Ishmael," or Jews and Arabs, and argued that the conflict in the Middle East reflected ancient spiritual animosity more than contemporary political problems. In time, these two conservative focal points—dispensationalism and missions to Muslims—would begin to clash because of the dispensationalists' innate sympathy toward Israel.

While much of American Christians' thinking about Islam has focused on non-American Muslims, in the post–World War II era Christians also had to contend with a domestic Muslim presence, which is the subject of chapter 6. This new Islamic factor has come in two primary forms: the American-born Nation of Islam, and after 1965, Muslim immigrants and students coming to America from overseas. Some conservative American Christians have considered these new Muslims as frightening domestic threats, while others have called for sympathy and kindness toward American Muslims, even as they have maintained the imperative to evangelize them.

Chapter 7 shows that after the collapse of the older American missionary system, evangelicals began to show interest similar to Zwemer's in organizing evangelistic efforts toward Muslims (and other non-Christians) globally, with the goal of fulfilling Christ's command to make disciples in all nations before he returned. Again, the heightened expectations for missionary breakthroughs among Muslims sometimes operated in tension with the burgeoning eschatological fascination with Jews and Muslims in the Middle East. Each new crisis in the Middle East, from the Six-Day War of 1967 to the Persian Gulf War of 1991, gave prophecy writers new opportunities to reflect on the fate of Israel and her Muslim neighbors. Active missionaries realized, however, that one could not bring dispensational views of Israel into the mission field with Muslims, where those ideas would become a barrier to effective witnessing.

The effect of the terrorist attacks of September 2001 on American Christian thought about Islam, the subject of chapter 8, is not yet entirely clear, but it seems that the attacks primarily re-energized familiar themes of Muslim conversions and Islam's place in the end times. These hopes gave some comfort that the dangers coming from jihadist Islam would be defeated. Among the most revealing developments since 2001 has been a new type of dispensationalist literature that places Islam at the center of end-times scenarios, with a Muslim Antichrist leading attacks against Israel in the last days. This kind of eschatology demonstrates the way in which some conservative Christian theology shapes itself according to the latest crises in the news.

In writing these chapters, I have discovered three primary changes and tensions over time that surprised me and should interest readers. First, there has historically been a major difference between image and reality in Americans' view of missionary work among Muslims. Cheery eschatological optimism about the inevitable conversion of the Muslim world to Christianity, and the assumptions that Muslims were spiritually empty and waiting for an introduction to Jesus, masked the fact that Western missions to Muslims have, at least until recent decades, been a near-total failure. Some missions advocates like Samuel Zwemer addressed this disappointment head-on, but others have often pointed to scanty anecdotal evidence of Muslim converts as a substitute for realistic assessment of Muslims' hardy resistance to the Christian gospel.

A second change that I did not fully grasp upon entering this study was the dramatic transition among conservatives from historicist to dispensational eschatology, and the great difference this alteration held for views of Islam's role in the last days. Before the mid-nineteenth century, Anglo-American conservative theologians always identified a clear place for the rise of Islam in Bible prophecy. With the rise of dispensationalism and its futurist emphasis, Islam lost much of its natural place in dominant Anglo-American prophetic thought. That central position could only be reasserted when news about the nation of Israel seemed to make Arab Muslims the Jews' great eschatological opponent. Only since 2001 has political Islam assumed a role as the leading villain in some Americans' scenarios of the last days.

Finally, it has become evident to me that two of the salient themes in conservative American Christians' writing about Islam in the twentieth century—dispensationalism and missions—have often explicitly clashed. In light of the Arab-Israeli crisis, many American prophecy writers have claimed that Christians were required to support Israel because God would always defend Israel and bless the nations that supported her. Many missionaries among Muslims found such views embarrassing, and feared they would obstruct evangelism. Although many dispensationalists participated in missions, there seems to have been an inverse relationship between direct involvement with missions to Muslims and zeal for the political eschatology of the dispensationalists. This split between conservative Protestants represents one of the most fascinating findings of this book.

The key themes of American Christian thought about Islam serve reassuring purposes for their articulators. Eschatological writing on Islam seems to have surged at times of Christian fear or anger related to Muslims, while the interest in missionary activity and Muslim converts suggested confidence in Christianity's final triumph over global competitors. The blending of political conviction and Christian theology, similarly, serves to affirm the rectitude of one's temporal and eternal views. Traditional American Christians' views of Islam illustrate the grave difficulties of maintaining exclusive religious views in a pluralist global society. How can a person uphold the truth of his or her spiritual beliefs while not demonizing other religions' adherents? One might hope that the Christian obligations of charity and grace might offer some assistance in these matters, but unfortunately, American evangelicals' dealings with Islam seem often to have exacerbated, not alleviated, the problem of traditional religion in a pluralist world.

Acknowledgments

Many people helped me write this book. I'd like to express my thanks to Soren McMillan, Baylor colleagues Barry Hankins and George Gawrych, and the reviewers for Princeton University Press who read the manuscript and made many helpful comments. Thanks, as always, to George Marsden, who offered incisive criticism on the manuscript. My thanks also to the Baylor University history department, including especially my department chair Jeff Hamilton, for providing a congenial atmosphere in which to write and teach. Thanks as well to my research assistants at Baylor University, particularly Holly Young and Jonathan Reid, for their help in managing library resources and developing my base of sources.

I appreciate the assistance of the Baylor University Research Committee and Office of the Vice Provost for Research, who provided grants for travel and research funds. I would also like to thank the Louisville Institute for providing a generous 2006 Summer Stipend. In addition, I'd like to thank the Council of Christian Colleges and Universities for a collaboration grant that put me in closer touch with my friends Tim Larsen, Steve Alter, and Sarah Miglio, who have given me helpful suggestions about the project, and thanks, as always, to David Bebbington, too, for his comments during our CCCU collaboration session in Fall 2007, and for reading parts of the manuscript. I also wish to acknowledge the assistance of the National Endowment of the Humanities, whose 2006-7 Fellowship helped me not only finish an earlier project on the Great Awakening of the eighteenth century, but also make great progress on this book. The views expressed in this book do not reflect those of any of these funding agencies.

I appreciated the opportunity to present and discuss ideas from this book in various settings, including Gordon College's "Faith Seeking Understanding" series in October 2005; First Presbyterian Church, Waco, Texas, in September 2005; and the American Society of Church History conference in January 2007.

I also wish to express my appreciation to the librarians and archivists that assisted me in researching this book. The staff at the Billy Graham Center at Wheaton, Illinois, provided wonderful help in sorting through their fabulous collections of missionary records, as did the staff at the Presbyterian Historical Society in Philadelphia. The staff at the Scholars' Collection at Moody Library, Baylor University, graciously assisted me in working with the papers of Finlay and Julia Graham, and I especially want to thank the interlibrary loan staff at Baylor for their tireless pursuit of popular Christian literature on my behalf.

An earlier version of chapter 1 was published as "'Is It Worse to Follow Mahomet than the Devil?': Early American Uses of Islam," *Church History*, 72, no. 4 (Dec. 2003): 766–90. Material related to the book was also published as "Islam in American Protestant Thought," in *Books & Culture: A Christian Review*, 12, no. 5 (Sept./Oct. 2006): 39–41.

Thanks to the many people at Princeton University Press who worked hard on the book, including Fred Appel, Claire Tillman-McTigue, copyeditor Michael McGee, and others.

Finally, I wish to thank my family, including my invariably supportive and encouraging wife, Ruby. The book is dedicated with much love to my sons, Jonathan and Joshua Kidd.

AMERICAN CHRISTIANS AND ISLAM

CHAPTER 1

Early American Christians and Islam

IN THE LAST PUBLIC ACT before his death, Benjamin Franklin parodied a proslavery speech in Congress by comparing it to a fictitious proslavery address by a North African Muslim pirate named Sidi Mehemet Ibrahim. Like proslavery southerners, the Algerian argued that he could not accept the end of Christian slavery because it would hurt the interests of the Algerian state, unfairly deprive Muslim slave masters of property, and release dangerous slaves into a vulnerable society. Franklin's salvo against slavery was published in 1790 in major northern newspapers.[1] His polemical use of a Muslim character is one of the most famous from eighteenth-century America, but was not unique. Islamic references peppered the public documents of early America, demonstrating that many were not only aware of the religion, but also ready to use it as a rhetorical tool. A close look at the uses of Islam in Anglo-American writing before 1800 shows that Franklin's appropriation of a Muslim character represented a well-established tradition: citing the similarities between an opponent's views and the "beliefs" of Islam as a means to discredit one's adversaries. Over the course of the eighteenth century, Americans' uses of Islam became increasingly secularized. Early in the century, Islam was typically used for religious purposes in religious debates, while later commentators often implemented knowledge of despotic Islamic states to support political points. Although one should hesitate to describe early Americans as conversant with Islam, they certainly conversed about Islam regularly. In doing so, they established views of Muslims that would persist, in very different contexts, through our own day.

How did North Americans before 1790 become aware of Islam? Although there were perhaps thousands of Muslim African slaves working on colonial American plantations, most free white observers failed to realize their devotion, and their presence had little impact on the way elite Anglo-American colonists imagined Islam and the Prophet Muhammad. Prominent Boston pastor Cotton Mather once noted that "we are afar off, in a Land, which never had (that I ever heard of) one Mahometan breathing in it."[2] In the sixteenth and seventeenth centuries, Muslims interacted with Elizabethan and Jacobean Britons in business and seafaring contacts, and appeared as characters in plays and books. After migrating to North America, however, direct contacts with Muslims became much less frequent for British colonists, especially for those with no ocean-going business. It appears that the two main sources from which early Americans derived their impressions of Islam were the enslavement of Europeans and North Americans in North Africa, and widely circulated books and sermons related to Islam.

Colonial North Americans, though living in a provincial society far distant from the physical residence of most African or Asian Muslims, nevertheless included them in their mental array of conflicting world religions. They were able to do this because of the ways printed treatises allowed colonists to believe they had legitimate "knowledge" of Islam. Anglo-American colonists used their knowledge of Islam to reinforce the superiority of their brand of Protestantism over its challengers, such as Deism or Catholicism, and to de-legitimize Islam and Muslims religiously, morally, and racially.

European Christians entertained both a lurid interest in, and a "paranoic repugnance" for, Islam since at least the Crusades of the twelfth and thirteenth centuries, but that fascination took a new turn beginning in the sixteenth century as "Barbary" pirates began to seize Christian sailors and make them slaves.[3] The term "Barbary" itself suggests non-normative races, or those who refuse to cooperate with the dominant faith or commercial systems. Even the North African church leader Saint Augustine used the term "barbarian" to describe his fellow countrymen who would not accept Christianity. In the early modern period, Europeans also routinely used the term "Barbary" to refer to the states of North Africa that campaigned against Europe's seafaring tradesmen, including Anglo-American sailors.[4] Many escaped or redeemed Britons wrote about their experiences to satisfy a growing literature on captives' lives in Islamic cultures.

In 1675, the English captive William Okeley set a significant pattern for the Anglo-American Barbary captivity narrative with his *Eben-Ezer or a Small Monument of Great Mercy*. Okeley faced down his Muslim captors with insistences that the Prophet Muhammad had "patch'd up...Jewish, and Monkish Fopperies, which was now their Religion." He marveled at the hypocrisy of Ramadan, when by day the Algerians fasted with great solemnity, but by night gorged themselves on food, drink, and sex. He called this a "Hypocrisie so gross, that whether it be to be sampled any where in the World, unless, perhaps, by the Popish [Roman Catholic] Carnevals, I cannot tell." Okeley and his companions stole away from Algiers and were providentially delivered back to England, but not before witnessing many cruelties and tortures by their Muslim captors.[5]

North Americans too watched with horror as some of their sons were enslaved by "the Fierce Monsters of Africa," and "Mahometan Turks and
Moors, and Devils," as Cotton Mather called them.[6] Though there were
some North American captives taken earlier, the first case of Barbary captivity to generate significant public interest was that of Captain William
Foster of Roxbury, Massachusetts, who was captured with his son in 1671
and held for three years. Increase Mather (Cotton's father) mentioned this
case as evidence that prayer worked to deliver Christians from the hands of
their enemies, and noted that when Foster was in captivity the church at
Charlestown set aside a day of prayer and fasting to ask for his deliverance.
The situation looked dire as the "infidel King" was not inclined to liberate
them for money. God intervened, however, by causing the unexpected death
of their captor, leading to Foster and his son's liberation. Mather noted that
this was only one of many examples when prayer helped free "Captives
amongst the heathen," such as the nearly contemporaneous deliverance
of the pious heroine Mary Rowlandson from Native Americans. Direct
colonial encounters with Native American peoples surely helped British
colonists articulate stereotypes of supposedly inferior North African and
Turkish Muslims, as well, despite the lack of English colonial success against
Muslim powers.[7]

Several other Anglo-Americans were taken by the pirates during the
1670s, including Seth Southell, the appointed royal governor of Carolina,
who was abducted as he traveled to North America in 1679, and later ran-
somed so he could assume the governorship. Joshua Gee was captured in
1680 during a transatlantic voyage from Boston. His captivity narrative, now
extant only in incomplete fragments, seems to have generated much discussion in Boston, and helped confirm the cruelties of the Muslims. Gee recorded the viciousness of his master who once "swore he wo[u]ld the next
daye boare o[u]te my eyes with his knife" and gave him "many evell treatments." Gee used the narrative to highlight the comforting power of Scripture, and he portrayed his Muslim captors as influenced by his prayers.[8]

Stories of Barbary captivity were so common that alms-seekers among
the urban poor in colonial America occasionally used them to curry favor.
Artisan Joseph Bean of Cambridge, Massachusetts, noted in 1742 that he
met a beggar who claimed he had "been among the turks." When the sailor
would not "own th[eir] Imposter for to be Christ[,] they burnt his arms" so
he could no longer work. Bean suspected the man might have falsified the
story, but he considered him an "object of pitty" and gave him some money.
This brief encounter spoke to the popular resonance of the Barbary captivity narrative in America.[9]

The Barbary captives helped generate an interest in America in literature on the Muslim states of North Africa, reflected in former English captive Francis Brooks's *Barbarian Cruelty*. This text, which Cotton Mather used to describe the conditions of the captives, included a wide-ranging discussion of Islamic piracy and slavery in North Africa. Brooks addressed his narrative to King William and Queen Mary, with the purpose of letting them know "the deplorable and miserable Condition" of English subjects "under the barbarous Tyranny and Inhumanity of Mully Ishmael [Moulay Ismaïl] Emperor of Morocco." Brooks reported that the English "Christians were grievously hurried and punished by those Hellish Negroes" who regularly demanded that they "turn Moors," or Muslims. He filled his account with stories of the Emperor's cruelties, but perhaps none was more revealing than his account of an English virgin taken by the pirates. She was delivered up to Moulay Ismaïl, who pressured her to "turn Moor, and lie with him." The woman resisted, so the Emperor raped and impregnated her. Muslim leaders routinely appeared as sexual predators in the captivity narratives.[10]

In Brooks's account, the Emperor also constantly demanded that the Christian captives convert to Islam. In one case, a French and an English captive made a failed attempt to escape, and they were brought before the Emperor, who offered them their lives if they would convert. Exhibiting the typical anti-Catholic themes of British Protestant literature, the Frenchman (a Catholic) gave in to the pressure, but the Englishman would not, replying that "God's Power was greater than the Devil's." Enraged, the Emperor had his "Negroes" mutilate the English prisoner "till his Body was as full of Holes as possible." The English captives admired this man's fortitude and reminded one another that he had counted his faith more precious than life.[11]

Brooks attributed some of Moulay Ismaïl's brutality to his racial characteristics, noting that he was a mulatto, "begotten of a Negro Woman by a white Man." When Ismaïl became enraged, he became "as black as an Infernal Imp." The Emperor made a habit of killing at least a person or two among his Christian or native African slaves every day, a practice that Brooks explained by reference to his Islamic faith: "Mahomet their great Prophet possessing them with a Belief, that if he kills any one, he merits Heaven by so doing." Brooks considered Ismaïl selective in his obedience to Muhammad's teachings, as he did not abstain from wine, but if he found that any of his entourage had so indulged, he would kill them.[12] Brooks eventually escaped from captivity and made his way back to England. Captivity narratives like Brooks's helped frame the global confrontation between Islam and Christianity for Anglo-Americans. Though it does not appear that many Anglo-Americans took seriously, or even knew of, the Islamic polemic against Christianity, many Britons did know that some English captives in North Africa had abandoned Christianity in favor of Islam. Many more Christians actually converted to Islam during the early modern period than vice versa.[13] Perhaps some apostates did this only for material gain, but surely many did so in part because they favored Islam as a religion. The prospect of any Englishmen turning Muslim was disconcerting enough to help make captivity narratives popular assurances of the ultimate superiority of Christianity over Islam.[14]

Cotton Mather, following Gee and Brooks, helped frame New Englanders' understanding of Barbary captivity with regular comments on the pirates. In his history *Magnalia Christi Americana*, Mather noted that in response to the provoking sins of New England, "God hath given up several of our sons into the hands of the fierce monsters of Africa. Mahometan Turks, and Moors, and devils, are at this day oppressing many of our sons with a slavery, wherein they 'wish for death, and cannot find it.'"[15] Mather's two most significant works on Barbary captivity were *A Pastoral Letter to the English Captives in Africa* (1698) and *The Goodness of God* (1703). As was Mather's wont, he penned *A Pastoral Letter* as if he meant the captives themselves to read it, but the letter was actually meant for readers in New England itself. In it, he promoted Christianity as a superior religion to Islam, and warned the captives to stand faithfully against the "Mahometan Tempters." Mather demonstrated some knowledge of the Qur'an by citing an English translation to prove that if Muslims read their holy book correctly, they would see that it pointed to Christ as the true Messiah. He cautioned prisoners to realize that their captivity in Africa was temporary, but captivity to sin was much worse and only gave a foretaste of the eternal torment to come in hell. It was the Lord who gave the captives over to the "African Pyrates" as a judgment against their sins. Instead of giving in to the temptations of the captors, it was much better to contemplate one's own sin, hold tight to Christ, and wait for redemption.[16]

By 1703, New Englanders had received news of the redemption of several hundred English prisoners, and in response Boston held a day of public thanksgiving for which Mather wrote *The Goodness of God*. A number of the captives, "delivered. . .from the most horrible Captivity in the world," considered Boston their home port and attended the service in which Mather preached. To describe the horrific nature of their captivity, Mather included a brief by William and Mary (found also in Brooks) promoting their redemption. While noting the usual deprivations, the account ended with perhaps the most fundamentally disturbing element of the Anglo-Americans' captivity:

the enslavement of whites by black masters. The captives were "sometimes driven about by Black-a-moors, who are set over them as Task-masters; and some of them have been so severely Whipp'd, that they have dropp'd down Dead." Incongruities such as this could not help but destabilize the appearance of racial permanency in Anglo-American slave-owning. The Virginia House of Burgesses went so far as to make this scenario illegal by stipulating that no "Negros, Mulattos, or Indians, although Christians, or Jews, Moors, Mahometans, or other Infidels" could own white Christians as slaves.[17]

Mather noted that while "now and then a wretched Christian. . .Renounced Christianity and Embraced Mahometanism," none of the New England captives had done so. God's grace did not allow them to "stretch out their Hands unto the Impostor Mahomet, and his accursed Alcoran!" Mather recounted Brooks's story of the Frenchman who converted and the English martyr who would not as an example of the strong faith of the sufferers. He rejoiced that now the slaves had been redeemed and were back among loved ones in New England. What had secured their liberty? Mather insisted it was the prayers of the New England churches: "with all due Humility; This Deliverance never began thoroughly to operate, until God began to awaken a Spirit of Prayer in the Churches of poor NEW-ENGLAND for it." Because of their faithfulness, "thou, O Mully Ishmael, with all thy Diabolical Fury, art no longer able to with-hold from us, the Friends, about whom God gave thee an Efficacious Order, To let them go." Mather closed with a warning to the liberated captives to make much of their lives now that they were saved from the "Filthy Disciples of Mahomet."[18]

The Barbary pirates' activities declined during the middle decades of the eighteenth century, but Anglo-Americans' use of Islamic categories and images had become a staple of religious polemics. American pastors and academics borrowed from a burgeoning European literature on Islam. The most notable and influential treatment of Islam which Anglo-Americans read was Humphrey Prideaux's biography *The True Nature of Imposture Displayed in the Life of Mahomet* (see Figure 1-1). This book was published in London in 1697 and went through eight editions there by 1723. Many learned colonists either read or heard about *The True Nature of Imposture*, because in the colonies the habit of applying the epithet "impostor" to "Mahomet" became nearly ubiquitous (though this usage was not unknown before Prideaux). American editions appeared in Philadelphia in 1796 and Fairhaven, Vermont in 1798, times of resumed troubles with North African piracy and worries about the powers of the new United States government. Prideaux was Dean of Norwich Cathedral and an orthodox Anglican theologian whose writings often confronted the threat of Deism. In *The True*

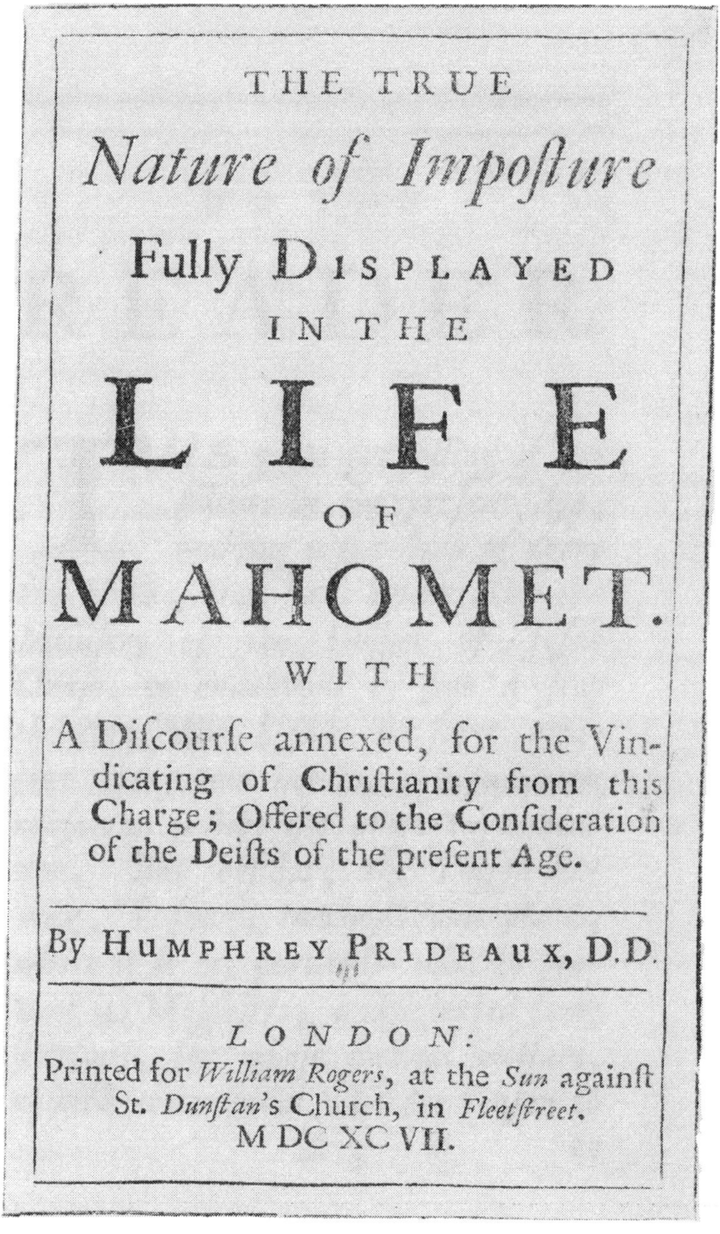

THE TRUE

Nature of Impofture

Fully DISPLAYED

IN THE

LIFE

OF

MAHOMET.

WITH

A Difcourfe annexed, for the Vindicating of Chriftianity from this Charge; Offered to the Confideration of the Deifts of the prefent Age.

By HUMPHREY PRIDEAUX, D.D.

LONDON:

Printed for *William Rogers*, at the *Sun* againft St. *Dunftan*'s Church, in *Fleetftreet*.

M DC XC VII.

FIGURE 1-1. Title page, Humphrey Prideaux's *The True Nature of Imposture Fully Displayed in the Life of Mahomet* (London, 1697). Beinecke Rare Book and Manuscript Library, Yale University.

Nature of Imposture he used Muhammad as a case study in religious fakery, as opposed to the authentic miracles of Christianity. Although Prideaux's book was derivative and full of errors, it shaped many American colonists' impressions of Islam's origins.[19]

Prideaux lamented how many Deists had charged Christianity with imposture, and he meant to hold up Islam as an actual fraud against which Christianity's legitimacy would become more apparent. Knowing that some might accuse him of painting Muhammad in the "foulest Colours," he insisted that he would approach Muhammad judiciously. Prideaux saw Islam as the judgment of God on the eastern churches that had been rife with bickering before the Prophet arose. Because the Christian churches turned their "Holy Religion into a Firebrand of Hell for Contention, Strife and Violence," God gave them over to the Muslims. He "turned their Churches into Mosques, and. . .forced on them that abominable Imposture of Mahometanism."[20] The rise of Islam, in Prideaux's formulation, was a cautionary tale against the disturbers of the church's peace.

As for the Prophet Muhammad himself, Prideaux argued that he hatched the scheme of Islam as a way to gain power over Arabia, and designed the new religion as a "Medley made up of Judaism, the several Heresies of the Christians then in the East, and the old Pagan Rites of the Arabs, with an Indulgence to all Sensual Delights." To authenticate his revelations, Muhammad soon began claiming visitations by the angel Gabriel. Prideaux noted that Muhammad began touting his prophetic authority at approximately the same time the Bishop of Rome asserted pastoral supremacy over the church. He thought the two developments not coincidental: "Antichrist seems at this time to have set both his Feet upon Christendom together, the one in the East, the other in the West."[21]

This association of the Roman church and Islam with Antichrist was common in the colonial period and the nineteenth century. Figures as various as Puritan lay leader Anne Hutchinson, the judge Samuel Sewall, and pastors Increase and Cotton Mather and Edward Taylor all commented on the connection, and New York's Lutheran leader Eric Tobias Bjorck noted that "the Scripture speaketh of Two great Anti-christs, one in the West, the other in the East. . .; one is called Mahomet, or Gog and Magog,. . .the other is the Pope." Prideaux also attributed much of Muhammad's successes to the promises of heaven's pleasure that he made to his followers, "which he cunningly framed to the gust of the Arabians." Because they lived in the "Torrid Zone," and because of the "excessive corruption of their Manners," his devotees responded eagerly to promises of cool drinks, shady glens, and abundant virgins.[22]

In the *Discourse for the Vindicating of Christianity*, Prideaux set out the fundamental characteristics of a fraudulent religion that set Islam apart from Christianity. An impostor religion would always (1) serve some "carnal Interest," (2) be led by wicked men, (3) have "Falsities" at the very heart of the religion, (4) use "craft and fraud" to accomplish its ends, (5) be backed by conspirators who would eventually be revealed, and (6) be spread by force.[23] Eighteenth-century Anglo-Americans widely attributed all these characteristics to Islam.

Prideaux's treatment of Muhammad was likely the most influential in eighteenth-century Anglo-America. The Library Company of Philadelphia had acquired a copy of *The True Nature of Imposture* by 1746, the New York Society Library owned one by 1758, and even the Wethersfield, Connecticut library listed a copy in a 1784 catalogue. Following Prideaux, anti-evangelical pastor John Caldwell once wondered "Is there any now hearing me but will own Mahomet was an Impostor?" He compared Muhammad's supposed deceptions to those committed by evangelicals in the Great Awakening of the 1740s. Both movements substituted overheated zeal for true piety, according to Caldwell. Thomas Wells Bray, pastor at Guilford, Connecticut, cited Prideaux in his *A Dissertation on the Sixth Vial* (1780) as an authority on the rapid expansion of Islam during Muhammad's life, explaining that "By cruel tyranny and over-bearing power, did that vile impostor Mahomet set up and propagate a false religion, which has been one of the greatest plagues to the christian religion, and filled all the eastern world with error and thick darkness, like the smoke of a bottomless pit." Charles Leslie's *A Short and Easie Method with the Deists* (originally published in London in 1698, with American editions in 1719 and 1783) used Prideaux to help show that Christianity was "incompatible with any imposture," saying that even learned Muslims knew that Muhammad's miracles were illegitimate.[24]

Anglo-Americans of various religious camps agreed with Prideaux and Leslie that the main flaws of both Islam and Roman Catholicism were irrationality and superstition. New Jersey's evangelical Presbyterian Jonathan Dickinson argued for "the reasonableness of Christianity" by contrasting it with Islam. "No wise man can trust in such a rhapsody of nonsense and confusion" as Islam, "and in such a medly of inconsistent, and absurd doctrines of religion and tyranny," with no proof other than the word of Muhammad. Dickinson noted that Islam offered no forgiveness of sins, and only promised sensual pleasures in heaven, which was "most disagreeable to a vertuous and rational mind."[25]

After Prideaux's, the next most important biography of Muhammad in Anglo-America appears to have been Henri de Boulainvilliers's *The Life of*

Mahomet, which was first translated into an English edition in London in 1731. It offered a more positive approach to Muhammad than Prideaux's. Boulainvilliers was a minor figure in the French Enlightenment, although he wrote some of the best French historical works in the age of Louis XIV. Boulainvilliers's Muhammad was much more enlightened than Prideaux's, and *The Life of Mahomet* was mostly written to counter Prideaux's view of Muhammad as impostor. Boulainvilliers argued that Muhammad no doubt misunderstood the nature of true Christianity, but he founded Islam as a reaction against truly un-Christian traits of the church, such as corruption and priestcraft, the same qualities that plagued the Roman Catholic church in the early eighteenth century. The Prophet was actually used by God to judge and purify the church. "Instead of chusing the Christian religion," he lamented, "Mahomet was so violently turned against it, by the abuses in its practice which he himself had seen, that he was rather excited to attack it, than to reform that which every true Christian bore with pain and sorrow." Boulainvilliers used Muhammad to shame Christians, whom he painted as partially responsible for the coming of Islam because of the deficiencies of the church. The success of Boulainvilliers's biography reminds us that British and European views of Islam were not homogenous or entirely negative during the eighteenth century.[26] However, Boulainvilliers's approach to Muhammad served polemical purposes within the French Enlightenment, as he appropriated Islam to promote anti-clericalism.

The Life of Mahomet was held in several colonial libraries, though it seems never to have come out in an American edition. It appeared in the Library Company of Philadelphia's catalogue in 1741, and in a 1772 accounting of the library of Robert Carter of Virginia. Tracing the exact reading habits of Anglo-Americans about Islam or Muhammad is perhaps not as important as realizing that they trafficked in an intellectual milieu ready to make use of Islamic categories. No matter how "knowledgeable" an author, his knowledge about Islam was located more in "internal apologetic concerns" than it was in the Islamic world.[27] Associating an opponent with Islam became a standard rhetorical move in religious debates, as it legitimized the accuser as a defender of righteousness.

A good early example of Americans' own uses of Islam was Rhode Island Baptist leader Roger Williams's attacks on George Fox in *G. Fox Digg'd out of His Burrowes* (1676). Throughout, Williams contrasted the Roman church, Islam, and Quakerism, all deceitful human systems, with the true religion of Christ. Williams hoped that "Old and New England may flourish when the Pope and Mahomet, Rome and Constantinople are in their Ashes," and that some of his Protestant readers might live to see "the Pope and Mahomet. . .

flung into the Lake that burns with Fire and Brimstone." Fox had argued that Quakerism proved its credibility by its quick growth and thousands of followers, but Williams noted that the same successes had marked Islam and Roman Catholicism. Williams reminded his readers of "the innumerable multitudes that followed after that stupendious Cheater Mahomet, even thirteen parts of the world, divided into thirty." He thought it remarkable that more people did not follow Fox, "this new Mahomet" of Quakerism since their religion was "so easie. . ., pretending so much from the Dove from Heaven as Mahomet did." Williams believed that both religions claimed a false inspiration from the Holy Spirit, and recalled the story that Muhammad trained birds to pick peas out of his ear to make it appear as though the Holy Spirit was speaking to him (a story which Prideaux rejected as apocryphal).[28]

As Williams's book indicated, English Protestants in America often included the destruction of Islam in their eschatological timetable, usually making it simultaneous with the future ruin of the Roman church. This belief was part of a "Judeo-centric" millennialism that was common, though not dominant, in seventeenth-century English Puritan thought. In this system, the mass conversion of the Jews would follow the destruction of the Ottoman Empire, and Islam generally. Increase and Cotton Mather, both of whom referenced Islam regularly, reflected on this prospect. Cotton Mather, excited in 1690 by the eschatological significance of William and Mary's "Glorious Revolution," predicted that the great victory for English Protestantism might also signal the coming destruction of Rome and the "Turkish Power," which he thought might soon become unable to wage war against the European states.[29] Similarly, Nicholas Noyes of Salem, Massachusetts, gave Islam a prominent place in the events of the last days in his election sermon *New-England's Duty and Interest.* He argued that the countries that had been Christian but had become "the Kingdoms of Antichrist & of Mahomet" would once again be won over to Christ in the last days. He took the resurrection of the witnesses discussed in Revelation 11 to mean that these nations would be liberated both from the Roman church and from "the Imposture and Oppression of the Mahometans." Despite the "fury and cruelty of the Arabian and Saracen or Mahometan Harpyes," Christ would rule the "East Empire" again some day. Likewise, the Harvard Hebrew instructor and Jewish Christian Judah Monis predicted that many Muslim countries would join with "King Gog" at Armageddon, and that Christ would there destroy them "with Pestilence and with Blood,. . . Hailstones, Fire, and Brimstone."[30]

It was not only New Englanders, more disposed than most to eschatological speculation, who held these opinions about Islam in the last days. Pres-

byterian pastor George Gillespie of Christiana Creek, Delaware, a future opponent of the Great Awakening, argued that the destruction of "Anti-Christ
and Mahomet" would precede the Jews' conversion to Christianity. He interpreted the pouring out of the sixth vial of judgment, the drying up of the
Euphrates River in Revelation 16:12, to mean the destruction of the Islamic
powers, specifically the Ottoman Empire. "The Mahometan Turk is as powerful as ever; but when his power is broken, then there shall be the Conversion of the Jews." Gillespie further asserted that Christianity was superior to
the "Mahometan Religion" because of the latter's focus on sensual pleasures
in heaven. Presbyterian Samuel Davies of Virginia had an expansive view of
the eschatological spread of the gospel, as it "shall triumph over heathenism,
Mahometism, Judaism, popery, and all those dangerous errors that have in-
fected the Christian church."[31]

Jonathan Edwards's son-in-law Aaron Burr also developed a speculative
eschatology with a special place for Islam. Burr's theology was much more
pessimistic than Edwards's, holding that the millennium would come not as
a progressive triumph but through divine deliverance in times of future
darkness. Burr saw Islam as one of the key persecutors of the true church,
and followed Prideaux in arguing that it grew largely because of the cor-
ruptions of the eastern churches. The "Rise of that false Prophet and great
Impostor Mahomet" came in the dark night of the church. Wherever it
spread, "it seemed as if the bottomless Pit had been opened, and Satan at the
Head of the Powers of Darkness, come forth." Reflecting Edwards's and others' interpretation of prophecy, Burr thought that Islam's appearance
fulfilled the mysterious image of smoke locusts coming from the abyss in
Revelation 9:2–3, because everywhere the religion went it spread "Misery
and Woe, stupid Ignorance and Superstition." Considering the future, he
noted that the Ottoman Empire still ruled much of Asia, Europe, and Africa,
and that the Muslims were for the time being "the greatest Obstacle in the
Way of spreading the Gospel." Burr thought that only a dramatic outpour-
ing of the Holy Spirit, at which recent awakenings might have hinted, would
remove the Muslim hindrance. Then the preaching of the gospel would be
attended with such "Light & Glory, as that the Remainder of Pagan, Popish,
& Mahometan Darkness, will flee before it."[32] Whether by conversion or destruction, many colonists agreed that Islam would be swallowed up by
Christ's kingdom in the last days.

Anglo-American colonists also assumed, as had Prideaux, that whatever
successes Islam had enjoyed only came by the sword. Thomas Paine of Wey-
mouth, Massachusetts, contrasted the plain truth of Christianity with the
imposed falsehoods of Islam: followers of "Mahomet perswade. . .by mas-

terly Evidence and Demonstration hurled about at the deadly Point of their victorious Swords, and most powerful Light and Energy, thundred forth by the mouth of their dreadful Engines of Cruelty and War." False religions like Catholicism and Islam, according to Paine, depended on bogus miracles and the threat of violence to keep believers in line. True Christianity, by contrast, demonstrated its truth by gentle persuasion and clear evidence. The Baptist leader John Walton similarly argued that Islam "was propagated by Force and Arms, and was partly borrowed out of the Christian Bible, and partly hatched out of the enthusiastical Brain of Mahomet." Islam succeeded through promises of sensual delights in heaven, including the assurances that "they should carnally enjoy beautiful Women in Heaven. This, together with many other ridiculous Notions, makes me prefer the Bible before the Alcoran," Walton concluded.[33] Many American Protestants like these, encountering new knowledge of the Islamic world, rushed to make the case that Christianity was superior to Islam.

Many argued further that the key to the distinctiveness of Protestant theology over Islamic, Catholic, or Jewish theology lay in the doctrine of grace. True (Reformed) religion depended on God's gracious intervention for salvation, while false religions put their hope in good works to justify man. The anonymous tract *The Sad Estate of the Unconverted* maintained that unconverted men are "exceedingly inclined to seek Salvation by our own Works. And this is the Way of the Mahometans." They believed that God gave Muhammad the law, so that anyone who obeyed those regulations would be saved. "The Papists seek Salvation in a like Manner," the tract noted, as they added all kinds of superfluous requirements to the divine law. The same was true for the Jews. Authentic Christians knew better: it was God's grace alone that saved and empowered them to do good. New Jersey revivalist Gilbert Tennent argued that false religions, including the "Mahometan imposture," focused on self-glorification. "Thro' the whole Alcoran there is a deep silence, about supernatural Principles of Worship." He believed that the Qur'an primarily taught "the Consideration of eternal Pleasures, to be afterward enjoy'd, as the Reward of good Works, and eternal Pains to be endured as the Punishment of bad."[34] Thus, Tennent's antirevivalist opponents, whom he believed had embraced works-righteousness, were no better than Muslims.

The most celebrated revivalist of the Great Awakening, the Anglican itinerant George Whitefield, seized upon the comparison of Christ and Muhammad in one of his most controversial and ill-advised public comments, saying in 1740 that the popular and deceased Archbishop John Tillotson of England "knew no more about true Christianity than Mahomet." Here was another typical use of Muhammad in Anglo-American discourse. Whitefield argued that "as to the method of our acceptance with God, and our justification by faith alone, [Tillotson] certainly was as ignorant thereof as Mahomet himself." The name "Mahomet" provided a rhetorical device with which adversaries could denounce one another. The association with Muhammad implied illegitimacy, infidelity, and likely damnation. In Whitefield's case, he realized later that he had overplayed his hand by using Muhammad to condemn Tillotson. These were "injudicious and too severe expressions," he admitted, as both in the colonies and in Britain he found that many who might have supported him now became his enemies because of his attack against the archbishop.[35]

But Whitefield's enemies used the accusation of similarity to Muhammad against him, too. Alexander Garden, the Anglican Commissary of Charleston, South Carolina, argued that Whitefield promoted rank enthusiasm, as had Muhammad. Whitefield and his defenders had claimed that his success and great following indicated the blessing of God on his ministry, but Garden thought this fallacious logic: "the same Effects, and in still greater Degrees, attended the Ministry of Mahomet." Popularity was not a reliable gauge for legitimacy. Enthusiasm bred heretical religions such as Islam. "Was not Mahometanism founded in Enthusiasm?" asked Garden. "And does not this run so strong in the Veins of that Religion, that all true Mussulmans [Muslims] firmly believe the greatest Ideots or Madmen are the greatest Saints?"[36] One can see in Whitefield and Garden's counter-accusations the multiple uses of Muhammad in early America: He could be portrayed as an example of a graceless legalist or a wild enthusiast, depending on the rhetorical need of the moment.

Some of Whitefield's opponents raised the prospect of imposture and used Prideaux's treatment of Muhammad as a way to criticize evangelical enthusiasts, too. In *The Wonderful Narrative*, an anonymous account of the French Prophets of London (a group of spirit-filled Protestants in the early eighteenth century), the author noted how many of the French zealots followed after their ecstasies as signs of God's presence. The Prophets, however, turned out (as, by implication, Whitefield would) to be "either Impostors, or under the Power of Delusion, or an overheated Imagination." One of the best historical examples of these deluded visionaries was Muhammad, and the author used Prideaux's account to show how "in the Course of a few Years, as ridiculous an Imposture as ever was invented, obtained in many Countries." The author also cited Meric Casaubon's *Treatise Concerning Enthusiasme* (originally published in London, 1654), which suggested that Muhammad may have had epilepsy, explaining his trances and visions.

This diagnosis seems to have had some currency in early America as a number of writers referred to Muhammad as "epileptick." *The Wonderful Narrative* asserted that Muhammad may have begun his imposture by means of a blameless affliction, but he used the disease as a device to achieve power. *The Wonderful Narrative* echoed Casaubon's warning that people should not too quickly "give Credit to such Fits and Revelations."[37]

Evangelicals could also use Islam for their own arguments, as demonstrated in the tract *The Conversion of a Mehometan*, published originally in London in 1757, and printed twice during the 1770s in New London, Connecticut. This tract contained a letter, ostensibly written by a Turk, "Gaifer," to his friend Aly-Ben-Hayton. Gaifer told how he came to England to learn more about Christianity, which he had first heard about from an English slave. The letter recorded the story of Gaifer's conversion to evangelical Christianity, but it is so formulaic and polemical that it seems almost certain that Gaifer was only a fictional vehicle for an evangelical attack. The target was not Islam primarily, however, but the established Church of England ministers. Gaifer acquired a Bible and realized from reading it that man could not be saved by good deeds, but only by the grace of Christ. He then discovered an evangelical church meeting where he was told that he must be born again to enter heaven. In light of these truths, Gaifer was dismayed to find that the established clergy "are, for the most part, the greatest strangers to the essence of the Gospel."[38]

As Gaifer wrestled with how he could be saved, he received a visit from an Anglican priest, who assured him that he need not be born again or receive the Holy Spirit. His melancholic state of spiritual wrestling, the minister assured him, was only a "religious distraction of mind, which we call enthusiasm, we have a great deal of this in England." But Gaifer would not listen to the established clergyman, and sought out the evangelical minister to help him find salvation. Finally, Gaifer realized that Christ could deliver him from his sins, and he was saved. He wrote the letter to his friend back in Turkey to plead with him to consider Christianity. Conversion "would soon wean you from your superstitious and fruitless pilgrimage to Mecca and Arafata in honor of a grand Impostor; and engage you to come and see the salvation of God."[39] Despite this assertion, the tract had little to do with evangelism to Muslims; instead, it used a supposed Muslim convert to attack the established clergy.

Like many other Anglo-American pastors, Jonathan Edwards gave a great deal of attention to non-Christian religions, including Islam. Edwards's thoughts on Islam were not unique but only more developed than most commentators'. Edwards's interest in Islam had primarily to do with its place in eschatology, its inferiority to Christianity, and its role in the on-going debates with Deists. He made Muslims prominent in his millennial theology, arguing that as the millennium approached they would be destroyed. In the "Notes on the Apocalypse," Edwards argued that Satan's earthly kingdom was made up of three parts: the false Christian kingdom (Roman Catholicism), the Islamic kingdom, which he called "the kingdom of the false prophet," and the heathen kingdom. Edwards did not think these three would join forces in an actual coalition in the last days, but he did believe they would be conquered nearly simultaneously, represented prophetically by the pouring out of the seventh vial of Revelation 16. "Then shall be their last overthrow; and with that overthrow, the millennium shall begin," he wrote.[40]

The major opponents of true Christianity would be defeated either through conversion or warfare, according to Edwards. In the late 1740s, Edwards began keeping a notebook that followed, among other items of eschatological interest, news of Islamic conversions. He delighted in the *Scots Magazine*'s 1751 report that "5344 persons, who were formerly pagans or Mahometans," were baptized into the Greek Orthodox Church. In 1748's *An Humble Attempt*, Edwards further anticipated "the Destruction of the Church of Rome, the entire Extirpation of all Infidelity, . . . the Conversion of all the Jews, and the full enlightning and Conversion of all Mahometan and Heathen Nations, thro' the whole Earth." Edwards, unlike some others, came to believe that these events were likely to happen soon, but that the millennium might begin around the year 2000.[41]

Edwards also used the comparison to Islam to demonstrate the superiority of Christianity as a religious system, countering the threat posed by other religions to Christianity's exclusive truth claims. In the "Miscellanies," Edwards contrasted the effects of Christianity's and Islam's propagation. Although he found that Islam did share in some truths of "natural religion," he thought the two religions were immensely different in their "goodness." Christianity brought a great increase of "light and knowledge," while Islam represented a change "from light to darkness" and a "propagation of ignorance," which only tended to "debase, debauch, and corrupt the minds of such as received it." Edwards argued that Islam only succeeded by playing to man's "luxurious and sensual disposition." In contrast to Christianity, which flourished in the intellectually advanced Jewish, Greek, and Roman cultures, Islam grew "in a dark corner of the earth, Arabia; and the people among whom it first gained strength, who sent out armies to propagate it to the rest of the world, were an ignorant and barbarous sort of people." Christianity was propagated by reason; Islam by the sword.[42]

Like Prideaux, Edwards argued that Christianity was based on observable facts (presumably including miracles), while Islam was based on "Mahomet's pretences to intercourse with heaven, and his success in rapine, murder, and violence." After the publication of Prideaux's biography, Deist skeptics such as Matthew Tindal, Thomas Chubb, and John Toland had continued to agitate against traditional Christianity, sometimes by comparing Islam favorably to it. Edwards agreed with Prideaux that Islam was demonstrably inferior to Christianity, and that in light of Islam, Christianity looked even more viable intellectually. Edwards argued that Islam's persistent success made its own case for the necessity of revealed (as opposed to natural) religion, and provided a "great demonstration of the extreme darkness, blindness, weakness, childishness, folly, and madness of mankind in matters of religion."[43] Again in Edwards we see a polemical interest in Islam as an apologetic tool for Christianity, especially against the Deists.

Benjamin Franklin's *Poor Richard* once wondered "is it worse to follow Mahomet than the Devil?" For most early American observers, no such question was necessary: to follow the one meant following the other. Before the period of the American and French Revolutions, Anglo-Americans typically used categories from Islam as rhetorical tools to discredit opponents, or as players in eschatological speculation. The Revolutionary era saw significant changes in the uses of Islam, however. In addition to using images of Islam for religious purposes, polemicists often used Islam and its states as the world's worst examples of tyranny and oppression, the very traits that the Revolutionaries meant to fight.[44]

Calvinist minister Nathanael Emmons revealed the subtleties of the transition to more political uses of Islam in his sermon *The Dignity of Man* (1787). Emmons lifted up the potential of man to enlighten the world through reason and the gospel, and gave the Revolution a key place in Christian teleology. Charting the progress of reason and the gospel briefly through human history, Emmons noted Luther's Reformation, Newton's scientific discoveries, and included "Franklin in the cabinet, and Washington in the field, [who] have given independence and peace to America." Emmons thought these were only part of a greater process, as the "kingdom of Antichrist is to be destroyed, the Mahomedans are to be subdued, the Jews are to be restored, . . .and the whole face of things in this world, is to be beautifully and gloriously changed." Here, the subjugation of the Muslims was only part of a reasonable millennial process. This reflected the borrowing of traditional eschatological categories for America's republican ends, what historian Henry May has called "secular millennialism."[45] The main difference from earlier American uses was that Islamic categories now often served primarily political principles.

Defenders of Revolutionary ideals pointed regularly to Muslim states as models of tyranny that crushed essential freedoms. John Trenchard and Thomas Gordon's highly influential *Cato's Letters* (1723) made much of the Islamic governments' prohibitions on the free press and free exchange of ideas. The Baptist leader John Leland argued against state establishments of religion by saying these were more fit for Islamic states, because "Mahomet called in the use of law and sword to convert people to his religion; but Jesus did not, does not."[46] In the 1788 Dudleian Lecture at Harvard, Timothy Hilliard described Muhammad as "arrayed in armor and blood" and a "fierce invader of the sacred rights of mankind." Montesquieu's *The Spirit of the Laws*, influential among many Revolutionary leaders in America, depicted the Turkish state as uniquely despotic. A number of Americans picked up on Montesquieu's formulation that all governments fell somewhere on the continuum between absolute despotism and absolute democracy. The Baptist leader Enos Hitchcock quoted "the great Montesquieu" at length in his *Oration in Commemoration of the Independence* in 1793, arguing that a "state, in which the will of an individual is most frequently a law, and decides on the life or death of the subject, is called a despotic state. Such is the Turkish empire."[47]

By the end of the American Revolution, the American Protestant themes of Muslims converting to Christianity, Islam's place in the last days, and the blending of theological and political opinion regarding Islam had all become well developed. Theologians made a clear place for Islam in their visions of the last days, characterized Muhammad as an impostor, and deplored Muslim polities as despotic. More so than in later periods, most knowledge of Islam in the colonial American period serviced intra-Protestant polemical needs. One important facet of American Christian engagement with Islam that had yet to fully develop, however, was the ideology behind missions to Muslims. Many Americans already entertained hope that in the last days Muslims would convert to Christianity in large numbers. Joseph Bean noted excitedly in his diary in 1741 that he had heard in the news that a Muslim leader had "Resolved for to have the Bible translated into the Per[sian] to[ngue] for he himself was dissatisfied as to th[eir] turkish al[c]oran." Bean joyfully prayed that by these means the gospel might spread among Muslims, and he looked forward to the time when Christ would receive "the heathen for his Inheritance."[48] It remained for American Christians to begin sending missionaries to Muslims to try to fulfill that eschatological hope.

CHAPTER 2

The Barbary Wars, the Last Days, and Islam in Early National America

IN HIS 1776 BESTSELLER *Common Sense*, leading patriot Thomas Paine denounced the evils of monarchy and called on America to become the world's new "asylum for liberty." To make the case against kings, Paine drew on America's wells of anti-Catholic and anti-Islamic thought. "Monarchy in every instance is the Popery of government," he wrote. He considered the doctrine of divine right a fable. It was a "superstitious tale, conveniently timed, Mahomet like, to cram hereditary right down the throats of the vulgar." It was high time for Americans to throw off all such superstition, according to Paine, and enter a new era of enlightened democracy. Islam proved one of the most readily available foils for that envisioned American republic. The pirates of the Barbary states remained one of the primary forces constraining the free growth of America's republic in the Atlantic world. Many in America's early national period perceived Muslims as both a military threat to their fledgling mercantile democracy, and one of Christianity's great eschatological enemies.[1]

The post-Revolutionary uses of Islam followed the pattern of appropriating "knowledge" of Islam and Islamic societies to make political points about America. An excellent example of this came with the second American printing of Humphrey Prideaux's *The True Nature of Imposture* by James Lyon of Fairhaven, Connecticut. Lyon was the son of Congressman Matthew Lyon, who was languishing in jail for violation of the Sedition Act, which in 1798 prohibited American citizens from writing or speaking maliciously against the national government. James Lyon tellingly omitted Prideaux's original preface, which had discussed English Deism, and let the book speak for itself about the dangers of centralized power and religious zeal for silencing dissent. To the Lyonses, President John Adams, who signed the Sedition Act, was the new Muhammad. Conversely, John Adams had worried in his "Discourses on Davila" that the excesses of the French Revolution would eventually lead to tyranny and people would "follow the standard of the first mad despot, who, with the enthusiasm of another Mahomet, will endeavor to obtain them." John Quincy Adams, similarly, once compared Jefferson to "the Arabian prophet," and imagined Jefferson's followers bellowing "There is but one Goddess of Liberty, and Common Sense is her Prophet."[2]

Anti-Muslim texts continued to foster these kinds of uses of Islam and the Prophet. A new biography of Muhammad by an anonymous British author, *The Life of Mahomet; or, The History of that Imposture Which was Begun, Carried on, and Finally Established by Him in Arabia* was published in American editions in Worcester, Massachusetts in 1802, and New York in 1813. This aggressively anti-Islamic and anti-Arabian text starkly contrasted the pure rationality of Christianity with the violent duplicity of Islam. The author portrayed Muhammad as a fiend of deception, who intentionally crafted a false religion suited to "ignorant barbarians, to whose lusts it promised to administer everlasting fuel." The growth of Islam came by the sword, as "rapine and murder were the darlings of [Muhammad's] soul." Although he produced little evidence confirming his prophetic office, the Arabians' reception of Muhammad's religion proved "the stupidity of the multitude, in believing the very worst of crimes can be the offspring of religion." Nothing less than "the conquest of Mahometan countries, by which the sentiments of men may be freed from their fetters, will ever be the destruction of that system of blasphemy and iniquity by which they are at present enslaved," the writer proclaimed. The author doubted that sending missionaries would help Muslim countries, as this would only be "conducting [the missionaries] to a slaughterhouse." Before Christian power alone "the monstrous blasphemy and absurdities of Mahomet must fall. . .The contest is between barbarity and benevolence, between Jehovah and a monster in the shape of a man." Anticipating late twentieth-century American opinions, *The Life of Mahomet* asserted that the global clash between the two religions was inevitable.[3]

The anti-Islamic rage behind publications such as *The Life of Mahomet* can be partially explained by the post-Revolutionary renewal of Barbary piracy in the Mediterranean. Incursions against American ships became one of the first great foreign policy challenges of the early republic, and a considerable source of anxiety about America's military impotence. Immediately after the end of the American Revolution, North African corsairs began attacking newly vulnerable American vessels that had lost the benefit of British naval protection. Algerian raiders seized two American ships in 1785, and eleven more in 1793. American diplomatic bungling and naval weakness allowed the North Africans repeatedly to embarrass the new nation, and a 1796 agreement to free eighty-eight American sailors in Algiers cost the federal government one million dollars, or about one-sixth of the national budget. When the ruler of Tripoli declared war on the United States in 1801, President Thomas Jefferson ordered a blockade of the North African port. A new disaster came in 1803 when the U.S. frigate *Philadelphia* ran aground and was captured by Tripolitans. This delivered more than three hundred American sailors into the North Africans' hands. A fiercer naval assault eventually forced Tripoli to concede victory to the Americans for a modest payoff of sixty thousand dollars in 1805. Algerian corsairs resumed attacks on American merchantmen during the War of 1812, and James Madison began a new war against Algiers in 1815. A formidable American fleet forced not only Algiers, but all the Barbary states, to give up piracy and ransoms against American interests by the end of 1815. This impressive victory signaled America's emergence as an independent commercial power in the broader Atlantic world.[4]

Thirty years of struggle against the Barbary pirates led to renewed popularity for captivity narratives, further refining American images of ostensibly typical North African Muslims. One American captive in Algeria, John Foss, kept a journal of his experience that was published in his hometown of Newburyport, Massachusetts, in 1798. Foss's narrative supplied lurid details of the horrific violence committed against Christian slaves in Algeria, and painted Islam as a bloodthirsty religion. The corsairs who boarded Foss's ship were "like a parcel of ravenous wolves" who stripped the Americans of all their belongings and clothes. One "old Turk" offered Foss a shirt to cover himself, but Foss thought that "this was the only Mahometan I ever met with, in whom I had the least reason to suppose the smallest spark of humanity was kindled." The pirates' captain told the captives they must be treated as slaves because of their "bigotry and superstition, in believing in a man who was crucified by the Jews, and disregarding the true doctrine of God's last and greatest prophet, Mahomet."[5]

Foss emphasized the Muslims' brutal treatment of Christian slaves, explaining at length the excruciating means of torture and execution their tormentors used. He noted that a Christian slave found in the company of a Muslim woman would be beheaded, while the woman would be tied into a sack with heavy rocks and thrown into the sea. Similarly, for speaking ill of the "Mahometan Religion," a slave would be burnt or impaled. These and many other horrors revealed the desperate situation of those slaves "persecuted by the hands of merciless Mahometans." Their demoralizing confinement stood in sharp contrast to the liberty these whites would enjoy in America.[6]

One can make the case that the conflict between the Barbary pirates and the United States did not originate in religious differences, and American diplomats had reasons not to emphasize the religious factor in these wars. In a 1797 treaty with Tripoli, in fact, the United States specifically pronounced that it was not a Christian nation, so that religion would not present a barrier in American–North African relations. On a popular level, however, many Americans seem to have viewed the contest with the North Africans as a spiritual battle. Foss and other interpreters certainly saw the clash that way. The Christian slaves were subjected to religiously inspired persecution and told that they would be treated viciously because, as Christians, they deserved no better. The North Africans acted as they did because they were "genuine children of Ishmael," given to violence against God's chosen people. A poem published with Foss's narrative, "The Algerine Slaves," wondered

> Ye sons of Ishmael, how long shall ye remain
> The scourge of Christians, robbers of the main?
> How long, ye vile, ye worse than savage crew,
> Must all the world bow down and stoop to you?

Strikingly, the poet called not just on the Christian God, but on *America's* God to destroy this Muslim threat:

> Columbia's God! unsheath thy glitt'ring sword,
> Ride on and conquer—speak, O speak the word...
> Send quick destruction on this cursed land,
> This more than vile, this worse than murd'rous band.

To supply even more background on the North Africans' faith, James Wilson Stevens's *An Historical and Geographical Account of Algiers* (1800) included an extended biographical account of Muhammad, who, as usual, was "styled the Impostor" and who made "his disciples swallow whatever he pleased to impose on them." Between the leaders of the North African states and American politicians, the conflict revolved around money and America's weak national defense. But in American popular imagery, the contest seemed equally to involve religion. In American Christian views of Islam, images have often supplanted secular realities as the shapers of opinion.[7]

Most captivity narratives did not touch on the subject of western Christians converting to Islam, despite the apparent regularity of such conversions in the seventeenth and eighteenth centuries. However, the *Narrative of the Captivity of Joseph Pitts* (1815) recorded how Pitts, an Englishman, did convert to Islam after being subjected to repeated torture sessions by his master. All Pitts had to do to stop his torment was to raise his finger and proclaim "There is but one God, and Mahomet is the prophet of God," but because he was a modestly serious Christian, he resisted. Finally, he made his confession of Muhammad as prophet, and was given more favorable treatment by his captors. Pitts gave a very detailed description of prayers in a mosque, and of his participation in the *hajj*, or the pilgrimage to the sacred shrine at Mecca. He promptly renounced his pragmatic commitment to Islam upon his liberation from Algiers.[8]

Very popular, and sometimes fictional, narratives of female captives in North Africa further contrasted western Christian civilization with North African Muslim barbarism. The most popular, Maria Martin's *History of the Captivity and Sufferings of Mrs. Maria Martin*, appeared in twelve widely differing editions (suggesting their fictional nature) between 1807 and 1818, including versions in such far-flung locales as Rutland, Vermont, and St. Clairsville, Ohio. In the first edition, the shipwrecked Martin was enslaved in Algeria and forced to witness the most brutal punishments of slaves imaginable. She marveled at how white slaves were forced to quarry rocks with "large collars about their necks, made much after the form of those worn by the West-India slaves." By contrast, the Moors of the city, "of a tawny complexion, of a lazy, idle disposition," lorded over the Christians. "They style themselves musselmen, or true believers, yet their word is not to be relied on. They abominate the christians. . .and are continually seeking means to destroy them." Martin noted that the Prophet Muhammad had assured Muslims that all who died fighting Christians would immediately enter paradise.[9]

In the city of Ténès, Martin was given to a particularly sadistic governess, who once killed a girl "by strewing her naked body with hot rice." Later, she witnessed a captured runaway being butchered by a nightmarish execution machine, so that afterward "there appeared nothing of him but a mass of goared flesh cut into a thousand pieces." Hints of illicit sexuality ran throughout the narrative, so that it was not surprising when Martin's master urged her to become his concubine. She refused his advances, which earned her months of solitary confinement in heavy chains and near-starvation conditions. As she despaired for her life, she confessed that "God the Creator was the disposer of my fate," and believed that he would give her strength to withstand her captivity. Seemingly having passed her test of spirit, she was almost immediately freed by the British consul.[10]

Eliza Bradley, in the likely fictional account, *An Authentic Narrative of the Shipwreck and Sufferings* (1820), used her story of captivity for more explicitly devotional purposes (see Figure 2-1). Reminiscent of Mary Rowlandson's famous Indian captivity narrative *The Sovereignty and Goodness of God*, Bradley's (or the unnamed author's) book filtered all her experiences

The Arabs conveying Mrs. Bradley into Captivity

FIGURE 2-1. Frontispiece, Eliza Bradley's *An authentic narrative of the shipwreck and sufferings of Mrs. Eliza Bradley* (Boston, 1823). Beinecke Rare Book and Manuscript Library, Yale University.

through Scripture, which she was providentially allowed to read during her enslavement. The account was intended to provide "convincing proof of the omnipresence of the Allseeing Eye" of God. Shipwrecked on Morocco's coast, Bradley, her husband (the captain), and the crew were captured by Arab Muslims. She described her new master as "savage and frightful. . . about six feet in height, of a tawny complexion. . .his hair was stout and bushy, and stuck up in every direction like brustles upon the back of a hog; his eyes were small but were red and fiery, resembling those of a serpent when irritated; and to add to his horrid appearance, his beard (which was of a jet black and curly) was of more than a foot in length!" He was, in short, a "monster, in human shape." This portrayal recalled older racial descriptions of American Indians, whose skin was "tawny" and whose hair was black, too.[11]

Bradley noticed the Arab men's devotion to Allah, as every morning when they assembled, they "strip themselves nearly naked, and then with dry sand rub every part of their bodies, after which, bending their bodies nearly to the ground, they cry aloud 'Allah Hookiber'—'Allah Sheda Mahomed!'" She was hardly impressed with their prayers. "What a pity it is that they are not taught the superior excellence of the Christian religion, and to worship the blessed Jesus, instead of the impure and idolatrous worship of objects prescribed by Mahomet—weep, O my soul, over the forlorne state of the benighted heathen!" She prayed that missionaries might come and deliver this "race of idolaters, on whom no light of revelation beams." To Bradley, the Arabs' spiritual destitution seemed both religious and racial in origin.[12]

Unlike Bradley's and other treatments, some newer captivity narratives focused less on the religious and moral failings of the Islamic captors and more on the political and social lessons to be learned from Barbary slavery. These captivity narratives, and the burgeoning popular literature based on slavery in North Africa, sometimes assisted the early American abolitionist movement. Susannah Rowson's play *Slaves in Algiers* (1794), for instance, featured an Algerian master, converted to democratic principles by his American slaves' bravery, who decided to end slavery in Algiers.[13]

The anonymous poem *The American in Algiers* (1797) juxtaposed the enslavement of a Revolutionary War veteran in Algiers with the enslavement of a West African man in America. After the war, the veteran was captured on a merchant ship and transported to Algiers, where he was presented to the "Dey,"

> A wretch austere! whose haughty looks, denote
> A soul more savage than the forest brute.

The Dey told the sailor that

> My God commanded, and Mahomet gave
> Full leave to make each infidel a slave;
> But if you'll turn Mahometan at once...
> My princely favor shall to you extend,
> And break the chains that o'er your limbs impend.

Here the Muslim Dey of Algiers was presented as a savage slave master, and the poem called for the United States to exact harsh retribution against the Barbary pirates, and to free the American captives. In the poem's second canto, however, a "sable bard" sought to "trump the inconsistency of those Feign'd friends to liberty, feign'd slavery's foes." How could white Americans express outrage at their own sons' enslavement in the Barbary states, when they enslaved Africa's sons and daughters in their own land? The United States' "Vile Christians perpetrate [murders] to serve their God," the poet raged. In a country devoted to the proposition that "all men are created equal," "Afric's sons continue slaves." In this poem, African Muslims were used as a brutish mirror image to shame Americans for their own sin of slave owning.[14]

Royall Tyler's *The Algerine Captive* (1797) was the most popular of the anti-slavery novels based on Barbary captivity, and it posited that the Algerian masters were no worse than those in the American South. If anything, they were probably more benevolent, despite being Muslims. Tyler's narrator Updike Underhill visited a southern church before his captivity and noted with bewilderment how the pastor beat and cursed his slave just before mounting the pulpit to preach on the text "I said I will take heed unto my ways, that I sin not with my tongue."[15] After he was taken captive, Underhill confronted a very bright and rational "mollah," who insisted that his faith "disdained the use of other powers than rational argument," and that he would not use the tactics of Rome—namely torture—to convert him. The mullah proceeded to bring into serious question the divine inspiration of the Bible, the peaceful nature of Christianity, and the clear distinction between the two religions. Underhill was befuddled, writing that "after five days' conversation, disgusted with his fables, abashed by his assurance, and almost confounded by his sophistry, I resumed my slave's attire, and sought safety in my former servitude."[16] Despite Tyler's later protests to the contrary, he used Islam to undermine Christianity's divine sanction. This was a far cry theologically from the typical American usage of Islam, but Tyler still meant primarily to contribute to intra-Protestant debates.[17]

Protestants also continued to use Islam as a way to associate theological opponents with imposture and infidelity. Antebellum American polemicists routinely associated Mormonism with Islam, for example. An 1851 *American Whig Review* article, "The Yankee Mahomet," commented that Mormonism "bears considerable resemblance" to Islam, in that both endorsed "arbitrary power" and "forcible dissemination." Observers often classed Mormonism's founder Joseph Smith and the Prophet Muhammad as deceitful, violent demagogues, and pointed to their successful leadership as evidence of the dangers of religious deception. The Mormon-Muslim association persisted well into the twentieth century. Literary critic George Seibel wrote in *The Mormon Saints* (1919) that both religions claimed to supplant Christianity and filled "the flesh-pots of the faithful." Seibel saw Smith as even worse than Muhammad, with the former being a "cunning impostor" and the latter a "sincere fanatic." Early Mormons rejected comparisons of their faith to Islam, but accepted the dominant anti-Islamic thought of American Protestants as a way to promote the legitimacy of their own religion.[18]

The traditional Protestant eschatological approach to Islam hardly vanished in America's early national years, either. Yale College President Timothy Dwight, a contemporary of Royall Tyler, anticipated the impending destruction of Islam. As he observed the dismaying anti-Christian reverberations of the French Revolution, he still held out hope for Christianity's fate in America and in the world. "How strongly do the events of the present day shew this awful advent of the King of Kings to be at the doors?" Some Jews on the Continent looked ready to convert to Christianity, new missions had targeted "heathens" for conversion, and African slavery seemed threatened. As for Islam and its states, Dwight made the absurd claim that "Muhammadism is nearly extinct in Persia, one of the chief supporters of that imposture." He also anticipated the near approach of the Ottoman Empire's fall. Dwight believed that the Catholic powers were under severe attack as well, making him think that "the advent of Christ is at least at our doors."[19]

In the 1780s and '90s, a number of Anglo-American writers spurred a renewed interest in the imminent eschatological downfall of the Roman Catholic church and the Islamic powers, especially Turkey. These prophecy writers conventionally used a "historicist" model of eschatological interpretation, which saw much of the prophecy in the books of Daniel and Revelation as already fulfilled in history, with some yet remaining to happen, and perhaps quite quickly. Historicist schemes (as opposed to later dispensational "futurist" eschatology) made a clear place for the emergence of Islam. Historicists routinely viewed the "smoke locusts" of Revelation 9:2–3 as a description of the rise of Islam. Similarly, one of the most anticipated events among historicist exegetes was the drying up of the Euphrates River referenced in Revelation 16:12, which many eighteenth- and nineteenth-century writers associated with the ruin of the Turkish Empire.[20]

The new eschatological fascination with Islam and the Roman Catholic church was no doubt spurred by unsettling events such as the French Revolution and ongoing Barbary piracy. Charles Crawford, a poet from the West Indies living in Philadelphia, argued that the destruction of Catholicism would be followed quickly by the collapse of the Ottomans, the conversion of the Jews, and the return of Christ. Referencing Daniel 11:36–45, Crawford asserted that "upon the downfall of Antichrist the Turkish empire will be annihilated, which abominable empire Daniel describes." Crawford identified Daniel 11's kingdom as the Turkish Empire because of geographic clues like "he shall have power. . .over all the precious things of Egypt." Also, he suggested that the phrase "neither shall he regard. . .the desire of women" spoke to rampant homosexuality among the Turks, as Crawford believed that the elite Turks often had a "seraglio of boys as well as women." He also thought that the "smoke locusts" of Revelation 9 referred to the Turks, and that Revelation 9:6's phrase "in those days shall men seek death, and shall not find it" might prophesy "the unhappiness of those who have been made captives by the Mahometans, which unhappiness has arisen from the unbridled or unnatural lust of the captors." Crawford attributed the widespread occurrence of the plague among the Turks to "sodomy" as well. The Turks represented one of the two great eschatological enemies of God, evidenced in part by their supposed homosexual practices.[21]

Many other students of prophecy concurred with the argument that the "smoke locusts" represented Muhammad's armies and/or the Turks. Congregational pastor and former Harvard president Samuel Langdon wrote that Revelation 9:1–12 described "the appearance of Mahomet, and the great armies of the Saracens. . .This impostor made his appearance suddenly, coming out of a cave, in all the darkness of a new invented, confused, false religion, and with all the rage of enthusiastic frenzy." Like many later Christian polemicists, Langdon believed that Muhammad had received his revelations straight from the devil. Islam spread quickly over Arabia, "like a black cloud of smoke belched out from the infernal pit; and the armies of the false apostle, like innumerable locusts thrown up in the darkness of his religion, subdued the countries all around." Prophecy writer Benjamin Farnham concurred, claiming that the locusts "distil the venom of a false religion which was calculated to suit the vicious passions of mankind."[22]

Eliphaz Chapman, minister on America's northern frontier at Bethel, Maine, also paired Islam and Catholicism as the eastern and western Antichrists in *A Discourse on the Prophecies* (1797). He accepted Humphrey Prideaux's idea that the papacy and Muhammad had risen to power simultaneously, suggesting their future simultaneous fall. He added a novel twist by seeing the rise of Islam also described in Daniel 11:40–45. In that passage, the "king of the south" represented the "Saracens" (Arabs), while the "king of the north" represented the Turks. The passage predicted the Islamic nations' conquest of large parts of North Africa and the Middle East. "Daniel's prophecy relative to the rise of the eastern Antichrist, hath already been fulfilled," Chapman wrote. While accepting the conventional interpretation of the smoke locusts, Chapman also believed that the prophecy of smoke darkening the sun in Revelation 9:2 had literally been fulfilled by a long-lasting eclipse recorded in the year 626, just as Muhammad was gaining power. He believed that the Catholic church and the Turkish Empire would both be destroyed around the year 2000. Political Islam would be ruined by "the conversion and restoration of the Jews, an invasion of the northern nations upon his dominions, and civil wars among the subjects of that empire."[23]

Connecticut physician Benjamin Gale concurred with other writers' readings of the smoke locusts, and also associated the Muslim nations with "Gog and Magog" of Ezekiel 37–38. "The Persians, Turks, and all other nations who have imbibed that imposture, as they are one part of mystical Babylon, will meet with a compleat and finished destruction on the mountains of Israel," Gale asserted. He believed that the Muslim nations and the Roman Catholic church would meet instantaneous ruin at the sounding of the seventh trumpet and pouring out of the seventh vial. He similarly thought that the "false prophet" of Revelation 19:20 represented "Mahomet and his imposture," and that the end of the Ottoman Empire would be followed by the return of the Jews to the land of Palestine.[24]

Congregational minister Thomas Wells Bray also paired Muslims and Catholics as the "two grand deceivers of mankind, and implacable enemies of Christ." He, too, saw Revelation 9 as describing the "rise and progress of the Mahomitan impostor, in the Arabian locusts." He disputed earlier interpretations, however, that had read the sixth vial of Revelation 16, "the drying up of mystical Euphrates," only as the downfall of the Turks. Other observers, such as Jonathan Edwards, had seen the sixth vial as representing the exhaustion of the "temporal supplies, wealth, revenues and incomes" of the Roman Catholic church, but Bray took a broader view, suggesting it anticipated the eradication of "civil and ecclesiastical tyranny," generally. Nevertheless, the drying up of the Euphrates would include the "overthrow of the Turkish empire," which would help clear the way for the mass conversion of the Jews. Following Prideaux's *True Nature of Imposture*, Bray posited that the Papal and Islamic impostures both commenced around the same time, roughly the year 606, and "so will they end nearly together." He argued that Daniel 11:36 showed that both would be destroyed "when the indignation against God's antient people [the Jews] shall be accomplished." Observers like Chapman, Bray, and others paired Catholicism and Islam as the pillars of political and religious tyranny in the West and East.[25]

Some American prophecy writers did not see a reference to Islam or the Turks in the pouring out of Revelation's sixth vial, however. Like Jonathan Edwards, pastor David Austin of Elizabethtown, New Jersey, believed that the sixth vial indicated the "drying up of the fountains and streams of the wealth and temporal incomes and supplies of the antichristian church and territories." Timothy Dwight believed that the "symbolical Euphrates" represented a "source of wealth, strength, and safety" to the "Romish spiritual Empire." Others maintained that the sixth vial did refer to the Turks, despite such arguments. Pastor Timothy Allen of Connecticut wrote in 1762 (at the end of the Seven Years' War, a time of great anti-Catholic eschatological expectation) that he was "not convinced that 6th vial means popish Revenues—cant see but Turk is meant—& must be broken before Jews the Kings of the East can come—but as soon as their 2 stumbling Blocks viz. popery & Turkish Power are removed that will come in suddenly." Even

David Austin expected that the "full enlightening and conversion of all Ma-hometan and heathen nations" would occur before the return of Christ.[26]

Some commentators also read Muslims into the prophet Daniel 8's image of a he-goat's little horn, and attempted to calculate the return of Christ from the predicted time of Islam's dissolution. This vision in Daniel 8:8–9 describes how a male goat's broken horn produced four new horns, and out of one horn grew "a little horn, which waxed exceeding great, toward the south, and toward the east, and toward the pleasant land." Popular British prophecy writer George Stanley Faber, whose *Dissertation on the Prophecies* was published in Boston and New York, saw Islam represented in that little horn. He paired this little horn with another little horn mentioned in Daniel 7:8, which he saw as representing the Roman Catholic church. He predicted that Islam and Roman Catholicism would "reign precisely 1260 years." Here he used the conventional formula that read Daniel 7:25 ("a time and times and the dividing of time") as 1260 prophetic days, meaning years. "Both these apostacies commenced in the same year [606]," so "they are both likewise to begin to be overthrown in the same year," probably 1866. That would set the stage for the conversion of the Jews to Christianity, the rise of an atheistic Antichrist, and the battle of Armageddon.[27]

Faber believed that the prophecy of the little horn waxing great toward the south, east, and north (toward the "pleasant land," or Israel) had been fulfilled by the spread of Islam. "Its conquests extended southward over the peninsula of Arabia; eastward, over Persia and in after ages over Hindostan; and northward, over Palestine, Asia Minor, and Greece." Its expansion west-ward had been rejected in Spain, and Faber thought the Barbary states too insignificant to be mentioned alongside the other Muslim powers. Faber concurred with other commentators who saw the smoke locusts as the rise of Islam, and the drying up of the Euphrates as the ruin of the Turkish Em-pire, which he believed was imminent.[28]

Citing Faber, Ethan Smith of Hopkinton, New Hampshire, argued that "Muhammadism has been predicted, under the emblem of the little horn of the he-goat." Similarly, Elijah Parish of Byfield, Massachusetts, followed Faber in seeing the goat's little horn as "a symbol of the Muhammadan im-posture." Parish believed that interpreters could calculate the coming of the millennium from the rise of Muhammad and the papacy in 606. In that year, according to Parish, "the tyrant Phocas made a grant of supremacy to Pope Boniface." Simultaneously (borrowing language directly from Faber), "the crafty impostor Mahomet retired to the cave of Mount Hara to consult the angel of fraud and enthusiasm, to fabricate that delusion, which to this day darkens the oriental nations." If one added 606 to the prophetic 1260 years of Daniel 7:25, then "may we not infer. . .that in three score years [1866] the glorious reign of Jesus Christ will cover the earth?" Parish asked. In the early nineteenth century, many Anglo-American Christians speculated that the millennium might begin in 1866. Parish addressed his forecasts to the Massachusetts Missionary Society, and believed that the approach of the last times should inspire vigorous new missionary efforts. Jedidiah Morse, pastor at Charlestown, Massachusetts, speaking before the Society for Propagating the Gospel among the Indians and Others in 1810, also believed that Islam and Roman Catholicism would be destroyed almost simultaneously, and soon. The beginning of the missionary movement heralded the beginning of the end for the "eastern and western antichrists." Their overthrow was "probably near at hand, even at the door," according to Morse.[29]

Although George Faber's text exerted great influence in early nineteenth-century British and American eschatological thought, at least one American observer felt Faber had gotten most of his predictions wrong. Enoch Shepard, a deacon in Marietta, Ohio's First Presbyterian Church, suspected that Faber's Anglican faith led him to downplay the Roman Catholic church's role in the last days. By denying that the Roman church was Antichrist, Faber was "palliating and excusing many of the blasphemous abominations of the apostate Church, the Man of sin." Because a single-minded anti-Catholicism drove his eschatology, Shepard may have given Islam the most limited role of any prophetic writer in the period. Like others, Shepard saw the drying up of the Euphrates as fulfilled in the French Revolutionaries' attacks on the church. Most distinctively, he denied that the smoke locusts of Revelation 9 represented the rise of Islam, seeing it instead as the rise of the papacy. He did concede that the second woe trumpet of Revelation 9:13–21 referred to "Mahomed's desolating, and destructive wars, in connection perhaps with the Turkish conquests." Normally, anti-Catholic and anti-Islamic thought coexisted in these eschatological systems, but anti-Catholicism seemed to push Islam to the margins of Shepard's last days scenario.[30]

Popular American historicist millenarianism culminated in the pre-Civil War era with the predictions of the farmer and Baptist layman William Miller (see Figure 2-2). Miller is most famous for his mistaken predictions of Christ's return in 1843 and 1844. He and his followers also commented extensively on the place of Islam and Muslim countries in the last days. Although Miller took unique risks by giving dates for Christ's second advent, the Millerites' views of Islam simply followed the swelling eschatological

FIGURE 2-2. William Miller, from Joshua Himes's *Views of the Prophecies* (Boston, 1842). Widener Library, Harvard College Library.

interest in Muslims that began in the late eighteenth century. Miller took exception, however, to some of the conventional readings of prophetic Scripture that supposedly foretold the rise of Islam.[31]

Pastor Josiah Litch, who became a Millerite in 1838, advanced one of the boldest predictions aside from Miller's own when he asserted in 1838 that the fall of the Turkish Empire, as forecast by the sounding of the sixth trumpet in Revelation 9:13, would occur sometime in August 1840. Litch adopted the conventional reading of Revelation 9's smoke locusts as the rise of political Islam, commenting that this passage's meaning was "so obvious that it can scarcely be misunderstood." Following an obscure calculation based on Revelation 9:15 (which he later repudiated), Litch concluded that the Ottoman Empire would be overthrown sometime during August 1840. "The prophecy is the most remarkable and definite, (even descending to the days) of any in the Bible," he wrote. When the month passed, Litch discovered that a diplomatic ultimatum from the major European powers, suggesting war if rejected, had been delivered to the Turkish Sultan on August 11, 1840. Litch took this as irrefutable confirmation of the prophecy's fulfillment: "According to previous calculation, therefore, Ottoman Supremacy did depart on the ELEVENTH OF AUGUST into the hands of the great Christian powers of Europe." As was typical of such readings of prophecy, just about any news item relevant to the Turks could seem portentous.[32]

Miller accepted Litch's interpretation of the sixth trumpet, and believed that the destruction of the Turks would signal the "closing of the door of mercy." Although Miller tended to place the devastation of the Roman Catholic church at the center of biblical prophecy, he nevertheless followed earlier observers who read the sixth vial as the destruction of the Turks, and the smoke locusts of Revelation 9 as the rise of Muhammad. The drying up of the Euphrates, according to Miller, referred to the "power and strength of [the Turkish] kingdom being diminished, or taken away." He saw plenty of evidence in recent news to suggest that the sixth vial had started to pour out on the Turks, indicated by the beginning of the Greek war for independence (1821), followed by the Russo-Turkish War (1828–29). He also associated the "false prophet" of Revelation 16:13 with Islam. The false prophet would "fill his party with notions of infidelity, lust, and conquest," and would make war against the people of God in concert with the Papacy (the beast) and the "kings of the earth" (the dragon). But all these powers would ultimately be vanquished at the battle of Armageddon.[33]

Miller did not accept the common interpretation of Daniel's little horn as Islam. He saw this little horn as the Roman Empire, and castigated Ethan Smith and other writers for identifying the little horn as Islam "without any intimation from God, the angel, or Daniel." He believed that all the descriptions of the little horn suggested it existed before the time of Christ. Smith had also anticipated the pouring out of the sixth vial and the overthrow of the Turks by 1844, if not earlier, but Smith did not expect the millennium to begin until around the year 2000. Miller commended Smith for his correct timing on the sixth vial, but he believed that the disintegration of Islam would be accompanied by the downfall of the papacy and the return of Christ, all in 1843.[34]

Many prominent evangelical leaders cringed at Miller's date-setting, but many otherwise did not take a substantially different approach to eschatology. For instance, leading New School Presbyterian George Duffield, Jr., of Detroit scolded Miller in 1842 for his "confidence and boldness of assertion, not sustained by sufficient proof," in claiming that Christ would return in 1843. Nevertheless, Duffield argued that "somewhere from 1843 to 1847, will be marked by very clear and decided movements in God's providence...and prove that we are advanced one stage nearer to the time of the end." One sign of the approaching end, according to Duffield, was the "rapid progress of dissolution which is now going on in the Turkish empire," which heralded the symbolic drying up of the Euphrates. Furniture merchant and prophecy author George B. Stacy of Richmond, Virginia, noted in 1860 that "we are now living under the Sixth Vial," because the "peculiarities of Muhammadanism are disappearing, one after another." Prophecy writer Pleasant E. Royse maintained in 1864 that the Euphrates of Revelation 16 represented the "great Muhammadan empire of Asia," but much different from Miller, Duffield, and Stacy, he did not expect its overthrow to happen until a far-distant period between A.D. 2580 and 2760.[35]

The embarrassment associated with the Millerites' failed predictions destabilized the previous dominance of historicist eschatology in conservative American Protestant circles. Many, though not all, of the historicist prophecy writers had also believed in a postmillennial advent of Christ, meaning that Christ would only return to earth after a thousand-year reign of peace, inaugurated by strenuous Christian efforts at reform and evangelism. Postmillennialism allowed for the combination of an optimistic view of human progress and a literal interpretation of the judgment of God in the end of days. Although postmillennialism remained dominant among conservatives through the end of the nineteenth century, the Millerite trouble damaged historicism's reputation and helped open the door for a new mode of conservative Protestant eschatology—the futurist schemes of premillennial dispensationalism. This system of theology, promoted in its earliest forms by British theologian John Nelson Darby, held that most of the last days prophecies in the Bible remained to be fulfilled. This meant that dispensationalists interpreted passages like Revelation 9:2–3 and Revelation 16:12 as descriptions of the Great Tribulation, that period of antichristian rule shortly preceding the return of Christ. The "smoke locusts" of Revelation 9 were read, not as the rise of Islam, but as a sign of "unprecedented activity of demons" during the Antichrist's reign, according to C. I. Scofield's reference Bible, the most popular text on dispensational theology in America. (Much later, Salem Kirban's sensational dispensationalist novel *666* (1970) took a more literal reading of the smoke locusts: he speculated that they represented an antichristian army of flying men with "jet belts.") Scofield believed that almost everything in Revelation chapters 4 to 22 was to occur in the future, after the mysterious rapture of true Christians by Christ.[36]

Among the most anticipated events of the last days for both historicists and futurists was the physical restoration of the Jews to Palestine, a belief that became common among British millenarians by the 1820s. The Anglican prophecy writer Edward Bickersteth, a well-known author in both Britain and America, lamented in 1841 that Jerusalem's Temple Mount was the site of a "Mahometan mosque," while Mount Calvary bore Catholic churches poisoned by the "superstition of Popery." Thus, "the two feet of Antichrist. . .tread down Jerusalem," but Bickersteth foresaw a better day when the Jews would return to Jerusalem. The concept of literal restoration of the Jews also became popular in America, as evidenced in 1844 when the theologian and Hebraist George Bush of New York University (a distant relative of the Bush presidential family) promoted the idea in his book *The Valley of Vision*. Bush noted that Christians had no special role to play in the return of the Jews to Israel, "except so far as governmental action may be requisite in removing the political obstacles that stand in the way." For many American Christians, these "obstacles" meant Turkish or Arab Muslims.[37]

For dispensationalists, political Islam's role in the last days became resigned to the neighboring Arab and Muslim states' supposedly inevitable opposition to the restored nation of Israel. Nevertheless, some premillennialists (those, including dispensationalists, who believed Christ's return would precede the promised millennium) maintained certain historicist distinctives. The popular evangelical minister A. J. Gordon still assumed in 1889 that the "smoke locusts" referred to the rise of Islam. Historicist premillennialism persisted into the late nineteenth and early twentieth centuries, especially among popular evangelical writers from the British Isles like Grattan Guinness (of the Guinness brewing family of Ireland). In his *Approaching End of the Age* (1878), which appeared in multiple editions in England and America, Guinness explicated recent historical evidence that the pouring out of the sixth vial of wrath, the drying up of the Euphrates, was being fulfilled historically in the decline of political Islam. The weakness of the Ottoman Empire, especially in Palestine, signaled to Guinness that Christ's return was near. But the English dispensationalist and Plymouth Brethren writer T. B. Baines saw Revelation 9 as having a "secondary" fulfillment in the rise of Islam, but believed that the "main application" of the smoke locusts was "something quite different, and still future," when "direct demoniacal power" would be "let loose." He also chided historicists for discerning the meaning of apocalyptic passages in "minute antiquarian research."[38]

While the Millerites were nearly unique in specifically forecasting the return of Christ to come at a date that was close enough to be verified, their eschatological views of Islam were fairly common, reflecting a long discussion reaching back to the Revolutionary period and earlier. From the Revolution to the 1840s, a remarkable burst of prophetic writings filled American presses, as eschatological speculations became more widely acceptable than ever before in American society.[39] Much of that prophetic writing paired fears of Roman Catholic and Islamic power, and anticipated the destruction of both. By the 1840s, the belief that Islam would play a central role in the events of the last days had become even more widespread among American Christians. Although the details of the scenarios would change, conservative Christians have remained fascinated with how Muslims fit into eschatological theology. American anger over the Barbary wars probably helped move Islam even closer to the center of eschatological thought in the early republic. That anger also made Christian slavery under Islamic power a useful trope in the growing antislavery debates. One can see, then, that views of Islam in the early American republic continued serving theological and political agendas, carrying assurances that Christianity would eventually triumph over any Muslim threat. The early nineteenth century would also see the first American missionaries carrying that hope of ultimate victory into Muslim lands, with dreams that the missionaries' appearance would lead to the downfall of Muslim power and the correlated conversion of the Jews. American missionary societies, often emboldened by eschatological confidence, found that their expectations of quickly ushering in the end of days did not easily conform with the enormous difficulties of evangelizing Muslims and Jews in the Middle East.

CHAPTER 3

Foreign Missions to Muslims in
Nineteenth-Century America

On October 31, 1819, aspiring missionary Pliny Fisk stood in the pulpit of the Old South Church in Boston and preached on Acts 20:22: "And now, behold, I go bound in the Spirit unto Jerusalem, not knowing the things that shall befall me there." The American Board of Commissioners for Foreign Missions (ABCFM) believed that the population of the Middle East—Jews, Muslims, and nominal Christians—was "in a state of deplorable ignorance and degradation," and "destitute of the means of divine knowledge, and bewildered with vain imaginations and strong delusions." Thus, the ABCFM commissioned Fisk and his colleague Levi Parsons to take the gospel to Palestine. Fisk told his audience that the "Mahommedans, who are masters of the country...are, as you well know, the followers of that artful impostor, who arose in Arabia." For American Christians "to make spiritual conquests from them" would require unprecedented effort. If the Christian gospel succeeded among the Middle Eastern Muslims, "some of the strongest fortresses of error and sin will be taken," Fisk proclaimed.[1]

Fisk and Parsons represented the vanguard of a new American missionary movement that flourished in the 1810s, highlighted by the founding of the ABCFM in 1810. Driven by New England evangelicals, heirs of Jonathan Edwards who were inspired by the fervor of the Second Great Awakening, the ABCFM began to contemplate a new American Christian role in evangelizing the non-Christian world. British evangelicals associated with the Church Missionary Society and other organizations had already begun to go on mission to the "heathens." Following their British colleagues' suggestion, the first five ABCFM missionaries departed for India in 1812. Widely held eschatological views fueled the missionary impulse, as organizers believed that missions could hasten the destruction of the Roman Catholic church and Islam, the conversion of the Jews, and the beginning of the millennium. As an ABCFM fundraising appeal put it, "Prophesy, history, and the present state of the world seem to unite in declaring that the great pillars of the Papal and Mahometan impostures are now tottering to their fall. . .

Now is the time for the followers of Christ to come forward boldly and engage earnestly in the great work of enlightening and reforming mankind." Before his departure for Palestine, Levi Parsons told an audience at Park Street Church in Boston that he did not expect "the conversion of the Jews by a miracle" but "with the word of God, and with the instruction of Missionaries." The military destruction and/or evangelization of Middle Eastern Muslims might prove a key to the ingathering of the Jews to their ancestral homeland, as well. "Destroy, then, the Ottoman Empire," Parsons said, "and nothing but a miracle would prevent [the Jews'] immediate return" to Palestine.[2]

The proposed evangelization of Muslims was integrally connected to the future conversion of the Jews. American Christian observers never seemed quite clear whether prophecy indicated that the destruction of Islam, or the mass conversion of Muslims to Christianity, would transpire before the establishment of the Kingdom of God. American missionaries to the Middle East assumed, however, that all people, regardless of race or religion, stood in need of forgiveness through Christ, so they targeted Muslims for evangelization. Or at least they said they did. Significant barriers stood in the way of reaching Muslims, beyond simple cultural and philosophical obstacles. Ottoman law prohibited Christian missionaries from proselytizing among Middle Eastern Muslims. Therefore, American missionaries in the Middle East usually worked first among Orthodox Christians, who were a legal object of evangelism, and who the missionaries assumed were not actually converted, but only nominally religious. The ABCFM turned the evangelization of Orthodox Christians into an ostensible foundation for eventually converting Muslims. Rufus Anderson, the secretary and historian of the ABCFM, held that Turkish Muslims would not convert "unless true Christianity can be exemplified before them by the Oriental Churches."[3]

Because of the Ottomans' strictures against proselytizing Muslims, and because of the limited resources of the ABCFM (despite its being the largest American missions organization before the Civil War), the actual evangelization of Muslims seemed at times almost totally neglected by American missionaries in the Middle East. Most attention fell on "native Christians [who] have so far departed from the truth that they do not feel the power of the Gospel," as Anderson put it. If the American missionaries could revive the eastern churches, then the "followers of Mohammed would look on with wonder," and although they might respond with hostility at first, they soon would realize the superiority of Christianity. This plan represented an "indispensable means of Christianizing the Moslems of Turkey and Persia."[4]

Anderson no doubt sincerely believed in this strategy, and it is hard to imagine how American missionaries could have publicly proselytized among the Turks given the legal restrictions on evangelism. Nevertheless, this policy meant that for a century or more, the distance between the image and reality of missions to Muslims was vast. Although eschatology and popular literature implied that great evangelistic progress among Muslims must be at hand, American Christians won only tiny numbers of converts from Islam during the nineteenth century. The eschatology buttressing the early missions efforts seems to have bred unrealistic expectations that evangelism in the Middle East would be relatively easy. Forcing Muslims into prophetic categories may also have created a kind of conceptual dissonance between Muslims as essentialized players in the drama of the last days, and as individual persons representing a substantially different and challenging faith. The missionaries also struggled with unstable political situations, and fell prey to illness and disease. By 1825, both Parsons and Fisk had died on the mission field. An undergraduate at Middlebury College wrote an elegy upon Parsons's death, wondering "Who now like him shall toil for Judah's race? And who like him destroy Mohammed's sway?" The difficulties of nineteenth-century missions did not cool expectations on the home front that the Americans' ministry in the Middle East could ultimately devastate Muslim power there.[5]

New American missionaries tried to set up a permanent base in Beirut, but in 1827 they had to flee to Malta. The ABCFM and their friends in New England became consumed in the 1820s with converting Greeks to authentic Christianity, seeing in the Greeks' revolt against the Ottoman Empire (which began in 1821) a new opportunity to damage the political might of Islam. Boston's Sereno Edwards Dwight (Jonathan Edwards's great-grandson) predicted that the successful Greek independence movement, along with the evangelization of the Greeks, would lead to the downfall of the Turks. Then, "missionaries loaded with bibles will feel their way into the farthest retreats of Mohammedan darkness." Although the ABCFM reopened the Beirut mission in 1830, and pioneered new works at Constantinople in 1831 and Smyrna in 1833, focus remained on evangelizing eastern Christians, not Muslims or Jews. The ABCFM could be quite frank regarding their short-term neglect of missions to Middle Eastern Muslims. In 1836, the agency called such missions "premature" because of Ottoman opposition to them.[6]

The missionaries in Turkey still watched Muslim and Jewish leaders with keen interest, filtering news through their eschatological beliefs. William Goodell, an ABCFM missionary in Constantinople, noted in the April 1841 issue of the *Missionary Herald* that Turkish authorities, both religious and political, had encountered unprecedented turbulence and opposition in recent months. He believed that these troubles revealed that "the golden period of their thousand years is drawing to a perpetual close." The Millerite Josiah Litch cited Goodell's views of Islam as support for his predictions of the Turkish Empire's imminent collapse. The Jews of Constantinople also appeared more interested than ever in scriptural prophecy, according to Goodell. They seemed unconsciously to be preparing for the time "when they can publicly profess the Messiah. . . . Great events seem to be at hand." Despite their relative inattention to Jews and Muslims, the missionaries still held hope for the future significance of their work in those communities.[7]

ABCFM representatives were not the only American missionaries to interpret Middle East missions through eschatological categories. The Disciples of Christ sent physician James Barclay to Jerusalem in 1851, where he hoped not only to reach eastern Christians, but also Muslims and Jews. At the outset, he was enormously optimistic, especially about evangelizing Muslims. He was under the impression that common Muslims actually wanted Protestants to conquer the Ottoman Empire, and were begging for more Christian missionaries. Officials in Constantinople were slowly beginning to tolerate Muslim conversions to Christianity, which to Barclay represented a clear indication of the prophesied drying up of the Euphrates. "The last sands of the prophetic period assigned to the Moslem Desolater," he exulted, "are now running out! The 'Little Horn of the East' shall gore no more!" Despite his awareness of the lack of missionary success among Muslims, he expected that the "swarthy sons of Ishmael" would soon convert in large numbers. Barclay struggled, however, to gain proselytes, and he returned to America within four years.[8]

Other American travelers filtered their impressions of the Muslim world through prophetic categories. Josiah Harlan, an enigmatic Quaker from Pennsylvania who spent fifteen years adventuring in India and Afghanistan, wrote in his memoirs that the destruction of the Turkish Empire was imminent, and that it had been prophesied by Daniel 11:45 ("Yet he shall come to his end, and none shall help him"). Harlan, raising a connection that modern prophetic writers would exploit after the 9/11 attacks, explained that even the Muslims' eschatology forecast the second coming of Christ, who in their view would assist the "Immaum Meihdee" (Imam Mahdi) in defeating the forces of Antichrist and establishing Islam as the true religion. "Mahomedan tradition and Christian faith unite in the belief of" the second coming, Harlan noted. He thought that political turmoil and financial difficulties would soon lead to the collapse of the Ottoman Empire, the restoration of the Jews to Jerusalem, and the battle of Armageddon.[9]

In the context of this kind of eschatological anticipation, the ABCFM also began sending missionaries to Persia in 1833, where much of the focus was on Nestorian Christians. One missionary to Persia, James Merrick, became disgruntled with the lack of attention given to direct evangelization of Muslims. Even before entering seminary at Princeton, the young Merrick dreamed of "a holy crusade to Mahomedan Persia" that would "lay open for easy conquest the whole Mahomedan world." The ABCFM commissioned Merrick to work among the "degenerate oriental churches" of Persia, as well as to assess how the "Mohammedan mind in Persia" might be penetrated. The commissioners particularly recommended that Merrick become familiar with Islam, the Qur'an, and the differences between various Muslim sects. Prior to leaving Constantinople for Persia, Merrick impatiently exclaimed in a letter that "if Christians wait until the adversary [the devil] shall himself open the gates of Mohammedanism, millions of ages will not bring even an approximation to the time of their conversion." Merrick admitted that no open proselytizing could be permitted, but private, personal witnessing promised "abundant labor" for any willing to risk it. He also conceded that some individual Muslims displayed admirable characteristics. Although he considered Islam a fundamentally flawed religion, he saw the Turks of the city of Bursa as "liberal and tolerant." He found that they cordially welcomed Christians into their mosques and engaged them in conversation. This open-mindedness represented a "golden door for the entrance of truth," yet he lamented the lack of any Christian missionaries among Bursa's Muslims.[10]

Merrick expressed mixed views regarding the eventual conversion of Muslims in Turkey and Persia. On one hand, he spoke optimistically of the immediate possibilities of western Christian evangelism. He wrote to Anderson in 1836 that "even among the blinded adherents of Islam a door of hope seems opening with the prospect of better things for future days." In the same letter, however, he expressed the fear that "an awful cloud of curses hangs over this people, which no merciful wind from heaven can wholly dissipate." He speculated that Muslims' persecution of Jews and Christians had brought the wrath of God against them. "Mohammedism" had from its beginnings represented "the most dreadful scourge of the Christian name." Just as it gained power by the sword, so also Merrick thought Islam might collapse through military force. He still hoped that God would "have mercy on the followers of the false Prophet, & save at least a remnant of them." Without the influence of the Holy Spirit, "we must utterly despair of ever seeing a single Moslem turn from the error of his belief," he concluded.[11]

As he continued his work in Persia, Merrick found the Shi'is there considerably less tolerant than the Sunnis of Turkey. He also found their religious devotion quite formidable, and repeatedly warned his sponsors that it would not be easy to convert the Persians. "Perhaps the general impression in Europe and America respecting Mohammedism," he wrote, "is, that it is such a flimsy, frost-work structure, that a few rays of science, a smattering of literature, or a modicum of the arts would annihilate it at once." Such notions were badly misleading, as the Islam he encountered in Persia seemed "a master-piece of skill and power." He also noted that Islam had a venerable tradition of learning, so that education alone could not be expected to crack the religion's defenses. Nevertheless, in 1835 he still believed that "the very foundations of Mohammedism in Persia are evidently crumbling away," and that the "spiritual redemption of the Persians is hastening on." Merrick became quite pessimistic about the expediency of public proselytizing, which undoubtedly would lead to violence against Christian missionaries. Expectations should be kept low, he recommended, and the ABCFM should wait patiently for God to initiate a breakthrough. Merrick eventually settled at Tabriz in northern Persia and began language study for his mission. He worked there for five years, but won no converts, so the ABCFM transferred him to work among the Nestorians, expressing doubts about whether a direct mission to Persian Muslims was advisable.[12]

In 1845, Merrick was recalled from Persia altogether, as the ABCFM had grown frustrated with his focus on private evangelization among Muslims, not Nestorian Christians. For his part, Merrick believed that the eschatological urgency behind the ABCFM's work had made its leaders naive. In 1835, Merrick pointedly told Anderson that American supporters "should be as patient in waiting for the harvest of the world, and for the jubilee which shall crown its ingathering, as those who toil thro' anxious years for this consummation." Merrick's critique of the ABCFM foreshadowed the turning away from apocalyptic views of Islam's near future by many American missionaries in the late nineteenth and early twentieth centuries. The Board had "yet much to learn on the great subject of evangelizing the world," Merrick chided Anderson in 1845. American missionaries had only begun the work of spiritually cultivating Muslim lands. Conversions would take many years, and would not "be speedily consummated by splendid plans and thrilling appeals." The missions were difficult and slow, Merrick acknowledged, but that gave no warrant for the Board to turn "wholly away from the Mohammedans," or especially the Persians, whom Merrick regarded as "the most hopeful class." Merrick feuded publicly with Rufus Anderson and Board officials upon his return to the United States, writing that the Board must "answer at the judgment to the cry of Moslim souls lost for lack of knowl-edge, through the withdrawal of a feeble but devoted instrumentality."[13]

Merrick's attacks on the ABCFM represented a dissenting voice in the missions community, but accurately reflected Americans' substantial ne-glect of Muslim evangelization through most of the nineteenth century. He was not the only critic of the American churches' policy toward Muslim evangelization, though. Merrick was echoed and specifically cited by Epis-copal missionary Horatio Southgate, whose *Encouragement to Missionary Effort among Mohamedans* (1836) turned the ABCFM's logic of evangelizing the eastern churches on its head. America's Protestant Episcopal Church in-augurated its missionary work in 1829, and from the start the liturgically minded Episcopalians took a more positive view of the eastern churches than their more conversionist evangelical colleagues in the ABCFM. Upon receiving his commission as a missionary to Persia, Southgate delivered a sermon on Isaiah 60:7 ("All the flocks of Kedar shall be gathered together unto thee; the rams of Nebaioth shall minister unto thee"). Because Kedar and Nebaioth were Arab tribes, he interpreted this passage as "predictive of the final overthrow of that false religion" of Islam. Southgate countered the idea that Muslim evangelization could only follow the conversion of the eastern Christians. He acknowledged the common belief that the eastern churches must be reformed before westerners could reasonably hope for Muslims to accept Christianity. Would it not be quicker, he reasoned, if western Christians presented the gospel and true Christianity to Muslims themselves? As of 1836, Southgate believed that the ABCFM's strategy of evangelizing eastern Christians in order to reach Muslims had failed.[14]

Southgate held a typically low view of Islam as a religion, but he had a sanguine opinion of evangelistic prospects among Muslims, particularly the Shi'is of Persia. He considered the Persians to be extremely intelligent as a race, and unlike Merrick, he found many of them religiously open-minded. As for Islam, it was a "religion of malice, cruelty, and violence," and shot through with sectarian divisions. The faith had devolved into "mere obser-vance of external rites" for many Muslims. Muslims were just waiting for western missionaries to come and help them, but "they have always been, and still are, almost entirely neglected by the Christian Church." Re-markably, Southgate lamented the history of the Crusades as the only no-table engagement of the western church with Muslims. "The Church has sent against them. . .slaughtering armies. . .under the sacred banner of the Cross; but no messenger of love, bearing the glad tidings of peace and good-will." Western missionaries in Muslim countries remained focused almost exclusively on the eastern churches. "This seeming indifference of the Church to the salvation of the Mohammedans" resulted from the false assumption that they were "inaccessible" to the gospel. "The one hundred and fifty millions who are in bondage to the false and pernicious faith of the Koran look to you," Southgate told his audience.[15]

Even Southgate was sobered by his initial journey to Persia, and in a wholesale reversal of his position in *Encouragement to Missionary Effort*, he returned to America in 1838 convinced that direct evangelization of Muslims in the Middle East was impractical. He moved to Constantinople in 1840, committed to lifting up the eastern churches and increasingly convinced of their compatibility with the Episcopal tradition. He publicly feuded with ABCFM missionaries over their attempts to convert eastern Christians, efforts which he saw as rude and unnecessary. His Episcopal Church sponsors commissioned him to "promote a friendly intercourse between the two branches of the one catholic and apostolic church." Accordingly, he did not encourage Orthodox Christians to leave their churches, as some other Protestant missionaries did. Moreover, he tried to convince eastern church leaders that the ABCFM missionaries meant to split their churches, despite the ABCFM's protests to the contrary. In 1844, Southgate was consecrated as the missionary bishop of Constantinople. His labors in Turkey were badly hindered by a lack of financial support, however, and he resigned his position in 1850.[16]

Like Southgate, many American observers of Islam contrasted the promising potential of the races of the Middle East with the debilitating effects of their religion. In the nineteenth century, westerners made a pseudo-science of discerning the ostensible intellectual and moral characteristics of the world's races. Some American Christians like Hartford, Connecticut pastor Joel Hawes, who visited the Middle East with his friend Rufus Anderson, made a point to distinguish the Turks' race from their religion. While the Turks were "naturally" a "noble race," Islam destroyed their hope of civilization or salvation. Islam was a "dreadful curse" on the empire. It made Turks fatally sensuous, stubborn, and corrupt, and drew its followers further and further from saving religion. The eastern Christians and their dead formalistic religion were hardly better. But if the Turks were not racially consigned to their inferior degraded state, then Christian missions could hope for success.[17]

Through the mid-nineteenth century, apologists continued to claim that Muslim evangelization represented a major goal of missions to the Middle East, and that the corruption of the eastern churches represented a primary barrier to reaching Muslims for Christ. Cyrus Hamlin, an ABCFM missionary to Constantinople, wrote in 1851 that it "is self-evident that the Mo-hammedan, who abhors some of the most important and essential truths of redemption, can have no saving knowledge of God or truth. It is also equally true of the nominally Christian races of the Empire." Among the eastern churches, he asserted, "there is actually no recognition of our Lord Jesus Christ." Both Oriental Christians and Muslims focused exclusively on exter-nal ritual rather than internal transformation.[18]

Experience told Hamlin that "we have not the slightest reason to believe, that Mussulmans can now be reached by argument and persuasion." Only true Christianity modeled before the Muslims could convince them. Be-cause the eastern churches maintained a nominal adherence to the Bible, the missionaries had hope of appealing to them with the "truth." Hamlin warned the ABCFM missionaries that good works and civilizing education were not enough: the "renovation of Oriental society can be accomplished by Bible Christianity alone." From his vantage point, "Bible Christianity" appeared most likely to be received first by the Oriental churches, not Mus-lims. Hamlin and many of his colleagues placed enormous importance on proselytes' rational appropriation of biblical precepts for conversion, and subtly downplayed the power of the Holy Spirit to convert people regard-less of cultural preparation. Nevertheless, Hamlin ended on an optimistic note that "we live in those latter days, when the residue of the Spirit is to be poured out upon all flesh. We are to labor for and expect those Pentecostal seasons, when thousands shall turn to the Lord in a day." Hamlin simply ex-pected the people of the eastern churches to convert first, followed by the Muslims. Nevertheless, his eschatology suggested that "Mohammedanism hastens to destruction," and he expected that some of his missionary col-leagues might "live to rejoice in the utter subversion of the false prophet's cruel dominion." But by 1878, Hamlin soberly estimated that no more than fifty Turkish Muslims had ever been converted and baptized by American missionaries.[19]

Isaac Bird, one of the first American missionaries to Syria, substantially agreed with Hamlin's views. Bird wrote in his 1872 history of the Syrian mis-sions that the images and icons used by the eastern Christians led Muslims to think they were polytheists. If the Muslim "could be convinced that the *true* disciples of 'Esa' (Jesus) believed in only one God as truly as himself, and that his prophet was under a gross mistake in supposing that Christian-ity had anything of idolatry in it," he might convert, leading to "the gaining of a great nation." Such motivations originally inspired the ABCFM to send out Parsons and Fisk, according to Bird. D. Stuart Dodge, professor at the Syrian Protestant College, agreed, recalling that the "Syria mission was

originally planned to evangelize the non-Christian sects, especially the Mohammedans; its work among nominal Christians was only a means to this
end." Nevertheless, very few Muslims converted to Christianity by way of
western missions in the nineteenth century, and probably only a few hundred eastern Christians became Protestants. Although precise numbers are
hard to come by, there may have actually been fewer Christians in the
Middle East at the end of the nineteenth century than at the beginning.
Hope for quick, eschatological change seemed unwarranted by 1900.[20]

One can see from Hamlin, Bird, and others' writings that "Bible Christian" missionaries saw both Islam and Eastern Orthodoxy as enemies to
the gospel, reflecting pre-Civil War eschatology that paired Islam and
Catholicism as twin Antichrists. Although the eastern churches possessed
less political might than Roman Catholicism, many conservative American
Protestants saw the two ecclesiastical communities as essentially the same:
dead, formalistic, and associated with the spirit of Antichrist. William Bird,
an ABCFM missionary in Lebanon, reported in 1858 that the Protestants
constantly battled local Orthodox priests and Roman Catholic missionaries
for the allegiance of proselytes. He called Jesuit missionaries in Lebanon "a
trained & faithful band in the service of the Man of Sin." The Catholic and
Orthodox clergy challenged the American Protestants' evangelistic efforts
on every front, but Bird found that unsurprising: "For centuries, have the
legions of darkness gloated over the scene in this land undisturbed, & held
diabolical carnival in view of the success of the Beast and the False Prophet."
But, Bird believed, Catholicism and Islam hastened to their end. The
"undisputed reign of the great red dragon is at a close." He envisioned a day
of ultimate Protestant triumph: "for the *convent* shall be the *seminary,* for
the *minaret* the *steeple,* for the *Jesuit* & the *imaum* the *preacher of righteousness* & for the *crescent* & the *crucifix* the glorious *Cross of Christ.*" Converting Catholics and Muslims promoted the final devastation of the great spiritual powers opposing Christ.[21]

Although much of the ABCFM's attention was given to "Bible lands" like
Palestine, Syria, and Turkey, missionary agencies noticed the large Muslim
populations outside of the Middle East as well. American Presbyterians entered India in the 1830s, where tens of millions of Muslims lived who were
"as fanatical" as those in the Middle East, according to a Presbyterian missions historian. Their lack of connection to the Turkish Empire or "Bible
lands" no doubt made these Muslims of lesser publicity value for missionary agencies. One of the Presbyterian missionaries to India, Joseph Warren,
wrote in his 1856 memoir *A Glance Backward at Fifteen Years of Missionary
Life in North India* that his work in North India focused on Hindus and

Muslims, and that the doctrines of both "are well suited to the corrupt propensities of human nature." Unlike in works dealing with "savages," the missionaries in India had to contend with the country's "pseudo-civilization." "We have something more to do than to clear the ground and build: we have first to pull down." Warren seemed slightly more optimistic about the prospects for evangelizing south Asian Muslims than did his Middle Eastern counterparts, but he also remained bitterly hostile toward Hinduism and Islam, concluding his memoir with the observation that "thirty-five millions of people, within the field of our North India mission. . . are following idols and Mohammed, and are under the influence of systems that lead them as directly and completely away from God as the arch-enemy of mankind could desire." The ABCFM, which sent its earliest missionaries to India, did comparatively more there to evangelize Hindus than Muslims. The ABCFM's *Missionary Herald* occasionally noted conversions of Indian Muslims to Christianity, commenting in 1878 that in the "northern part of India much more has been done among the Mohammedans than elsewhere."[22]

English Baptists entered India in the 1790s, and Adoniram Judson pioneered the American Baptist work in Burma in 1814. American Baptists enjoyed particular successes among the largely Buddhist Karens of Burma, but still kept their eye on Muslim targets in the region. Francis Mason, one of the key American missionaries to the Karens, wrote in 1830 that because of the Muslims' common Abrahamic faith with Christians, they were "a most interesting people to the Missionary." Mason believed that Islam was superior to Hinduism, which he saw as idolatry. "Great as is the evil of Mahometanism," he wrote, "it will be made a blessing, should God use it as an instrument for the destruction of idolatry. But Mahometanism itself totters." Baptists' missions work, like other denominations', tended to focus only indirectly on Muslims.[23]

G. Winfred Hervey, the author of *The Story of Baptist Missions in Foreign Lands* (1886), reflected on the challenge of Islam after seventy years of American Baptist global missions. He noted that Muslims were serious evangelistic competitors, as "the Mahometans are almost the only false religionists who are making proselytes among the heathen." Muslims, to Hervey, still seemed more an obstacle to missions than an evangelistic target. In India, China, the East Indies, and Africa, the presence of Islam hindered the Baptists' efforts. Offering a novel twist on Islam in eschatology, Hervey believed that the Muslims' proselytizing among pagans had been predicted in Revelation 9:13–21, which spoke of judgment against idolaters. The "serpent-like tails of the horses having heads" (v. 19) suggested to Hervey the

"Mahometan Fakirs or Dervishes, that have ever followed the track of Moslem conquest to make proselytes, are truly serpent-like in their cunning compliances and insinuating ways." Although these Muslim evangelistic efforts had seriously obstructed Christian missions, Revelation 9 predicted that the Muslims would "subdue only a third part of idolaters," and that their superficial influence could be removed instantly by God, Hervey maintained.[24]

By the 1860s and '70s, some American observers had become seriously concerned about the "problem" of Muslim evangelization. Muslims had begun to develop a reputation as uniquely exclusive and closed-minded, which excused the fact that missionary agencies had done comparatively little to evangelize Muslims. Henry Jessup (see Figure 3-1), an ABCFM and Presbyterian missionary in Syria, by 1860 took a deeply negative view of Islam and Middle Eastern religions in general, as civil war in Syria's Mount Lebanon loomed. "Islamism," he wrote, "is not a spiritual faith. It has no way of reconciliation with God." The typical Muslim "is a man of unrestrained passions, full of falsehood and blasphemy. . . . He has no love of God, and no hope of heaven. And the moral character of the Moslem is a fair representative of the character of *all* the different religious sects of the East. They are all, alike, corrupt and immoral. Not one of them gives evidence of a saving knowledge of Christ." After forty years of American missions in the Middle East, there still seemed little reason for optimism.[25]

In America, Jessup did a great deal to popularize his views of degraded Arab culture and the difficulties of proselytizing among Muslims. He and many other American missionaries to Syria were embittered by the 1860 war in Mount Lebanon in which many Maronite Christians were killed by local Druzes (members of an offshoot of Islam based primarily in Lebanon). Shortly thereafter, a large number of Damascus's Christians were also massacred. A horrified ABCFM missionary wrote that like "wild beasts," the Muslims "joined in mercilessly slaking their thirst in the blood of Christians." Most missionaries in Syria tended afterwards to elevate the status of the nominal Christians, and to denigrate Muslim culture. In *The Mohammedan Missionary Problem* (1879), Jessup outlined factors unfavorable and favorable to Christian labors among Middle Eastern Muslims. Among the key unfavorable factors, Jessup pointed to rampant hypocrisy and immorality, "Ishmaelitic intolerance," and the degradation of women. About the Islamic treatment of women, to which Jessup devoted a separate book, he said that all Muslim women are "uneducated, profane, slanderous, capricious, [and] never trained to control their tempers or their tongues for a moment." Regular beatings were their only form of discipline. "Women are

FIGURE 3-1. Portrait of Henry Jessup from *Fifty-Three Years in Syria* (New York, 1910). Moody Memorial Library, Baylor University.

treated like animals, and behave like animals." Jessup believed that women in the home were the critical players in American Christianity, so no female basis existed on which to build a Christian culture in Muslim society.[26]

By the early twentieth century, Jessup's view of the ostensibly miserable place of women in Muslim societies had become a typical justification for sending civilizing Christian missions to Muslims. In *Western Women in*

Eastern Lands (1910), Helen Barrett Montgomery expressed a common missionary opinion when she averred that the "darkest blot upon the prophet Mohammed" was his low estimation of women. Across the variety of Muslim cultures, Montgomery argued, debasing situations for women appeared: almost all women were veiled and "secluded behind barred windows in the harem." Muslim women suffered from easy divorces, polygamy, and a lack of education. Ruth Frances Woodsmall, a Middle East worker with the Young Women's Christian Association, similarly blamed the "spirit of fatalism" in Islam for keeping women oppressed and quiescent. She hoped that education would help Muslim women "bring religion into accord with modern needs."[27]

Despite its typically grim perspective on Muslim society, Jessup's *Mohammedan Missionary Problem* pointed to some theological affinities between Islam and Christianity, including monotheism and a reverence for Jesus, as reasons for optimism. Jessup saw that the growth of the British Empire meant that political Islam was "completely encircled by Anglo-Saxon, Christian political and civil power." Many American and British observers in the late nineteenth century built hope for missionary success on the expansion of the British Empire's scope. When Western-style education, government, and business penetrated Islamic cultures, the West inevitably would triumph. In unapologetically imperialistic language, Jessup asserted that "in the conflict between civilization and barbarism Islam must be the loser." With the successful translation of the Bible into Arabic, Jessup predicted the opening of a great new era of missionary success in the Middle East. "God's word is ready; the promises of Christ are ours; God is overturning among the nations. . ., while Mohammedan prestige and power sink rapidly out of sight." The political strength of the West in the region had become crucial to the success of the missions in the Middle East. With British and American funding, the Syrian Protestant College opened in 1866, but it would quickly drop its evangelistic emphasis and only focus on civilizing Syrians.[28]

As of 1910, Jessup estimated that there had been forty or fifty Muslim converts to Christianity in the Syrian mission. Sensitive to accusations that the Syrian mission was doing little to evangelize Muslims, Jessup highlighted the supposed deceptions of an American Baptist missionary, E. F. Baldwin, as a cautionary tale against sensational mass evangelism. Jessup met Baldwin in 1889, five years after Baldwin had moved from North Carolina to Morocco. Baldwin had come to Syria to recruit native converts to help him in his work. Jessup uncomfortably noted Baldwin's native "John-the-Baptist-in-the-wilderness appearance," as he listened to Baldwin's claim that he had baptized dozens of Moroccan Muslims. Baldwin promoted what he called the "Matthew 10" philosophy of missions, which meant that missionaries would depend on the generosity of the evangelized for support, as Jesus told the disciples to do in the Gospel of Matthew chapter 10. After returning to Morocco, Baldwin published criticisms of the Syrian mission, claiming that nothing was being done there for Muslims. As usual, Jessup countered that the "whole system of missions" in Syria was designed to reach Muslims eventually. Soon, what Jessup dismissively called the "Baldwin Bubble" burst, as visitors to Morocco found that Baldwin had made no converts at all. Baptists in Morocco subsequently abandoned the Matthew 10 philosophy. When Baldwin later returned in disgrace to Syria, he began teaching that "the dispensation for preaching the Gospel had come to an end" and that Christians should "sit down and wait the appearing of the Lord," according to Jessup. He believed that Baldwin's bubble taught that Muslim evangelization was not going to be easy, and anyone who suggested otherwise should not be trusted. Jessup also reflected many missionaries' turning away from eschatologically freighted readings of missions, and toward greater confidence in the slow but inexorable march of the Christian gospel and western civilization as the means to transforming Muslim lands and eventually ushering in the millennium.[29]

Despite the lack of substantial effort directed toward the actual evangelization of Middle Eastern Muslims in the nineteenth century, readers in America enjoyed a number of popular accounts of Muslims converting to Christianity. The perceived difficulty of missions to Muslims ironically boosted the attractiveness of accounts of Muslim converts. The fictional English tract *The Conversion of a Mahometan*, originally published in America in the 1770s, remained widely read in the United States through the early nineteenth century. It appeared in at least seventeen American editions between 1773 and 1829, including a German translation in Harrisburg, Pennsylvania, in 1801.

Another conversion narrative with far-reaching fame was the account of Abdallah and Sabat, originally related in a sermon titled "The Star in the East" (1809) by Claudius Buchanan, a former chaplain to the British East India Company whose studies of the Orient inspired a generation of American and British missionaries.[30] As told by Buchanan, the zealous Muslims Abdallah and Sabat were good friends in Arabia. The two men traveled together to Kabul, Afghanistan, where Abdallah had secured an administrative post. Sabat left to tour Tartary, while Abdallah procured an Arabic-language Bible, and through reading it converted to Christianity. Abdallah tried to conceal his conversion for a time, but then fled for Tartary, hoping to find refuge among Christians there. He met instead with his old friend Sabat, who knew of Abdallah's turn to Christianity. Sabat betrayed Abdallah to the authorities for torture and execution.

Abdallah refused to renounce Christianity and peacefully accepted his fate. Afterwards, Sabat was wracked with guilt and wandered through south-central Asia, eventually coming to India, where he also came into possession of an Arabic New Testament. "At length the truth of the word of God fell on his mind. . .like a flood of light," and he was converted and baptized in Madras. Sabat began translating the Scriptures into Persian, and writing evangelistic literature in Arabian. He also became a student of Henry Martyn, a prominent English missionary in India. But an 1818 report in the *Christian Observer* claimed that Sabat had renounced Christianity and returned to Islam.[31]

Abdallah and Sabat's narrative caused a sensation in Anglo-American evangelical circles, generating an epic, at least two published poems, and a play. One of the poems inspired by Abdallah and Sabat, *The Power of Christianity*, rhymed

No more the Koran can its votaries warm,
No more Mahomet's paradise can charm;
When God who holds the destiny of man,
In his good time reveals his mighty plan.

"The Star in the East" was published all over Britain and America, often as an individual tract or in Buchanan's collected works. The tract saw editions not only in major American cities but also in smaller towns of the early republic like Newark, New Jersey (1809), Winchester, Virginia (1810), and Lexington, Kentucky (1813). Adoniram Judson, the first American foreign missionary, was deeply influenced by the story in 1809, and it helped prompt his decision to go to Burma. A condensed version of the story (including Abdallah's torture and dismemberment) was appended to John Campbell's children's book *Alfred and Galba* (1812). As late as 1887, their account was being reprinted in American missionary periodicals. In 1922, Abdallah and Sabat were included in Basil J. Matthews's *The Book of Missionary Heroes*, a collection of short biographies.[32]

Adding to the popularity of Muslim conversion narratives was *The Life and Conversion of Mahomed Ali Bey*, which went through at least six American editions over more than forty years. Its first edition was produced by the American Sunday School Union in Philadelphia in 1823, and the last by a Presbyterian press in Richmond, Virginia, just after the Civil War. Muhammad Ali Bey was the unlikely product of the Scottish Missionary Society's work along the Caspian Sea in Russia. Muhammad Ali was enlisted by the Society as an Arabic language teacher, and through conversation with the missionaries "the Spirit of God began. . .to shake his belief in the absurdities of Islamism." The missionaries gave Muhammad Ali a copy of Abdallah and Sabat's narrative, which affected him deeply.[33]

The young teacher knew that his conversion to Christianity would lead to ostracism and persecution, but he found the missionaries' answers to his questions convincing. Touching a common theme among Muslim proselytes, Muhammad Ali had a hard time fathoming the doctrine of the Trinity, but became more convinced that God could be both one and three. Finally, he came to the conviction that he was "poor, wretched, miserable, and undone; that all my prayers, my worship, and obedience, in time past, were vain and unprofitable," and he turned to Christ for forgiveness. The news reached his father, who disowned him. Muhammad Ali began to receive a stream of Muslim visitors who intended to win him back to Islam, but the convert's arguments proved incontrovertible. Muhammad Ali received baptism and was renamed Alexander Kazem Bey, and the missionaries hoped that his conversion would become the first of many that would begin to break Islam's hold in the Caspian Sea region. The Scottish missions did not meet with much success generally, although Alexander Kazem Bey went on to become a professor of Persian, first in Kazan, and then at St. Petersburg University.[34]

Although Henry Jessup's Syrian mission did little to evangelize Muslims, he nevertheless made one Muslim convert the subject of a grandly titled book, *The Setting of the Crescent and the Rising of the Cross* (1898). Kamil Aietany, known as Kamil Abdul Messiah after his conversion, approached Jessup at the Syrian Protestant College in Beirut, telling him "I am not at rest. I find nothing in the Koran to show me how God can be a just God and yet pardon a sinner." After studying the Bible with Jessup, Kamil overcame typical Muslim objections to the Trinity and became a Christian. As Kamil Abdul Messiah, he joined with Samuel Zwemer, a missionary of the Reformed Church in Arabia, who encouraged Kamil to preach the gospel publicly. This likely led to Kamil's mysterious death in 1892, probably from poisoning by hostile Muslims. According to Jessup, "Kamil's history is a rebuke to our unbelief in God's willingness and power to lead Mohammedans into a hearty acceptance of Christ." Although Kamil had originally resisted the doctrine of the Trinity, God broke through and convinced him of his need for Christ, according to Jessup. Jessup hoped that Kamil would be the first of many converts, but he represented only a tiny group of Middle Eastern Muslims who had become Christians by the end of the nineteenth century.[35]

Prompted by the success of Muslim conversion narratives and the grow-
ing interest in foreign missions, biographies of, and memoirs by, missionar-
ies became increasingly popular in England and America at the end of the
nineteenth century, including many accounts by missionaries to the Middle
East. Several American editions of ABCFM missionary William Goodell's
Forty Years in the Turkish Empire were printed in the late nineteenth century.
In it, Goodell's biographer primarily described his work among Turkish
Christians, but also noted that Goodell did what he could to witness to
Turkish Muslims under the erratic Ottoman policies regarding proselytizing and conversion. After an 1856 edict seemed to guarantee freedom of religion in Constantinople, the ABCFM missionaries became more privately
aggressive in their overtures to the city's Muslims. By 1859, Goodell was
quite encouraged, as the mission had sold hundreds of Bibles to Muslims,
and more than twenty former Muslims had been baptized. Goodell blamed
missionaries from the English Church Missionary Society for stirring up
trouble by publicly disparaging Islam, however. That landed a number of
native converts in jail in 1864. The polite Goodell chose to work behind
the scenes, and fellow missionary Isaac Bird commended him for remaining a "man of peace" despite being "surrounded by bigoted and fanatical
Moslems and papists."[36]

Cyrus Hamlin was the head of the ABCFM school and seminary in
Bebek, Turkey, until he broke with the ABCFM in 1860 over the primacy of
education as opposed to direct evangelism. He published his autobiograph-
ical book *Among the Turks* in New York and London in the late 1870s. His
memoir included extended reflections on Islam, which he regarded as an
admirable religion marred by centuries of corruption. In Hamlin, one can
begin to see the emergence of a non-evangelical modernist Protestant perspective on Islam, which did not necessarily denounce Islam or the Prophet,
but argued that Muslims primarily needed civilization, not spiritual conversion. Hamlin considered Islam's sensuality its worst feature, lamenting its
doctrine of a paradise where "true believers shall quaff the most delicious
wines from flowing bowls, with no possibility of intoxication or of even a
headache." In essence, Islam represented a monotheistic repudiation of
idolatry, but "tradition has introduced an immense mass of error and superstition into the Moslem world, of which the Prophet was not guilty." Commerce and education were keys to destroying Islam, as the "general progress
of civilization, the railroad, the steamboat, the telegraph, the expansion of
commerce, the increase of travel, have all united in softening the prejudices
of the Moslem mind." Hamlin assumed that all these developments went
hand-in-hand with Christianity. He specifically noted the Sunni Wahhabist

revival as a sign of Muslim resistance against modernity. "It is a revival of ig-norance, darkness, and fanaticism," Hamlin wrote. Betraying a turn toward secularization in missions, Hamlin ended his volume with a three-fold pre-scription to alleviate the Turks' deficiencies: "Peace, Time, and Education!" No mention of Christ seemed necessary. Civilization equaled Christianity to many modernist missionaries. In time, evangelicals would revolt against this kind of civilizing non-conversionist strategy.[37]

Missionary books like Presbyterian missionary James Bassett's *Persia: The Land of the Imams* (1886) gave American readers a reasonably accurate description of the various sects within Islam. Bassett's memoir, published in New York and London, described the faith and practice of the Twelver Shi'is who dominated Persia and parts of present-day Iraq. "The essential and dis-tinguishing tenet of this sect" was that the eldest living representative of Ali, the cousin and son-in-law of Muhammad, was by divine right the spiritual and political ruler over Islam, down to the twelfth generation. The twelfth imam, Muhammad al-Muntazar, disappeared while still a child, in the year 874, and Twelvers believed that this hidden imam would return as the mes-sianic Mahdi in the last days. "The doctrine of the Mahde has given abun-dant occasion for the pretensions of impostors," Bassett observed. Overall, Bassett considered the faith of the Twelver Shi'is to be both fanatical and weak. Belief in the Mahdi "has prepared the minds of the people for change, and the absurdities of the system of the Twelve Imams has gone far to shake the faith in Islam." This knowledge of Persian Islam both informed western readers of its doctrines, and assured them of its ostensible irrationality, de-spite the lack of western missionary success among Muslims.[38]

These missionaries' memoirs from the Middle East helped spur the "Holy Land mania" that preoccupied many nineteenth-century Americans. Not all of the Holy Land literature was explicitly Christian, but most of it fed into the dominant Western view of Middle Easterners, and especially Arab Pales-tinians, as a degraded people occupying a most important land. When the tottering Ottoman Empire fell, Western Christians would presumably re-claim those Bible lands for Christ and Western civilization. While other Muslim parts of the world, like Africa or East Asia, might not command the same public interest, the combination of Bible lands and Arab culture proved an alluring mix for American and British readers. This view of Pales-tine and the Ottoman Empire through the lens of the Bible helps account for the prominence of Middle Eastern Muslims, as well as Jews and eastern Christians, in the American Christian imagination.[39]

The key Christian text fueling the Holy Land mania was Presbyterian missionary William Thomson's *The Land and the Book*, which only Harriet

Beecher Stowe's *Uncle Tom's Cabin* surpassed in popularity in its time. *The Land and the Book* certainly ranks as one of the all-time bestselling books by an American missionary, and appeared in many different American and English editions after its initial publication in 1859. Thomson worked for the Presbyterian mission board in Syria from 1832 to 1877, but made a greater mark by narrating his travels in the Holy Land for a vast American and British audience. The whole book (which by its 1908 edition encompassed three volumes of more than five hundred pages each) was strangely strained, as the "land and the book," but not the land's current inhabitants, formed its central concern. Thomson portrayed the Arabs and other residents of Palestine as unwelcome interlopers on the "scenes and scenery of the Bible," and on the hills where Jesus taught and prayed.[40]

Nevertheless, Thomson's account made a number of comments about the Arab Muslims in Palestine, and about Islam in general. Quoting Sir William Muir's popular *Life of Mahomet and History of Islam* (1858–61), Thomson agreed that the "sword of Mahomet and the Coran are the most fatal enemies of civilization, liberty, and truth which the world has yet known." In an odd conversational style, Thomson described daily Muslim prayers and invited the reader to "see those men in that mosk. . . . They are preparing to say prayers—perform them, rather—in this most public place, and in the midst of all this noise and confusion. That man, standing with his face towards Mecca, raises his open hands till the thumbs touch the ears, exclaiming aloud, Allah hu akbar—'God is most great.'" After describing the Muslim prayers in great detail, Thomson asked "You think, then, that this solemn ceremony is mere hollow-hearted hypocrisy?" In a slight concession, he answered, "Not exactly that; at least not necessarily so, nor in all cases." Thomson's chief interest in these Muslim prayers was their correspondence to "those of the Hebrews in the olden times." But Thomson, embittered by the massacre of Christians in Mount Lebanon and Damascus in 1860, warned that the Muslims' "kind of piety is associated with the most tiger-hearted fanaticism. Just such men planned and guided those diabolical butcheries and massacres in 1860." To Thomson, the Muslims' devotion might help Christians understand the religious practices of the ancient Middle East, but he regarded the praying Muslims themselves as contemptible. That impression was passed on to hundreds of thousands, if not millions, of American and British readers of *The Land and the Book*.[41]

Although his book did not match *The Land and the Book* in popularity, Mark Twain also made a great commercial success out of his Holy Land travel narrative *The Innocents Abroad* (1869). In it, the decidedly non-evangelical Twain joked about Muslim culture in a way that many American Christians surely appreciated: in Turkey, "Mosques are plenty, churches are plenty, graveyards are plenty, but morals and whiskey are scarce. The Koran does not permit Mohammedans to drink. Their natural instincts do not permit them to be moral." As reflected in these travel and missionary texts, Middle Eastern Muslims were of intense interest to American readers and missionaries. The American literary uses of these Muslims during the nineteenth century further convinced American Christians of their cultural and religious superiority, and also assured them that Western Protestants were making a good faith effort to evangelize the supposedly stubborn disciples of Muhammad. Early in the century, optimism about missions was stoked by apocalyptic hopes for the quick downfall of Islamic powers, especially the Ottoman Empire. Protestant eschatology both promoted and hindered the cause of missions. It seemed to motivate some missionaries eager for the millennium and the second coming of Christ, but it also put even more conceptual distance between actual Muslims and American Christians lost in the haze of last days scenarios. To missionaries like James Merrick, eschatology might make for effective fundraising, but it also bred terribly unrealistic anticipation of how easily Muslims and others would be won to Christ. Later Christian missionaries like Hamlin and Jessup put more confidence in the expansion of Anglo-American Christian civilization by educational institutions and military power to reform Muslim societies. The reality of Muslim evangelization was far different from what cheerily optimistic missions literature in America suggested. By the late nineteenth century, the shame and frustration of the American missionary community over the neglect of Muslims elicited the first concerted planning to take the Christian gospel directly to them, instead of to Eastern Christians.[42]

Samuel Zwemer, World War I, and "The Evangelization of the Moslem World in This Generation"

In April 1906, delegates from twenty-nine Protestant missionary agencies met in an unprecedented conference in Cairo, Egypt, to formulate a coordinated plan to reach the world's Muslims for Christ. While the conference did not dwell on the nineteenth century's feeble attempts at evangelizing Muslims, there was a clear sense among attendees that missions to Muslims had been almost entirely ineffective. Robert Speer, the secretary of the Presbyterian mission board, bluntly admitted that "we do not have. . . a campaign for the evangelization of Moslems." At the end of the conference, Samuel Zwemer, the conference organizer, pointed to a map of the Muslim world and told the conferees that God would raise up an "army of volunteers" from America's and Europe's universities to fulfill the aim of Christian missions to Islam: "The Evangelization of the Moslem World in this Generation."[1]

This chapter will consider the increasingly strategic efforts by American Protestants to evangelize Muslims in the late nineteenth and early twentieth centuries, with a primary focus on the remarkable and understudied career of Samuel Zwemer. It is difficult to overstate Zwemer's importance in American missions to Muslims, or his role in popularizing religious knowledge about Islam among American Christians. He was certainly the most influential American Christian missionary to Muslims of his time, if not ever. He became the most prominent shaper of American Christians' views of Islam for three main reasons: first, he was an active missionary in Muslim countries for several decades. Second, he was the first American systematically to organize efforts to reach the world's Muslims. Finally, Zwemer was one of America's leading scholarly writers on Islam. He produced a host of books on Muslim culture and religion, and served as the first editor of the *Moslem World*, the leading periodical in America devoted to global evangelization of Muslims. Missionary writings like Zwemer's exercised great influence over American Christians' views of Islam. As a historian in 1924 wrote, missionaries' presentations "made a large proportion of [the American] people familiar with events and conditions in the Near East."[2]

Zwemer was a Reformed Church evangelical, and consistently viewed Islam as a flawed religion that could not save its adherents. He also believed that the "Moslem world" was in deep cultural crisis, requiring a winsome Christian witness, lest a great moment of opportunity be lost. Over time, Zwemer developed a deeper respect for certain aspects of Muslim intellectual and spiritual life. He made the first major strategic departure from American missionaries' earlier policy of focusing evangelistic efforts mostly on Middle Eastern Christians. Zwemer's ascendancy also revealed that before World War I, the influence of premillennial eschatology on actual missions to Muslims was limited. Premillennial dispensationalists anticipated that Christ's return could be imminent, and that upon his return Christ would establish an earthly kingdom and inaugurate the millennium, or thousand-year reign of peace. Instead of the expectation of imminent apocalypse, Zwemer and his colleagues tended to embrace a postmillennial confidence that a rotted Islam must gradually crumble under the pressure of Christian witness and Western civilization. For a number of respected missionaries and scholars like Zwemer, postmillennialism continued to serve as a mediating position between the literalistic forecasts of the premillennialists and the abandonment of prophecy by the Bible's liberal critics. To postmillennialists, the return of Christ was not likely to happen soon, but instead would follow the millennium, which would be established in part by the church sending missionaries to convert the world. The postmillenialist view had certainly lost some of its former dominance, as the new fundamentalists found it overly optimistic, and liberals believed it conceded too much to ostensibly outdated prophetic interpretations of Scripture. Postmillennialism retained enough strength to shape the evangelical, scholarly, and moderate Zwemer.[3]

Zwemer (see Figure 4-1), born in 1867 in Vriesland, Michigan, was a child of Dutch immigrant parents. He attended Hope College in Holland, Michigan, where he joined the Student Volunteer Movement (SVM), a key new advocacy group promoting global missions by American college students. The SVM had first been organized at a summer conference in Northfield, Massachusetts, in 1886, and soon made its slogan (or "watchword") "the evangelization of the world in this generation." Inspired by the thought of systematically fulfilling Jesus's "Great Commission" to preach the gospel to all nations (Matthew 28:19–20), hundreds of students like Zwemer soon committed themselves to the mission field. In 1887, Zwemer went to New Brunswick Seminary (Reformed Church) in New Jersey, where he began to study Arabic. He became convinced that God was calling him to work in Arabia, the birthplace of Islam, which had largely been ignored by Protes-

Figure 4-1. Samuel M. Zwemer and an Inquirer, from J. Christy Wilson, *Apostle to Islam: A Biography of Samuel M. Zwemer* (Grand Rapids, MI, 1952). Moody Memorial Library, Baylor University.

tant missionaries. In 1890, he joined his fellow seminarian James Cantine in Beirut, where they continued to learn Arabic. A year later, they opened the first mission station at Basra, in southern Iraq. Soon they had opened several stations along the east coast of the Arabian peninsula, and in 1894 their mission was officially adopted by Zwemer's Reformed Church.[4]

Zwemer did not restrict himself to local missions work and evangelism, as he became a prolific writer. By the end of his career, he had written or edited at least forty-nine books, in addition to his editorial work and many articles for the *Moslem World*. In his early works, he spoke unabashedly of the need for evangelical Christians to wage spiritual war, or a new crusade, against Islam. To the extent that Zwemer saw missions to Muslims as the fulfillment of prophecy, he focused on Old Testament passages that seemed to suggest the turning of Arab nations to God. In his first book, *Arabia: The Cradle of Islam*, he interpreted Isaiah 60:7 ("All the flocks of Kedar shall be gathered together unto thee; the rams of Nebaioth shall minister unto thee") as a sign that Arab Muslims would "have a large place in this coming glory of the Lord." Zwemer, while still extremely negative about contemporary Muslim culture, was more positive than earlier American Christians about the prospects for direct evangelization of Muslims, partly because of his optimistic postmillennial views.[5]

By the turn of the twentieth-century, missions apologists had begun to divide between social gospel and direct proselytization advocates, with the former emphasizing service and education, and the latter maintaining focus on evangelism and conversion. Zwemer blended the two approaches. He believed all Muslims needed to accept Christ personally, but he also believed that the march of Christian civilization would prepare the way for large-scale Muslim conversions. Rufus Anderson, as leader of the ABCFM, had worried that such a civilizational approach would eventually threaten the goal of training a "native ministry," able to reach indigenous populations. Later fundamentalist missionaries would also see an emphasis on civilization and education as signs of social gospel liberalism. But Zwemer showed that a combination of the two could hold.[6]

Zwemer and an international roster of organizers held the Cairo conference in order to plan the evangelization of the Muslim world. The perceived crisis among Muslims across the globe, as well as a belief in new opportunities among animistic peoples in Asia and Africa, catalyzed the assembly. Organizers said almost nothing about eschatology, but warned that continued neglect by Christian missionaries would risk a resurgence of global Islamic power, and the successful proselytization of unaffiliated polytheists by Muslims instead of Christians.[7]

The Cairo conference produced three volumes of essays printed in America that publicized Zwemer's and his co-laborers' views of missions to Muslims. The venerable Henry Jessup, in the introductory essay to *The Mohammedan World of To-Day*, seemed to still hold the nineteenth-century assumption that Muslims within the Turkish Empire were essentially closed off from Christian evangelism. But most of the missionaries were moving beyond Jessup's view and resolving to take the Christian message, and Western civilization, straight to Muslims. E. M. Wherry, a Presbyterian missionary to Muslims in northern India who helped Zwemer organize the conference, hoped that the assembly would awaken Western Christians to their duty of evangelizing the world's Muslims, as well as the "ignorant savages" in Africa, China, and India who were the targets of Muslim proselytization. Wherry expressed a common view in Anglo-American missionary circles when he forecast that all the world's "idolaters" would soon accept either Islam or Christianity. Islam was Christianity's only serious rival for the religious "conquest of the world." Accordingly, he advocated developing a specific plan for the direct evangelization of Muslims wherever they might live.[8]

The Cairo assembly precipitated an unprecedented flood of Anglo-American missionary treatises on Islam. Wherry was one of several key participants at the Cairo conference who subsequently wrote books popularizing the missionary view of Islam. He published a series of lectures given at Princeton Seminary titled *Islam and Christianity in India and the Far East* (1907). Wherry, like Zwemer, believed in a strategy that combined philanthropy, education, and direct evangelistic appeals. He considered Muslims in India regressive and depraved, even in comparison to Hindus. Christian schools had been the most effective means of reaching Indian Muslims. Summarizing the findings of the Cairo conference, Wherry proposed that some missionaries should learn Arabic in order to identify more closely with Muslims' religion and traditions. Zwemer and Wherry both modeled this approach, becoming far more advanced scholars of Arabic and Muslim history than most Western missionaries before or since. He also believed that Christians should acknowledge some measure of truth in Islam, such as the idea of monotheism. Wherry pointed to the need to depend on the Holy Spirit, the proclamation of the Bible, and intercessory prayer as the chief means of converting Muslims. While Wherry's and others' emphasis on education might have betrayed a modernist trajectory, the focus on the Word and the Spirit showed that the modernist/fundamentalist split had not yet separated the civilizing and proselytizing goals of missionary work.[9]

James Barton, a missionary to Turkey, and Foreign Secretary of the

ABCFM, also promoted these combined evangelistic and reforming goals of missions in books following the Cairo meeting. In *The Unfinished Task of the Christian Church* (1908) Barton asked what "the evangelization of the world," from the SVM's "watchword," actually meant. He argued that it entailed a broadly tailored program of social uplift, as well as the promotion of individual conversions. He insisted that conversion, including repentance and "the new birth" of salvation, remained essential to missions. He saw the "Mohammedans," a target of Christian missions that he knew well, as a unique challenge on the global scene. Sharing the deeply hostile views of previous commentators, Barton averred that Islam "rests like a blight upon every country, race, or individual it masters." Despite its corrupt, debilitated nature, no other religion's adherents were harder to reach. He admitted that few direct efforts had been made to evangelize Muslims. Following Zwemer's and the Cairo conference's evidence, Barton lamented the fact that seventy-eight million Muslims entirely lacked a Christian witness. He also warned of the dangers of Muslim evangelization among polytheists in Africa and Asia. In his historical *Daybreak in Turkey* (1908), Barton still endorsed the idea that the corruption of the Eastern churches posed a major obstacle to Muslim evangelization. He expected that the conversion of Muslim Turks would only be achieved by a demonstration of the "true Christian life," which included Western benevolence and education. Soon the highly influential Barton would become consumed with relief efforts for the brutalized Armenian population in Turkey, one of the ABCFM's long-time objects of attention in the East.[10]

Wherry's and Barton's efforts notwithstanding, Zwemer emerged from the 1906 Cairo assembly as the most influential American missionary to, and scholar of, Islam. In his 1907 *Islam, A Challenge to Faith*, which was translated into German, Danish, and French, Zwemer argued that the Muslim world could be reached on multiple fronts. He commended Bible distribution as a subtle but effective way to spread the knowledge of Christ. Educational and medical missions could also break down misunderstanding and resentment between Muslims and Christians, but these must remain a means to an end in converting Muslim people. Above all, Zwemer advocated verbal witness to Muslims, both individually and through public preaching, where legally possible. "Islam as a religion is doomed to fade away in time before the advance of humanity, civilization and enlightenment," but whether authentic Christianity would replace it depended on whether enough missionaries would take on the challenge.[11]

Fresh off the Cairo conference, Zwemer was able to take a global view of the missionary problem that Islam represented. He particularly highlighted regions of the world with large Muslim populations but no effective Christian witness. Among these were Sudan, Afghanistan, and parts of China and Siberia. The call to reach Muslims was not only urgent because the task had lain neglected for so long, but also because Muslims were Christians' most aggressive evangelistic competitors on the world stage. The "Moslem peril" threatened vulnerable animists who had yet to be contacted by Christian missionaries. Particularly in West Africa, Zwemer predicted that "heathenism" would die out within fifty years, and its adherents would split between Islam and Christianity. "It is now or never," he insisted, "it is Islam or Christ!" He called for a "Holy War," fought not with earthly weapons, but "with the Sword of the Spirit," to take the Muslim lands for Jesus.[12]

Zwemer's Cairo meeting was an important precedent for the great World Missionary Conference in Edinburgh (1910), which Zwemer attended. This conference, which represented a seminal moment of Western missionary confidence and organizational zeal, was suffused with a sense that dramatic religious change could be on the global horizon. Randall Davidson, the Archbishop of Canterbury, predicted at the meeting that the evangelization of the world might result in the inauguration of the Kingdom on earth within a generation. But there was nothing inevitable about the Christianization of the world, and Islam presented one of the chief obstacles to the goal. Commission I of the conference, on which Zwemer sat, dealt with taking the gospel to non-Christians. In its report, the commission expressed a combination of optimism about the "world-wide opportunity" of evangelism, and regret that the goal of effective global missions remained so far from completion.[13]

Using language reminiscent of today's globalization-talk, the commission noted optimistically that for missionaries, "the whole world is remarkably accessible." New exploration, communication, and transportation had all integrated the world's communities like never before. In Muslim countries, Islam showed signs of losing its grip on the educated classes. Nevertheless, the commission pointed to Islam as exhibiting the "greatest solidarity and the most activity and aggressiveness" of all non-Christian religions. As of 1910, Christian missionaries clearly regarded Islam as the greatest threat to Christian expansion, especially in Africa, South and Southeast Asia, and the Middle East. Again, the commission viewed animist Africa with particular concern, and asked "whether the Dark Continent shall become Mohammedan or Christian"? The great challenges were to defeat Muslim evangelistic efforts among native polytheists, and to find an effective means of proselytizing Muslims. The commission blamed a century of ineffectiveness in reaching Muslims almost entirely on the lack of religious liberty in Muslim countries. It also called for a serious effort, in light of liberalizing political situations, to place missionaries who would directly appeal to Muslim peoples. They hoped Christian agencies would expand their work across the Middle East from Arabia to Afghanistan, where in large areas no Christian influence existed.[14]

By January 1911, when he and his missionary colleagues assembled at a new congress on Muslim evangelization in Lucknow, India, Zwemer had become almost giddily optimistic about the prospects of converting the Muslim world. This confidence sprung in large part from recent successes in collecting and publishing knowledge regarding Muslim societies. Conferees heard Zwemer preach on his view of Islam as a prodigal son of the Christian church for whom believers should wait and pray with the tender love of a father. He suspected that missionaries might not have to wait much longer, as "stupendous changes" had revolutionized governments in Iran and Turkey since the Cairo conference. Zwemer looked on the overthrow of Turkey's Sultan Abdul Hamid by the "Young Turks" in 1908 as a major step toward religious liberty. (Unfortunately, he and many other Westerners failed to anticipate that the Young Turks would soon perpetrate the Armenian genocide in 1915.) He believed that prayers offered during, and because of, the Cairo conference, may have helped induce the political upheavals. The progress of civilization and education presented an unstoppable threat to traditional Islam. Zwemer hoped that the new political leaders of the Middle East would turn not to secularism, but to Christian faith, because the "supreme need of the Moslem world is Jesus Christ."[15]

The Cairo and Lucknow assemblies led George Herrick, longtime ABCFM missionary to Turkey, to publish *Christian and Mohammedan: A Plea for Bridging the Chasm*, which was one of the most positive assessments yet of Islam by an American Christian. Clearly influenced by modernist ideas regarding missions and evangelism, Herrick downplayed conflict and emphasized Christian brotherhood with Muslims. Although Herrick still believed that Islam always produced "depressing" social and ethical effects, he hinted at a kind of universalist ecumenism when he insisted that there was a lot of truth in Islam, and that there had always been Muslims who sought after God and "who, it is reasonable to hope, have found him." Herrick took a very negative view of the history of the Crusades, and any kind of crusading mentality among Western Christians. "Mohammedans are not our enemies," he wrote, "they are our brothers." Herrick was dismissive of the SVM's watchword, and encouraged "Christianization" instead of evangelization as the primary task of missionaries. Instead of trying to "snatch a soul here and there," he called for "the enlightenment, the education, the uplifting of entire races of men. . .by the power of Christian civilization." Still, Herrick had not given up the idea that Muslims ultimately should accept Jesus as their "Redeemer and Reconciler with God." Soon these two goals of social uplift and evangelization would seem contradictory to many Western Christians of both the theological right and left.[16]

Despite his sympathies for some aspects of Muslims' history and culture, Zwemer would never swing as far as Herrick toward relativistic ecumenism. Zwemer continued his remarkable productivity in 1911 by inaugurating his periodical the *Moslem World*, which for many years would serve as America's primary clearinghouse for information related to Christian missions to Muslims. In the magazine's opening editorial, Zwemer commented that if Christians were ever "to reach the Moslem world with the Gospel, they must know of it and know it." He planned for the *Moslem World* to be nonsectarian and open to all who shared the belief that the "solution of the Moslem problem" lay in the conversion of Muslims to Christianity. Zwemer assembled a distinguished list of American, German, and British pastors and missionaries as associate editors, many of whom had participated in the Cairo, Edinburgh, and Lucknow conferences.[17]

By 1911, Zwemer was indisputably America's, and perhaps the world's, leading Christian apologist with regard to Islam. He spoke across the globe at missions conferences, his many books and articles were widely distributed and translated, and he apparently persuaded a number of Western Christians to become missionaries among Muslims. One of the students that Zwemer influenced was the celebrated William Borden, an heir to the Borden milk family fortune, who became widely known as "Borden of Yale." His biography became one of the most widely printed missionary accounts of the twentieth century, with approximately twelve American, Canadian, and British editions (the most recent in 1988), and a Chinese translation in 1960. As a Yale freshman in 1906, Borden attended an SVM convention in Nashville where Zwemer spoke passionately on the two hundred million Muslims unreached for Christ. As usual, Zwemer came equipped with a map of the Muslim world, and lamented the legions "under the sway of Islam, held in a bondage than which none on earth is more relentless." Borden was particularly struck by the fact that fifteen million Muslims lived in the interior of China, with not a single Western missionary living among them. According to his biographer, Borden left the conference committed to becoming a missionary to Chinese Muslims.[18]

After Yale, Borden studied at Princeton Seminary, and in 1910 he attended the Edinburgh conference. In a meeting chaired by Zwemer, Borden announced his intention to go with the China Inland Mission to evangelize

Chinese Muslims. As was typical of the SVM ethos, Borden was drawn to these Muslims because they seemed "by far the hardest as well as the most neglected field for missionary enterprise. The very difficulties attracted him," his biographer wrote. Although coastal Chinese cities did have some Muslims, he decided to go to Gansu province, where millions of the "virile, dominating sons of Islam" had no access to the Christian gospel. Borden, like many other SVM-inspired missionaries, saw the evangelization of the world's darkest places as a test of his faith and Christian manhood.[19]

In 1913, Borden arrived in Cairo to study with Zwemer and other Western missionaries in Arabic language and Muslim culture. He and Zwemer canvassed the bazaars and markets of Cairo, handing out Christian tracts. Borden soon bought a red fez, which seemed to give him more anonymity among the Egyptians. He attended the emotionally charged dances of Muslim dervishes, which he found fascinating but ultimately regarded as attempts to "induce a state of ecstasy or auto-hypnosis." But Borden died soon after coming to Cairo, having contracted meningitis. The missionaries quickly produced an evangelistic pamphlet detailing Borden's life, which was translated into Arabic, Persian, Hindustani, Dutch, and Chinese, and distributed among Muslims.[20]

Although he had very few direct encounters with Muslims in his life, Borden's story, shaped heavily by Zwemer, became an inspiration for Western evangelicals to continue praying for, and sending missionaries to, Asian Muslims. William M. Miller, a future Presbyterian missionary to Iran, heard Zwemer speak for the first time at a convention in Kansas City in 1913, where Zwemer called on students to take Borden's place in China. Later, Miller had his own missionary call confirmed when he heard Zwemer speak at Princeton Seminary on the missionary neglect of Muslims.[21]

Like Zwemer, Miller represented a continuing evangelical impulse within the mainline Protestant denominations, and he worked for forty-three years as a missionary in Iran for the Presbyterian Church (U.S.A.). Upon arrival in 1919, Miller confidently asserted that "Mohammedanism is losing ground fast" in Iran, and that it was "time for a forward movement on the part of the forces of Christ." Islam in Iran seemed to him a hollow shell of ritual, and he thought that few Iranians actually believed Islam was true. Thirty-eight years later, Miller still believed that Islam was crumbling, but he feared that it would be replaced by Communism, atheism, and materialism instead of Protestant Christianity. As elsewhere, most of the converts he had seen during his tenure were among Eastern Christian Armenians or Syrians, not Muslim Persians.[22]

Americans like Borden and Miller began their missionary work in the

context of dramatic changes in the Middle East that would lead to the dis-
membering of the Ottoman Empire. Although missionaries like Zwemer
held their eschatological views lightly, the horrific news stories of the mid-
to late 1910s stimulated other American Christians with more apocalyptic
sensibilities. World War I transformed American Christians' views of Islam
by disrupting missionary efforts, requiring missionaries to face the horror
of the Armenian genocide, and reshaping American eschatological views of
the collapsed Ottoman Empire and Muslims generally. The editor of the
Biblical World exulted in 1913 at the Turks' defeat in 1912–13 by its European
satellites in the Balkans. "The fall of the Beast and the Harlot may not yet be
fully ours, but we can already see that Turkey can never again be the arch-
enemy of Christianity." By 1918, the Ottoman Empire would cease to exist,
and millions of Armenians, previously among the most important Christian targets of Western missions to the Middle East, would have been de-
ported or brutally murdered by Turks.[23]

Since the late nineteenth century, the Armenian minority's position
within Turkey had become increasingly endangered, as Turkish authorities
viewed them with a suspicion that was at least indirectly related to the
American missionaries' disproportionate attention given to the Armenians.
Between 1894 and 1896, Sultan Abdul Hamid ordered the massacre of tens
of thousands of Armenians. These killings stimulated the American publication of Frederick Greene's *Armenian Massacres, or, The Sword of Mohammed* (1896). Greene, an ABCFM missionary to the Armenians, secured
endorsements for his book from a host of luminaries, including William
Gladstone, Josiah Strong, Cyrus Hamlin, Julia Ward Howe, and Frances
Willard. Greene included testimonies from a variety of witnesses to the
killings. One insisted that Turkey had adopted a policy of "crushing the
Christians" in the empire, so that Christian Europe had a duty "to prohibit
Turkey from acting the part of Anti-Christ." Another attributed the violence
to "religious and race hatred." Greene downplayed religion and race, however, and argued that the Muslim failure to separate church and state meant
that the Turks enlisted state power to execute religious violence.[24]

Appended to Greene's book was popular religion writer Henry Northrop's
The Mohammedan Reign of Terror in Armenia, which attributed the Turks'
violence largely to their faith. He blamed "ignorant and intolerant" sheikhs
and imams, as well as dervishes and "howlers." These latter groups turned
their ecstatic religion into a motivation for killing Christians, Northrop believed. Dancing, chanting, and screaming, they worked themselves into fits,
and "most of them think that the killing of a Christian is a sure passport to
heaven." Allowing some room for Muslim moderation, Northrop com-

mented that these groups were "the cranks of Mohammedanism" and not representative of all Muslims. Nevertheless, he believed that the murders of the Armenians originated in Islamic theology and government, which could never tolerate Christian minorities for long. Frances Willard, president of the Women's Christian Temperance Union, was more blunt in the preface to another book on the killings of the mid-1890s. Islam was solely to blame for the atrocities, according to her, as Muslims had long believed that killing Christians would guarantee eternal bliss. "Under the insane spell of this awful fanaticism, they have come down like wolves on the gentle Christian people" and murdered them only because they were Christians. Given past understandings of Muslims' moral characteristics, Willard's views on the massacres were no doubt commonly shared in America.[25]

The killings of the mid-1890s were unfortunately only the beginning of the Turks' onslaught against Armenians. Fearing that the Armenians would revolt in the event of a Russian invasion, the Young Turks began systematically exterminating them in April 1915. Eventually a million or more Armenians fell victim to the genocide. Many Americans like missionary William Miller interpreted the tragedy as a product of "devilish Moslem fanaticism." Armenians were often tortured, violated, and killed by the most sadistic means imaginable. Many American missionaries fled Turkey, or died during the epidemics that followed the waves of violence, and by the end of 1915 the ABCFM's work had been reduced by half. Many American Christians recoiled in horror at both the German-Turkish alliance, and the Armenian slaughter. A satirical letter published in *The World War in Prophecy* (1917) by H. C. Morrison (the president of Asbury College, an evangelical Methodist school in Kentucky), featured Satan writing a letter to the German Kaiser in which he expressed amazement at the sight of German officers commanding Turkish armies to massacre Christians. Satan was so disgusted with the atrocities committed by the Turks that he abdicated his office to the Kaiser: "the great key of hell will be turned over to you," the devil wrote.[26]

Although the Armenian genocide confirmed Americans' worst stereotypes of Muslim brutality, the American missionaries' responses to the extermination campaign featured some heroic defenses of the imperiled Armenians. Among the most publicized accounts of American missionary bravery was that of Dr. Clarence Ussher, an ABCFM medical worker in the city of Van. The Turkish governor of Van province began a brutal killing spree in early 1915, with orders issued that the "Armenians must be exterminated. If any Moslem protect a Christian, first, his house shall be burned, then the Christian killed before his eyes, and then his [the Moslem's] family and himself." Ussher remained in the Armenian quarter of Van trying to

treat and save as many of the sick and injured as he could, and almost suc-
cumbed to typhus himself. The illness did kill his wife. But Ussher remained
confident that the Turkish government, not the Turks generally, was to
blame for the genocide. Through blatant deception, the Young Turks tried
to arouse the Muslim population against the Christians, but rank-and-
file Turks failed to trust the government, according to Ussher. Instead,
Turks saw the great charity of the missionaries, and the fortitude of the
Christian Armenians, who would rather lose their lives than convert under
duress to Islam. Ussher, exhibiting optimism bordering on naiveté, thought
these circumstances made the "hearts of the Turks" more open than ever to
Christianity.[27]

Led by former missionary and leader of the ABCFM James Barton,
American missionaries also launched an unprecedented fundraising campaign, named "Near East Relief," that sent millions of dollars in cash, food,
and supplies to help the "starving Armenians" in the 1910s and '20s. Barton
also used his close connections to Woodrow Wilson's administration to not
only secure help for the Armenians, but to keep the United States out of the
war against Turkey during World War I. Although Barton and his colleagues
may have truly feared that war would only worsen the Armenians' plight,
ABCFM officials also worried that a U.S. attack might further damage their
substantial property holdings in Turkey, worth more than a hundred million dollars.[28]

In Barton's *Story of Near East Relief* (1930), he followed Frederick Greene's
example by not identifying religion as the primary reason that the Turks
slaughtered the Armenians. Apparently, Barton felt that if he could make
the case that specific strategies concocted by a corrupt government had precipitated the tragedy, then he could also hope for reform of the Turkish government. If the Armenian genocide simply reflected Muslim hatred for
Christians, then the Turkish and Armenian problems would be inevitable
and unsolvable, a true clash of religions. He admitted that if the Armenians
had simply converted to Islam, the massacres would not have happened.
The complex connections between religion, nationality, and government
produced the crisis, and "differences of religion" did not sufficiently explain
what transpired, according to Barton. He quoted historian Arnold Toynbee,
a key player in British relief efforts, who wrote that "Mussulman fanaticism"
had nothing to do with the genocide. To the extent that Muslim intolerance
played a role, Barton said, it was only as a tool for Turkish political domination. These subtle distinctions may have been lost on an American public
who routinely read sensational newspaper accounts of "Turkish horrors" in
the genocide.[29]

Ultimately, the Armenian genocide did not seem substantially to change many American Christians' impression of Islam, as negative stereotypes of Muslims were only confirmed by the Turks' slaughter of Armenians. If anything, after 1915 ABCFM leaders like Barton, Greene, and Ussher tried to soften American Christians' revulsion against Turkish Islam by arguing that the genocide was fundamentally political, not religious in motivation.[30] The great changes emerging from World War I that influenced American views of political Islam, instead, were the Ottoman Empire's failed alliance with Germany, the Turkish Empire's dissolution at the war's end, and new hopes for a Jewish homeland in Palestine, publicly proclaimed in Britain's 1917 Balfour Declaration.

Even before the war concluded, American Christian observers were pronouncing that the Turks had sealed their own fate by their decision to ally with Germany. The Germans supposedly wanted to use the Turks to stir up a pan-Islamic jihad against the imperial powers of western Europe, "turning the hordes of Mohammedans loose in merciless rapine to deluge the whole Christian world with fire and blood," as H. C. Morrison put it. Most other Islamic countries and groups failed to follow the Ottomans' lead, leading James Barton to observe that all religious and political unity among the world's Muslims had been shattered. This situation presented, in Barton's view, a special new opportunity for Christian evangelization. Barton, the ardent Wilsonian, believed that the churches should enlist in the cause of making "the emerging democracies of the nations safe for themselves and for the world" through the civilizing effects of the gospel.[31]

Samuel Zwemer similarly argued that the course of the war, and all intellectual and cultural signs, pointed toward what he called "The Disintegration of Islam," the title of a lecture series at Princeton and a 1916 book. Zwemer believed that history was moving inexorably toward Islam's destruction, which was a "divine preparation for the evangelization of Moslem lands." Zwemer saw Islam as groaning under the weight of centuries of corrupt tradition. The most appealing Muslims to Zwemer were its reform advocates. Zwemer particularly admired eleventh-century Sufi theologian Muhammad al-Ghazali, who represented "Islam at its best" because of the way he tried to inject spirituality into cold tradition. Nothing, however, could save Islam except for Christ.[32]

In Zwemer's view, political changes seemed to be hastening Islam's demise. He regarded the Turks' alliance with Germany as "suicide," producing only failed hopes of a pan-Islamic jihad against France and Britain. As a result of that ill-fated union, the Ottoman Empire and its Islamic Caliphate (which held claim to religious leadership for the global Muslim community), seemed grievously threatened. Pan-Muslim unity had become irre-versibly fractured, and most of the Muslim world would soon lay under Western imperial control, which would likely bring religious freedom and the right for Muslims to convert to Christianity. Zwemer had no sympathy for the idea that Islam could become a stepping-stone to Christianity, or that Islam was somehow a primitive form of religion that Christianity fulfilled. Instead, he saw an unbridgeable cultural and theological gulf be-tween Christianity and traditional Islam, a gulf that was brutally exposed in the Armenian massacres. Modernized educated Muslims under Western imperial governments were the best targets for conversion to Christianity, because they saw the ostensible intellectual embarrassments in Muslim tra-dition and theology. He called for evangelistic efforts particularly to appeal to these educated classes and reformed Muslims, because soon "Reformed Islam will be Islam no longer, but an open door into Christianity." [33]

The postmillennial eschatology of key missions advocates like Zwemer and Barton played little specific role in their writings, only giving them a general confidence that Christianity's triumph was inevitable. Other Ameri-can Christian writers saw the events of World War I through a much more precise eschatological paradigm. World War I supplied more news fit for es-chatological speculation than any other event in the early twentieth century, and seemed to fulfill many premillennialists' expectations of what would happen as the last days approached. World War I was widely seen as setting the table for the physical return of the Jews to Palestine and the rise of the Antichrist. Critical to that process was the collapse of the Ottoman Empire and the end of Muslim control over Jerusalem. Even before those events transpired, American Christians like H. C. Morrison were anticipating that the end of the "times of the Gentiles" was at hand, when the British army would drive "the unspeakable Turk" from Jerusalem and Palestine, opening the door for the Jewish regathering. [34]

Two events in late 1917 electrified American prophecy scholars: first, in November, the British Foreign Secretary Arthur Balfour officially commit-ted Britain to the idea of creating a "national home" in Palestine for the Jew-ish people. Second, in December, the British captured Jerusalem from the Turks. These developments led dispensationalists to proclaim the imminent return of Jews to the ancient land of Israel, a development that several years earlier seemed almost impossible. C. I. Scofield called the seizure of Jerusa-lem a "real prophetic sign." Pastor A. B. Simpson, leader of the Christian and Missionary Alliance, wept as he read the Balfour declaration to his congre-gation, and told readers that the fall of Jerusalem was "a signal from heaven, and the marking of an epoch of history and prophecy." [35]

At a prophecy conference in Philadelphia in 1918, A. E. Thompson, who at the outset of the war had been the pastor of the American Church at Jerusalem, exulted over the British defeat of the Turks at Jerusalem. It was an event "to which students of prophecy have been looking forward for many years" and a "pivot in prophecy." It represented the "beginning of the downfall of Mohammedanism" and "the triumph of the cross." It also signaled the destruction of Muslim political power in the Middle East. The easy bloodless defeat of the well-defended city was another sign: "that was God," Thompson concluded. It heralded the state-sponsored return of the Jews to Palestine, and a great opening of the Muslim world to Christian proselytizing. Finally, the end of the war prepared the way for the rise of the Antichrist over the new ten-nation confederacy, which might well be represented by the new League of Nations, he believed.[36]

Adventists, although somewhat marginal to evangelical circles because of their Millerite origins and Saturday Sabbath, maintained eschatological views of Islam that were similar to other conservative Protestants'. The Adventist tract *World Peace in the Light of Bible Prophecy* (1919) took an even more specific view of the eschatological import of the Ottoman Empire's collapse. The anonymous author argued that the "king of the north" in Daniel 11 represented the Ottoman Empire. The prediction that "He shall come to his end, and none shall help him" (Daniel 11:45) was fulfilled in the empire's dismemberment. Following nineteenth-century historicists, the Adventist writer argued that the Ottomans' end also fulfilled the prophecy of Revelation 16:12 concerning the drying up of the Euphrates. He believed that these events set the stage for the battle of Armageddon, but because Daniel 11 also spoke of the king of the north moving his seat of government ("the tabernacles of his palace") to Jerusalem (the "holy mountain"), the writer also expected the "Mohammedan hordes" to make one final attack on Jerusalem and to move their capital there. This would elicit the great attack of the surrounding nations on Palestine, precipitating Armageddon.[37]

Texas fundamentalist Baptist pastor J. Frank Norris visited Palestine in 1920 and concluded that the Arab Muslims would inevitably lose the land to the Jews, both because of the Arabs' degraded racial characteristics and because of the biblical-prophetic mandate. Comparing the Arabs to Native Americans, Norris remarked that in Palestine "it will be the survival of the fittest," and "the Jew is industrious, the Arab lazy; the Jew is progressive, the Arab is only half civilized." Norris saw the providential purpose behind World War I as the return of the Jews to Palestine. Their arrival would set the stage for the national conversion of the Jews to Christianity, he believed, and the return of Christ. Fundamentalist Methodist writer Arno Gaebelein agreed, rejoicing that Jerusalem was "delivered from the bloody grasp of the hellish Turk." He speculated that the "unseen hosts of heaven" had fought on the British side in the battle, and declared that providence had used the war to "take away Palestine from the Turk and make it possible for the Jewish people to return."[38]

For decades to come, American observers would aver that the capture of Jerusalem marked the beginning of the end of the "times of the Gentiles" (Luke 21:24), and the start of the Jews' return to Palestine. Keith Brooks, editor of *Prophecy Monthly*, contended in 1937 that World War I was fought simply to "open the way for the Jew to return to the Holy Land." God had given the British a bloodless victory at Jerusalem to set the stage for the Jews' homecoming, which had precipitated Arab protests and rioting in Palestine. Brooks saw this as a continuation of the ancient hostility between "the seed of Ishmael and the seed of Isaac." He hardly anticipated peace between Muslims and Jews in Palestine, but believed that fighting and turmoil would continue until the "Mosque of Omar" (the Dome of the Rock) was "demolished" and the Jews were converted to Christianity. The "blood bitterness of Ishmael" would not permit the Arabs to tolerate the Jews' presence in Palestine.[39]

By the conclusion of World War I, many American Christians believed that the era of Muslim political power in the Middle East had ended, in accordance with prophecies regarding the "times of the Gentiles" and the return of the Jews to Palestine. In these scenarios, the Jews played a much more central role in God's redemptive plans than did Muslims, who seemed destined only to be swept aside by God in the last days. But in the segment of conservative Protestantism concerned with missions, the study of Muslim culture for the purpose of evangelism had become more scholarly than ever, thanks to the work of Samuel Zwemer and others. Zwemer and his colleagues exuded postmillennial confidence about Christ's inexorable triumph in the Muslim world, even though actual evangelization of Muslims remained very limited. The tendency that Presbyterian missionary-educator Charles Watson referred to as the missionaries' "strange fatality for turning away from Moslems," and evangelizing non-Muslims instead, persisted. Many conservative American Christians continued to expect Islam's destruction in the last days, or perhaps the widespread conversion of Muslims to Christianity. While dreams of the apocalypse flourished, actual efforts to see Muslims evangelized remained proportionately insignificant.[40]

w Missionary Overture to
ıslims and the Arab-Israeli Crisis

IN THE 1920S, the missionary consensus surrounding the "evangelization of the world in this generation" began to falter. R. C. Hutchison, a philosophy professor at a Presbyterian college in Iran, wrote provocatively in the *Atlantic Monthly* in 1926 and '27 that missions to Muslims had failed because Christians had not shown enough love to Muslims. Although Hutchison still believed in proselytization, he also believed that Christian missionaries should not demand that non-Christians convert in exchange for the Christians' benevolence. "Service to needy men requires no pay in the form of conversion," he wrote. He believed in the possibility of a "nonevangelical, nonproselytizing message of Christianity" that would supplement the good news of redemption through Christ. Hutchinson's and others' elevation of service-oriented missions confirmed the fear of conservatives that theological modernists were quietly betraying the great purpose of missions: the salvation of souls.[1]

The 1910s and '20s saw the outbreak of the Protestant fundamentalist-modernist controversy in America, in which theological conservatives stood against the rising tide of modernist thought. These religious controversies split denominations and were encapsulated for the nation in the 1925 Scopes Trial over teaching evolution in Tennessee's public schools. Theological squabbles had begun to affect denominational mission boards by the early 1920s, but among advocates of missions to Muslims, older models assuring Western Christians of Islam's eventual collapse remained dominant. Leading missions proponent John Mott's edited volume *The Moslem World of To-Day* (1925) pointed to the great changes among Muslims, highlighted by the abolition of the Caliphate that accompanied the end of the Ottoman regime. The "impending disintegration of Islam calls for an adequate substitute," Mott wrote. "Only Christ and his programme can meet the need." Despite his predictions of Islam's demise, Mott also called for Christians to take a "positive, constructive, fraternal, and co-operative" approach to Muslims and their faith. Robert Speer, secretary of the Presbyterian Board of Foreign Missions, confidently asserted in the volume that there was a deep theological divide between Christianity and Islam, and that ultimately the "Moslem peoples need to know and love and obey God as revealed in Christ." Mott recommended that social service should complement, but not replace, direct proclamation of the gospel.[2]

As sensible as the combination of service and proselytization may have seemed, the old strategies could not hold due to the growing schism between modernists and fundamentalists. Some modernists suggested that the desire to "convert" non-Christians was coercive and outdated. This view was expressed in the controversial "Laymen's Report" of 1932, which emerged from a commission sponsored by John D. Rockefeller, Jr. This commission produced a seven-volume report and a one-volume summary, titled *Re-Thinking Missions*. Chairman William Ernest Hocking, a professor at Harvard who was primarily responsible for the perspective expressed in *Re-Thinking Missions*, called for recasting missions as "world understanding on the spiritual level." Collaboration, education, and service were to be the new aims of missions, not proselytization and conversion.[3]

Re-Thinking Missions helped fracture irretrievably the Protestant missionary community. Robert Speer wrote to missionary William Miller and expressed fear that because of the controversy, missionary agencies were "in danger of being torn asunder between the ultra-modernists. . .and the ultra-fundamentalists." While the American Board of Commissioners for Foreign Missions enthusiastically sent copies of the book to its missionaries, the conservative magazine *Sunday School Times* called it a "strange, sinister, Satanic document." Many older missions advocates expressed reservations about the book's dismissal of conversionist preaching, but agreed that social service held an important place in missions. Samuel Zwemer addressed the Laymen's Report with reference to Christian work among Muslims in his *Thinking Missions with Christ* (1934). While maintaining his relatively irenic approach to Islam, Zwemer sided with Christian fundamentalists in arguing that there was no point in blurring the stark theological differences between Christianity and Islam (or other world religions). Active missionaries among Muslims knew these differences well, for Islam's "denial of Jesus Christ's mission, His Incarnation, His Atonement, His Deity, are the very issues of the conflict," he wrote. Although Zwemer had retired from the mission field to teach at Princeton Seminary, he cautioned academic theologians that they needed to keep thinking in "black and white" to maintain orthodoxy. The contrast between Christianity and Islam was clear to Zwemer: "it pleased the Father that in Jesus Christ should all fulness dwell, not in Mohammed."[4]

Zwemer's theological approach to non-Christian religions, including

Islam, would eventually win the day among most American missionaries, despite the fact that modernists seemed to triumph in many of the battles over mainline Protestant denominations and their mission boards. A relativistic view of religion gradually deflated the liberals' missionary impulse as many of them abandoned the quest to win converts. Evangelicals and fundamentalists, meanwhile, founded alternative agencies to continue reaching the world for Christ. Beginning in the 1930s, the mainline missionary agencies went into a protracted decline, while conservative missions groups began a steady ascendancy. By 1980, some 35,000 career missionaries from America were in the field, and conservative denominations and ministries employed more than ninety percent of them.[5]

In the Middle East, evangelical missionaries like the Christian and Missionary Alliance's Ralph Fried, pastor of the American Gospel Church in Jerusalem, took a hard-nosed approach to evangelism and deplored older missionary efforts that had dabbled with modernism and the social gospel of service and reform. Although many Western missionaries were in the Middle East, Fried argued that many of them did not share the goals of born-again Christians. First among the deceivers were those who worked for a "union of nominal Protestants with some of the idolatrous Oriental churches." Second were those who were "not preaching the Gospel." The final group was the representatives of "false sects." Minus all these, true missionary work in the Middle East was quite limited. "Combine the extreme impenetrability of the Moslem with the proud, quick-tempered, prejudiced and determined nature of the Arab and the task seems hopeless," Fried warned. Political rioting among Arabs and Jews made evangelicals' efforts in Palestine even more difficult. But he thought that through the power of God and missionary reinforcements, "trophies of grace" could be won among the Arabs.[6]

An excellent example of the new evangelical agencies, and one which brought new knowledge of African Muslims to American Christians, was the Sudan Interior Mission (SIM). This faith mission targeted the northern areas of sub-Saharan Africa, and originally focused only on proclamation of the gospel, not relief or educational programs. Later, the SIM focused more on medical care and schooling, which they used as a means to share the message of Christ. The agency reprised the nineteenth-century experiences of the ABCFM in the Middle East, as SIM missionaries ostensibly came to evangelize both animists and Muslims, but ended up winning most converts among non-Muslims. African Muslims usually faced intense pressure not to convert or even associate with the missionaries. SIM missionaries reported that some African Muslim converts to Christianity were poisoned and killed. Muslim leaders took on a menacing cast in the missionaries' minds, as opposed to the more innocuous "heathens." SIM founder Rowland Bingham recalled being horrified as a young man at the prospect of "Moslem kings of the north" raiding "pagan" areas for slaves. Bingham resolved to "reach the Central Sudan with the Gospel." Between the 1920s and 1940s, both the SIM's staff and its financial resources increased tenfold, despite the intervention of the Great Depression.[7]

In the view of SIM missionaries, expressed in reports to North American supporters, Islam represented "Satan's masterpiece," a deceitfully easy religion designed by the devil to trap its adherents. Engaging actual African Muslims and reading Samuel Zwemer's works softened many SIM missionaries' views of Islam in the 1930s and '40s. Nevertheless, they commonly described Muslims as nominal and functionally pagan, and considered Islam a social problem that degraded family life.[8]

SIM medical missionaries Douglas and Laura Hursh held common American views of Islam in sub-Saharan Africa. They wrote home from Nigeria during World War II, and wondered at the strange manners of the Muslims there. In contrast to the scantily clad "pagans," the Muslims "wear more clothing than they need with their long gowns and turbans," they noted. The Hurshes marveled at the Muslims' prayer rituals, and concluded that "they have Judaism and Catholicism beat when it comes to law and works." Nevertheless, they thought that "when saved, [the Muslims] make real Christians." Laura Hursh deplored the way that Muslims at their clinic attributed sickness in children to evil spirits. "Mohammedanism is as bad as paganism in some ways," she said. Despite their skepticism about unseen forces causing sickness, Douglas later recalled Kano, Nigeria, a heavily Muslim city where he worked in an eye clinic, as a place filled with evil spirits. The local Muslims were "lax" in their devotion, but once an Indian Muslim missionary associated with the fundamentalist Ahmadiyya movement appeared at the clinic and tried to proselytize among the patients. Hursh perceived that the man was "Satanic," and he and the clinic superintendent banned the missionary from speaking to patients. "There was just a feeling there of...the devil himself being in our midst," he remembered. Hursh also encountered many women patients who claimed to be demon-possessed and who could at times speak fluent English, of which they had no previous knowledge.[9]

By 1960, the SIM had become the largest Christian mission organization in Africa, with more than twelve hundred missionaries working across the continent's central region. In a popular account, *Splinters from an African Log* (1960), SIM medical missionary Martha Wall depicted Christianity and

Islam as locked in a great spiritual battle for Niger's and Nigeria's souls. The Muslim towns of Niger were Satan's "territory." At one of the great moments of dramatic tension in the book, the SIM missionaries tried to build a new mud-walled church in Muslim-dominated Tsibiri, but the "powers of darkness were set against that church and the Christ whose worship it would proclaim." Local Muslims prayed that the rains of the growing season would ruin the church, and the SIM team prayed that the rains would hold off. Indeed, the rains did not come until the roof was finished. It was like an Old Testament scene, such as Elijah's showdown with the prophets of Baal, with the same spiritual powers at odds.[10]

Wall expressed discouragement about the prospects of evangelizing African Muslims. They faced many of the same pressures and threats not to convert as Muslims elsewhere, and she felt an urgent desire to see "pagans" convert to Christianity before Muslim evangelists and their "fanatic missionary activity" got to them. She estimated that thousands of animists converted to Christianity for every one Muslim who did so. Nevertheless, in the penultimate chapter of the book she discovered a rural Muslim village that had largely converted to Christianity and been "delivered from the tentacles of Islam." She offered a warning that the progress of Muslim missions represented "everlasting death creeping subtly over the land and into the hearts of undying souls." Fifty years after the Edinburgh Conference, Wall and other SIM missionaries still painted Africa as a dark continent bound for domination by either Christianity or Islam.[11]

The concept of the Muslim as uniquely difficult to reach transferred easily to the new evangelical and fundamentalist missionaries of the post–World War II era. Chicago's Moody Press published Eric Fisk's *The Prickly Pear* (1951), which featured stories of evangelical missionary work in Morocco. Fisk presented missions to Muslims as an exercise in what many evangelicals would call "spiritual warfare." He lamented how many well-intentioned missionaries had been wrecked by the experience of trying to evangelize Muslims, and the workers returned home like soldiers with "chronic nerve shock." Why was Muslim evangelization so difficult? Because it represented an assault on the devil's stronghold. "Islam is the Devil's reply to Calvary and Pentecost," Fisk wrote. Because Islam seemed to honor God, but denied Christ's deity, it represented a "masterpiece of delusion." "Satanic pressure" constantly buffeted the Christian missionaries, who sometimes were tempted to believe the "pernicious lie that Muslims cannot be saved." Fisk argued that the missionary had to understand the nature of the devil's attacks in order to survive in a mission field like Morocco.[12]

Despite the perceived difficulties of Muslim evangelization, the American evangelical presence in Muslim areas continued to grow after World War II. It was not only the new non-denominational mission agencies like the SIM that maintained a presence in Muslim regions of the world. The doctrinally conservative Southern Baptist Convention's Foreign Mission Board, for instance, pioneered new evangelistic and publishing efforts in the Middle East during the early twentieth century. Following the establishment of the state of Israel in 1948, Baptist efforts increased significantly, but direct evangelization of Muslims was sporadic and generally unsuccessful. In 1948, Finlay and Julia Graham became the first resident Southern Baptist missionaries in Lebanon, having briefly served in several other Middle Eastern locations. Finlay Graham's early impressions of Middle Eastern Muslims were grim, and reflected earlier criticisms leveled by Samuel Zwemer and others. Western culture was slowly breaking down the rigid conservatism of Muslim culture, he believed, but there was little effective Christian witness among them to help replace Islam. Graham particularly worried about Muslim women, who seemed to live practically as "slaves." He hoped that the gospel of Christ would "emancipate them" and give them equal educational opportunities. Graham remained sober about the prospects for evangelizing Muslims because of the Muslims' own "fanaticism" and the poor example of eastern Christians. In the relatively freer environment of Lebanon, the Grahams did see some Muslim converts. The first, a teenage student named Alia Mikdadi, was baptized in 1954, and despite pressure from her father she seems to have stood fast in her conversion, which proved "a means of blessing and revival to the whole church," according to the Grahams. Mikdadi's father subsequently received threatening letters from the Muslim Brotherhood in Lebanon.[13]

The Foreign Mission Board published a host of books on missions in the mid-twentieth century, presumably for Southern Baptist adult and youth studies of the peoples among whom Baptist missionaries worked. These guides tended to be comparatively generous in their assessment of Islam, showing the influence of Samuel Zwemer's thought. For instance, despite the sensational title of Pen Lile Pittard's *Clash of Swords* (1952), she saw the conflicts in the Middle East as complicated by ancient and modern violence committed by Muslims, Jews, and Christians alike. She lamented that the founding of the state of Israel meant that Arab residents were "cruelly shoved out of the way to make room." As a result, "hundreds of millions of followers of Mohammed are ready to take up the sword in a holy war (*Jihad*) against the Western world." Pittard did not attribute the violence in Israel to prophetic inevitability.[14]

Similar in its relative nuance, *A World within a World* (1955) by high school teacher Elwyn Lee Means described global missions to Muslims as neglected, difficult, and short on results. She did not blame the lack of success on Muslims, but on a lack of Christian "stewardship." She also resisted singling Muslims out as particularly intransigent: they needed "to be saved, not because they are Moslems or the devotees of any other faith, but because they need Christ." Often citing Zwemer, Means gave a sober summary of Muslim history and doctrine, as well as Southern Baptist mission work in the Middle East and other Muslim regions. She concluded by calling on her readers to pray and give more money for Muslim evangelization, to learn as much about Islam as they could, and to remember that "each Moslem is of great worth in the sight of God." In contrast to Martha Wall's depiction of African Muslims as especially malevolent, in Means's estimation Muslims were like all other sinners in need of Christ—no better or worse.[15]

Finlay Graham's *Sons of Ishmael: How Shall They Hear?* (1969) struck a similar tone, commenting on "the tragedy of a divided Palestine" and "extreme Zionism" as barriers to peaceful relations and an effective Christian witness in the Middle East. He also cited Zwemer favorably, and called for Baptists to use a wide range of proclamation techniques, as well as educational and medical services, to help meet Christians' "greatest unmet challenge": the conversion of Muslims. The Southern Baptists' continuing commitment to missions in troubled areas of the Middle East has resulted occasionally in extreme violence against their missionaries, including episodes widely reported in America that reinforced popular stereotypes of Muslim fanaticism. In 1972, Baptist medical missionary Mavis Pate was shot and killed in Gaza. More recently, in late 2003, three Baptist medical missionaries in Yemen were killed in a terrorist's attack inside their hospital. Since World War II, the Southern Baptist Convention has become one of America's key denominational forces contending for Muslims' souls on the foreign mission field, complementing the contemporaneous ascendancy of non-denominational agencies like the SIM.[16]

Samuel Zwemer continued to frame most conservative missionaries' thoughts about Islam after World War II. No evangelical writer on Islam has yet surpassed the comparative influence of Zwemer in his time, as seen in part in his broad influence on missions thought among an array of Christian groups. Although American Catholic missionary writing with regard to Islam was relatively limited as of the mid-twentieth century, a key Jesuit text also showed Zwemer's influence. Thomas O'Shaughnessy's *Islamism: Its Rise and Decline* (1946) found Islam deficient in ways reminiscent of Protestantism: "Deprived of a teaching body infallible in the spiritual and moral guidance of its adherents, the Mohammedan religion is laid open to the inroads of emotion and caprice, to the whims and passions of men, [and] to bizarre interpretations of its deposit of belief." Similarly, "in the Mohammedan system, . . .as in that of the Protestant innovators of the sixteenth century, salvation depends on faith alone." Acceptance of the Muslim creed was essential for salvation, regardless of one's good works. Just as Protestant critics often compared Islam to Roman Catholicism, O'Shaughnessy compared Islam to Protestantism. Like Zwemer (whose *Moslem World* he commended), O'Shaughnessy anticipated "the waning of the crescent" as modernizing forces influenced Muslim culture. He hoped that the "evils of materialism and religious indifferentism" among them might prepare the way "for the coming of the true Faith." The decline of Islam appeared to be inevitable, but less certain was its replacement by Christianity.[17]

Despite Zwemer's unparalleled authority, some other Protestant writers did carry on Zwemer's tradition of scholarly yet popular writing on Islam, including his protégé J. Christy Wilson, Sr. Wilson worked as a missionary in Persia and wrote what remains the standard biography of Zwemer, *Apostle to Islam* (1952), published shortly after Zwemer's death. Wilson's most enduring work was the pamphlet *Introducing Islam* (1950), which appeared in at least five American editions between the 1950s and '80s. Zwemer's influence was clear in Wilson's approach to Islam and the Prophet, as Wilson spoke of the "great truths and high accomplishments in Islam," yet he maintained that Christianity was spiritually superior. He also believed that with growing Western influence in Muslim areas, the Islamic world stood at the edge of a "dramatic new era" of change. He hoped that the difficulties of Muslim evangelization would inspire a "great spiritual campaign of love." Revealing a postwar skepticism about state power and missions, Wilson carefully avoided a militaristic tone when describing the evangelistic campaign. He pointedly noted that "Jesus does not want political power, but does want the hearts and wills and souls of. . .the whole world of Islam." Wilson conceded that success in missions to Muslims seemed very distant.[18]

Perhaps the most influential scholar-missionary of Islam in the second half of the twentieth century, who assumed something approaching Zwemer's place in Islamic missions studies, was Kenneth Cragg, an Anglican bishop who held posts in Jerusalem and Cairo. Cragg's sway among evangelical American Christians was somewhat ironic, given his liturgical bent and suspicion of evangelical missionary tactics. Nevertheless, Cragg's learned yet accessible *The Call of the Minaret* (1956) has remained required reading for many conservative Western Christians interested in Islam. The book appeared in at least eight American editions, and remains in print today.

Cragg was an irenic high-church version of Zwemer, and in 1952 Cragg followed Zwemer as an editor of the *Muslim World* (so renamed from the *Moslem World* in 1948). Although he studied Islam closely and highlighted its positive aspects, Cragg believed that Muslims needed to convert to Christianity. This Christian conversionism, combined with his depth of scholarly insight, helps explain his work's enduring popularity among American conservatives. But some of his views also challenged the conventional opinions of many American Christians regarding Islam, the Middle East, and missions. *The Call of the Minaret* expressed deep reservations about the treatment of Arab Muslims in Palestine, lamenting their "deepening experience of deprivation, indignity, frustration, insecurity, expropriation, and tragedy," which he "laid squarely at the door of the current version of Zionism."[19]

Cragg also criticized Western missionary tactics in the Middle East, especially the preoccupation with numbers of converts. Quality of mission was more important than numbers, and prospective missionaries "should remember to think before they start to count." The Christian missionary among Muslims should expect to struggle and serve, often with few obvious results. Cragg even proposed downplaying the importance of baptism for converts, in order to avoid the implication that proselytes were abandoning not only their religion, but also their families and culture. Cragg still insisted that a "Christian mission that renounces the making of Christians has forsaken both its genius and its duty. Christ did not serve the world with good advice, and no more shall we." Cragg was not as dismayed as others by the difficulties of Muslim evangelization, for in his view suffering and patience represented normal aspects of the disciplined Christian life.[20]

As Cragg's references to the Palestinians indicated, Western Christians had growing reasons to be interested in the political relationship between Islam and Judaism in the Middle East during the post–World War I era. News from the Middle East may also have fueled some American evangelicals' sense of urgency regarding missions. To many conservative American Christians, signs seemed to point to Christ's imminent return, and as Samuel Zwemer noted at a 1943 prophecy conference, "those who are filled with the hope of His coming, are also on fire for world-wide evangelism." Following the 1917 Balfour Declaration, rapid Jewish immigration to Palestine and tensions over the use of sacred sites in Jerusalem fostered growing hostility between the Jewish and Arab populations. That resentment erupted in August 1929 with rioting and ethnic violence, leaving hundreds of Jews and Arabs dead and wounded. Rioting continued in the 1930s, and in 1939 the British pulled away from the Balfour Declaration when they called for an end to Jewish immigration and repudiated an independent Jewish state.

This stance lasted through World War II, even as the details of the Nazis' Final Solution were becoming known. Many American evangelicals saw Hitler as "energized by Satan himself," and believed that in light of the Nazi campaign to destroy the Jews, the need for a Jewish state in Palestine was even more urgent. In 1947, the British deferred the Palestinian situation to the newly created United Nations, and U.S. President Harry Truman called for the establishment of an autonomous Israel. Finally, in 1948–49, Jews and Arabs fought a vicious war over Israeli independence, resulting in the establishment of the nation of Israel and the displacement of hundreds of thousands of Arab Palestinian refugees.[21]

Many American Christian writers filtered these events through the lenses of dispensational theology, which held that the Bible's prophecies of the last days referred chiefly to future events in a reestablished Israel. Premillennial dispensationalism began to grow in popularity in America and Britain in the late nineteenth century, replacing older historicist modes of prophetic interpretation. Dispensationalists broke redemptive history into a series of distinct eras, or "dispensations." The final dispensation, which received a disproportionate amount of attention, would be the millennium, or thousand-year kingdom of God on earth, which would be preceded by Jesus's physical return to earth. By the early twentieth century, millions of American Protestants had come to view world events in the context of dispensationalism, which they received in Sunday sermons and popular publications, led by C. I. Scofield's reference Bible, published in 1909.

Dispensationalists looked on tumultuous political and military happenings as possible signs of the return of Christ. They typically expected that the Jews would return to Palestine prior to Christ's second coming, and so they excitedly tracked the Zionist movement's campaign to create a Jewish homeland in Palestine. Prophecy writer George T. B. Davis explained that the Jewish immigration to Palestine represented "the Lord's appointed hour to rebuild and re-people the land, and all the nations of the earth are utterly powerless" to stop it. He blamed the Arabs for the violence of 1929, and chastised them for not being more appreciative of the material blessings the Jews' return had brought. The SIM's Roland Bingham wrote of the Jewish immigration that "when God has opened a door, no man or set of men can close it." A. H. Carter, writing in *Bible Witness*, assigned demonic causes to the Arabs' resistance, saying "Whatever Satan and his instruments may attempt to do, they can never succeed in frustrating God's purposes regarding the children of Israel. The Arabs' present efforts. . .will never be successful." Evangelist Charles Price contended that the Arabs' removal from Palestine was biblically ordained, and that the Jews would receive temporary protection from European powers to tear down the Dome of the Rock and rebuild the temple. "Then the Moslem world will gnash its teeth in rage," but there was nothing it could do to stop the prophetic timetable, Price believed. Such assumptions of eschatological inevitability made it difficult for dispensationalists to take Arab Palestinians' grievances seriously.[22]

Charles Trumbull, editor of the *Sunday School Times*, expressed the conventional wisdom of dispensational theologians when he argued that the return of the Jews to Palestine represented the "budding of the fig tree" that Christ referred to in Matthew 24. Although some earlier prophecy writers had assumed that the Jews would not return to Palestine until after their mass conversion to Christianity, now writers like Trumbull became convinced that the Jews would come back to the land "in unbelief," preparing the way for the great assault on Israel during the Great Tribulation, and the Antichrist's occupation of the rebuilt Jewish temple. Dispensational prophecy experts still rarely gave Muslims a central place in the events of the last days because of the theologians' abandonment of historicist eschatology. In 1943, John Walvoord of Dallas Theological Seminary, the citadel of American dispensational theology, spoke on the drying up of the Euphrates in Revelation 16:12, and dismissed older interpretations that saw this passage as the waning of Turkish or Muslim power. Instead, Walvoord believed that the verse should be interpreted literally, suggesting that at some point during the Tribulation the actual Euphrates River would dry up, preparing the way, as the verse said, for an invasion of Israel by the "kings of the east." Walvoord speculated that the kings of the east would cross the dry river bed and attack restored Israel at Armageddon, but he hesitated to identify the kings' identities, suggesting that the Chinese, Persians, Indians, and Japanese were among the likely candidates. By the end of World War II, few placed the Muslim-Jewish conflict at the center of eschatological scenarios, but many American Christians did see the Jewish return to Palestine as biblically mandated, and the Arabs' opposition to it as a futile part of global anti-Semitism in the last days.[23]

Pastor Dean Bedford of Rochester, New York, speaking also at the 1943 prophecy conference, saw all anti-Semitism, including that harbored by Arabs, as having its roots in the ancient hostility between Ishmael and Isaac. As described in Genesis chapters 16 and 21, the patriarch Abraham fathered a child, Ishmael, by his maidservant Hagar, because his wife Sarah was barren. But God told Abraham that his promise to make him a great nation would be fulfilled through the son, Isaac, that Sarah would miraculously conceive in her old age. Ishmael, according to Bedford, was "Satan's substitute for Isaac," and Hagar and Ishmael came to despise Isaac when he was born. This episode "began in Ishmael not only a competing racial group" (presumably the Arabs), "but a competing religion" (presumably Islam). Bedford called on Christians to bless and pray for the Jews, for which they and their countries would receive divine protection. To the dispensationalists, to be anti-Jewish was functionally to be anti-Christian, as well. Thus, as *Prophecy* magazine editor Keith Brooks proclaimed, the "Arab and Moslem world is not only anti-Semitic, but is out and out anti-Christ." This view of the Arab-Israeli conflict as predestined hostility between the descendants of Isaac and Ishmael would become increasingly common among Christian conservatives in the late twentieth century, as would the belief that Christians had an almost unlimited obligation to support Israel against Arab Muslims.[24]

Other American religious conservatives in the mid-twentieth century, such as the Southern Baptist writers cited earlier, expressed a measured sympathy for the plight of the Arab Palestinians, and explained some of the Arabs' anger by reference to political circumstances, not prophetic inevitability. Paul Votaw, who worked in Palestine and Syria with the Presbyterian Board of Foreign Missions in the late 1940s, recalled that most of his missionary colleagues were pro-Arab. He admitted, however, that as a Dallas Seminary graduate he had a "little bias" in favor of the Jews "which is related to prophecy." Being pro-Palestinian did not necessarily relate to theological liberalism. J. Christy Wilson, for instance, insisted that Islam lacked the essential spiritual features of forgiveness of sin and eternal life. In assessing the Middle East crisis, however, he took an even-handed approach. He congratulated Israel for its independence and argued that Jews needed a homeland where they could enjoy freedom and peace. But "we must not lose sight of the Arab side of the question," he wrote. Palestine had long been overwhelmingly Arab, but during the establishment of Israel upwards of "one million Arabs, Moslem and Christian alike, were made homeless," Wilson noted. It would take years to solve this massive refugee problem. He also chastised Israel's Jews for their secularism, and suggested that God's covenant with Israel was contingent on their obedience to God, and did not represent a blank check of blessings under any circumstances. Wilson's measured assessment differed only slightly from the views of many liberal Protestants.[25]

Theologically liberal Christians tended to be more hostile toward Israel than conservatives were. Henry Sloan Coffin, Sr., the former President of Union Theological Seminary, wrote in 1947 that American support for Israel hindered missionary work among Muslims, creating a "violent anti-American feeling" around the Islamic world. Muslims regarded Americans as "aggressive meddlers" and "hypocrites" who expressed sympathy for Europe's Jews but pushed them into Palestine instead of welcoming them in America, Coffin lamented.[26]

Contrary to Coffin, the liberal but "neo-orthodox" Reinhold Niebuhr, America's most famous theologian of the World War II era, adopted an aggressive Zionist position before the war. He supported the American Palestine Committee in its efforts to promote the Jewish homeland, and frankly accepted the reality that establishing Israel would mean depriving the Arabs of certain rights, territorial or otherwise. He hoped that in the long run a solution could be made acceptable to Palestinian Arabs. In 1958, he described the founding of Israel as a "glorious moral and political achievement." He did express embarrassment over "Messianic claims. . .used to substantiate the right of Jews to the particular homeland in Palestine." He also worried about the harm done to the Arabs by the "Jewish ethic and faith" now "embodied in a nation." Niebuhr believed that religious ethics did not blend well with the political choices required of a nation.[27]

Among evangelicals, the key differences between views on the Arab-Israeli crisis lay in eschatological beliefs. Dispensationalists believed in a literal restoration of Israel to the biblical land of Canaan that would precede the Jews' persecution and nearly wholesale conversion to Christianity during the Great Tribulation. Accordingly, they thought Christians should support visible progress toward the accomplishment of these certainties. God had destined the Arabs to be removed from the land. Martin DeHaan, host of the "Radio Bible Class," wrote in *The Jew and Palestine in Prophecy* (1950) that the restoration of Israel represented the greatest fulfilled prophecy yet. The Balfour Declaration had heralded the Western powers' acceptance of prophetic inevitability, but Britain lost its way by allowing many Arabs to remain in Palestine, and by proposing to divide Palestine politically. In doing so, they foolishly fought against the prophetic tide and forced, symbolically speaking, Isaac and Ishmael to live in the same tent. This would only lead to bloodshed. "The present-day Arabs are direct descendants of Ishmael," and God had promised the land to Isaac, not Ishmael. What, then, would solve the Arab-Israeli conflict? Nothing, "until, in obedience to God, the sons of the bondwoman [Arabs] are put out to make way for the sons of promise." Compromise between Arabs (Muslim or Christian) and Jews was pointless, for God had promised the land to the Jews, and God would give them the land one way or the other.[28]

According to many dispensationalists like DeHaan, the biblical land of Canaan was much larger than even an undivided Palestine, implying that the restored nation of Israel would eventually displace many other Middle

Eastern Muslims from Egypt to Iraq. Very soon, DeHaan estimated, Israel would possess not only Palestine, but all land northeast to the Euphrates River, and west to the Sinai Peninsula and the Nile River. "This is the truth of God's Word," he asserted. This belief would make many American Christians sympathetic to Israel's desire to expand beyond its 1948 boundaries. To partition Israel, in this view, was entirely unacceptable. DeHaan prayed that "the nations would turn over to the true possessors of the land of Palestine their full rights and thereby receive the blessing of the Lord." Any nation that tried to limit Israel's prophetic right to the land invited the judgment of God on itself.[29]

The question of Israel's expansion first came to a head during the Suez crisis of 1956–57, when Israel temporarily occupied the Gaza Strip and the Sinai peninsula. When the United States did not support Israel's incursion, many American dispensationalists worried that abandoning Israel risked angering God. Evangelicals were divided over the crisis, however. The new flagship evangelical magazine, *Christianity Today*, tended to blame Arabs for starting the trouble, but also chastised Israel for being "ruthless and aggressive" by displacing hundreds of thousands of Arabs. The magazine hosted a debate over Israel in late 1956 between Fuller Seminary's Wilbur Smith, and Oswald Allis, who had taught at Princeton Seminary and later at the conservative breakaway Westminster Seminary.[30]

Allis, who was a Reformed evangelical and self-consciously anti-dispensationalist, argued that the Bible did not give Israel "clear title to Palestine." He stated that the Jews' possession of the land of Canaan was always conditioned on their obedience to God's laws, and their dispersion came because of their disobedience. Even if the Jews did accept Jesus, that still would not justify their violent expropriation of Palestine. Under the Christian gospel, land and place had become much less significant than it had been in the Old Testament. For Jewish and Gentile Christians, the land of Palestine had no more than "sentimental interest." Allis lamented how world powers had done nothing to "right the wrongs of the dispossessed Arabs, whose tragic condition fosters resentment and hate throughout the entire Moslem world." Veering toward darker anti-Jewish sentiments, Allis asked whether Christians should "be willing to plunge the nations into a third world conflict just to restore unbelieving Jews to, and maintain them in, a land from which they were driven nearly two thousand years ago?" Obviously, Allis thought not.[31]

Wilbur Smith, a professor at the key neo-evangelical Fuller Seminary in California, countered Allis's perspective with the premillennial view. He pointed to Old Testament verses that stated that God had given the Israelites the land of Canaan forever. Although the Old Testament anticipated Jewish exile from the land, it also forecast their return to Israel and the millennial era of peace and blessedness. As for the Arabs, they were only "a curse to the land." The Jews would inevitably possess Palestine and enjoy God's prosperity there. "No anti-Semitism, no wars, no unbelief, no pogroms, not Antichrist himself will be able to prevent the fulfillment of these divinely given promises," Smith concluded.[32]

Despite such confident assertions, Christian observers had to contend with the fact that Israel soon withdrew from the Sinai and suffered considerable diplomatic embarrassment over the episode, as did their backers Britain and France. William Hull, a Canadian Pentecostal missionary in Israel, demonstrated the flexibility of the dispensationalists' views when he explained in his *Israel: Key to Prophecy* (1957) that the Israelis' failed occupation of the Sinai, and the United States' opposition to it, actually set the stage for the imminent attack of Russia and allied Middle Eastern powers against Israel. This represented the prophesied incursion and miraculous destruction of Gog and Magog in Ezekiel 38 and 39. Hull anticipated that Russia would align with Egypt (bitter over the occupation of the Sinai), as well as Iran and Iraq, who would soon "come under Communist control" and "open the pathway...to the mountains of Israel." But God would rain judgment down on the invading "Communist hordes," and Russia would be eliminated from the eschatological stage. In the Cold War era, many evangelicals assumed that Russia would play a key role as the tormenter of the Jews in the last days, but not all pundits included Muslims in the Gog and Magog attack. Prophecy writer Charles Pont believed that the Arab states would ally with Britain and America in the last days. Pentecostal evangelist C. M. Ward went so far as to argue that Arab Muslims and Israelis would unite against Russia, perhaps setting the stage for Armageddon. The Jews' and Arab Muslims' common racial and theistic bonds would lead them to stand against the atheistic Soviet menace. "There is no real quarrel between these Semitic brothers," Ward wrote. Expectation of Jewish and Muslim unity in the last days was not a common position among American conservative Christians in the post-World War II era, however.[33]

Hull's *Israel: Key to Prophecy* marked an important departure in American evangelical literary culture as it provided one of the earliest fictional accounts that detailed the possible events of the dispensational last-days scenario (see Figure 5-1). Such books would grow enormously in popularity over the next half-century. Taking a vicious anti-Catholic perspective, Hull imagined that after the destruction of the Russians, a one-world Antichrist government would emerge, led by a Catholic American President who doubled as head of the United Nations. Sometime around the Russian inva-

FIGURE 5-1. William L. Hull, *Israel: Key to Prophecy* (Grand Rapids, MI, 1957). Author's collection.

sion of Israel, true believers would be raptured (taken up to meet Christ), so that only the godless would be left on earth to worship the Antichrist. Jews and Muslims would be allowed to continue worshipping in their way, but could not make any converts. The "vastness of [the Muslims'] numbers made them a power to be reckoned with," Hull noted. Writing in past-tense style, Hull noted that the Antichrist "permitted [Muslims] to continue their worship of Allah, but required at the same time a token recognition of himself as the earthly leader." Eventually the Antichrist demanded that the Muslims give up the *Haram Esh-Sherif* (Temple Mount) for the rebuilding of the Jewish temple, a deal which they accepted in exchange for their continuing status as an acceptable religion.[34]

Once the temple was rebuilt, the Antichrist set himself up as god and demanded that the Jews worship him. When they refused, he began a massive extermination campaign against them, in which Arab Muslims participated enthusiastically. Hull envisioned how under the reign of the Antichrist, the material fortunes of the Middle Eastern Muslims had dramatically improved. "One thing had not changed," however: "they never wavered in their hatred of Israel." Their displacement in 1948 as a result of "the unprovoked Arab attack on the Jews, had never been forgotten." Hull traced the Muslim refugees' animosity toward the Jews to Ishmael's ancient hatred of Isaac. Summoned by the Antichrist, the newly powerful Arab military attacked surviving Jews in their hideout at the ancient walled city of Petra, but God miraculously foiled the attack. The rest of the Arab Muslims, along with the Antichrist's great world army, would be destroyed at Armageddon, when the remnant of Jews, who had converted to Christianity, returned to Jerusalem with the triumphant Christ at their head. In Hull's eschatological scenario, Roman Catholicism and Islam became two key allies in the Antichrist's campaign to destroy the Jews, harkening back to older historicist Protestant models that had paired Catholicism and Islam as the twin Antichrists. Although dispensationalism did not naturally integrate Muslims as key figures in its events of the last days, news from the Middle East kept bringing Muslims back toward the center of dispensationalists' narratives.[35]

After the establishment of Israel in 1948, the most celebrated news event for American Christian observers was Israel's ostensibly miraculous triumph in the Six-Day War of 1967. The Israelis crippled Egypt, Syria, and Jordan's militaries and conquered Arab territory in the Sinai Peninsula, West Bank, Gaza Strip, Golan Heights, and most significantly, the city of Jerusalem. Dispensationalist observers immediately proclaimed that this victory not only affirmed the prophetic legitimacy of the state of Israel, but that it might also suggest the fulfillment of Jesus's prophecy in Luke 21:24

about Jerusalem being trod down until the "times of the Gentiles" had expired. Presbyterian L. Nelson Bell (evangelist Billy Graham's father-in-law) wrote soon after the war that it was a "thrilling thing to see a segment of prophecy being fulfilled!" But again, the evangelical Christian response was hardly uniform, as *Christianity Today* revealed by hosting another debate about Israel's role in Palestine.[36]

William Culbertson, president of Chicago's Moody Bible Institute, restated the prophetic argument that Israel's return to the land of Canaan was foreordained, and that this regathering might herald Christ's second coming. He refused to state definitively whether Israel's occupation of Jerusalem signaled the end of the "times of the Gentiles," but he thought it might. He suggested, "in view of the signs of the times, [that] it would be very foolish to live as though the end of the age could not possibly be upon us." Unlike some dispensational critics, Culbertson noted the grievances of Arabs, and warned that he was "not ready to defend every last action taken by Israel." Nevertheless, he tended to accept Israel's right of self-defense as justification for their military actions and handling of Arab refugees.[37]

In the opposing *Christianity Today* editorial, James Kelso, a former Pittsburgh Seminary professor and leader in the mainline United Presbyterian Church, excoriated Israel and her American Christian supporters, pointing to Israel's long history of abuses against Arabs. He especially lamented how the United States' support for Zionism had squandered the abundant goodwill among Arab Muslims toward the United States that had existed as of World War I. He believed that U.S. support for Israel made the Soviets the dominant influence in the Middle East, jeopardizing a key strategic region in the Cold War for little benefit in return. Finally, Kelso argued that America's backing of Israel had essentially destroyed what little missionary work existed in Arab Muslim areas of the Middle East. To many Muslims, American Christians seemed to support Israel unquestioningly, making conversion to the missionaries' faith even more unthinkable. Obviously, Kelso had no sympathy for claims of Israel's biblically ordained right to the land, and his editorial's inclusion in *Christianity Today* suggested substantial diversity in conservative Protestants' views of Arabs, Israel, and the Middle East crisis.[38]

Typical among American dispensationalists were the views expressed in Wilbur Smith's *Israeli/Arab Conflict* (1967), which quoted Luke 21:24 on its first page, commenting that it was the first time since 597 B.C. that an independent Israel had possessed Jerusalem. Smith chastised "reformed theologians" for believing that "there really is no future for the Jew as a nation." In a chapter called "The 'Perpetual Hatred' of the Arabs," Smith returned to the

Isaac-Ishmael theory, which posited that the Arab Muslims' rage against the Jews had essentially nothing to do with current political realities. "The Arabs have been hating Israel century after century," Smith reminded his readers. Dean Charles Feinberg of the Bible Theological Seminary of Los Angeles concurred, explaining in a 1968 article that the Ishmaelites sought "the complete extinction and annihilation of God's people Israel," and that "today these sons of Ishmael are among the greatest adversaries of the Gospel." The Arab-Israeli conflict represented a "living prolongation" of the struggle that began in Abraham's household. God will eventually "cast out the sons of Ishmael" and "settle the sons of Isaac." Smith believed that Jerusalem belonged by divine mandate to the Jews, and that the Jewish temple would be rebuilt on the Temple Mount. Although he did not comment on what should happen to it, Smith noted that the Dome of the Rock currently stood where the temple should go. The occupation of Jerusalem energized American dispensationalist speculations about the imminent rebuilding of the temple, and the resumption of temple sacrifices.[39]

Canadian Mennonite Frank Epp, representing a theologically conservative but pacifist and non-dispensationalist view, lamented that Smith's *Israeli/Arab Conflict* offered a presentist theological scheme "in which Christ and anti-Christ were related to the political powers of the day." As the news changed, so did the eschatological scenarios. Therefore, "at the moment many Christians see Christ allied with America and Israel and the anti-Christ with Russia and the Arabs," Epp wrote. Some American dispensationalists seemed authentically torn between their prophecy beliefs and their ethical convictions about the situation in Israel. Charles Ryrie of Dallas Theological Seminary argued in 1969 that "a concern for people, more than for politics or even prophecy, brings the Palestine problem into proper perspective." Although he endorsed the idea that the Six-Day War furthered "God's purpose for Israel," he also cautioned prophecy believers that the ends did not justify all means. "The State of Israel," he continued, "is not relieved of its obligation to act responsibly in the community of nations even though the secret purpose of God may be brought to fruition through its actions." He pointed to the suffering of Arab refugees, especially Christian Arabs, and the difficulties of Christian missionaries in the theater of war, as matters that should spur Christians to prayer and charity. Although dispensationalism exercised a heavy influence over many American Christians' view of the Arab-Israeli conflict, we should not imagine that dispensationalism rendered its devotees entirely incapable of critical reflection regarding Israel's treatment of the Palestinians or surrounding Arab countries.[40]

Popular dispensationalism usually featured less sober ruminations than

Figure 5-2. Jerusalem's Old City from Mount of Olives (2006), by Wayne McLean, Wikipedia Commons.

Ryrie's about the Arab-Israeli crisis, however. The key popularizer of dispensational eschatology after the Six-Day War, particularly regarding the status of the Temple Mount, was Hal Lindsey. Lindsey, a former tugboat captain in New Orleans, studied at Dallas Seminary and then became an evangelist with the parachurch organization Campus Crusade for Christ. His *The Late Great Planet Earth* (1970) became America's bestselling non-fiction book of the 1970s, and until the appearance of conservative pastor and author Tim LaHaye's *Left Behind* series in the 1990s, Lindsey's book stood unchallenged as the most popular American book on prophecy ever. Lindsey's breezy text presented a fairly conventional view of dispensational theology. Following the establishment of the nation of Israel, Lindsey argued that the possession of the Old City of Jerusalem and the rebuilding of the temple were the next two key prophetic events to happen in Israel. He instantly recognized in 1967 that the second step had been fulfilled, as the "Jews had unwittingly further set up the stage for their final hour of trial and conversion."[41]

As of 1967, Lindsey began waiting for Israel to rebuild the temple, but he noted that the Dome of the Rock (see Figure 5-2) stood in the way. He did not know what might happen to the Dome of the Rock, but quoted an Israeli historian who speculated that an earthquake could destroy it. Messianic Jewish Christian writer Milton Lindberg also suggested the possibility of an earthquake destroying the Dome of the Rock in his *The Jew and Modern Israel in the Light of Prophecy* (1969). Lindberg believed that the occupation of Jerusalem by Muslims had been foretold in Ezekiel 7:23–24 ("Wherefore I will bring the worst of the heathen, and they shall possess their houses; and their holy places shall be defiled.") Lindberg asked "who have deserved the title 'the worst of the heathen' more than the fanatical Muhammadan and the terrible Turk?" One way or the other, according to Lindberg and Lindsey, the Muslims and their sacred sites would be removed, the temple would be rebuilt, and Jewish sacrifices would resume, preparing the setting where the Antichrist would desecrate the temple and demand that all worship him. "Prophecy demands it," Lindsey wrote.[42]

Lindsey also placed "Egypt, the Arabic nations, and countries of black Africa" in the confederacy of Ezekiel's King of the South that would, in cooperation with the Soviet Union, attack restored Israel. Unlike some earlier dispensational writers, Lindsey predicted that the Arab nations would be "double-crossed" by the Soviet Union, which would briefly conquer the whole Middle East, only to be miraculously destroyed in Israel. Despite some differences in the details, dispensationalists in the Cold War era usually forecast that Arab Muslims would ally with the Soviet Union and be miraculously destroyed by God in the Gog and Magog attack, prior to the final battle of Armageddon and the return of Christ.[43]

Despite calls from missionary-scholars such as Zwemer, Wilson, and Cragg for deeper sympathy and understanding of Islam, the pressure of an increasingly polarized Middle East crisis, often viewed through the lens of dispensational prophetic schemes, worked against a charitable evaluation of Islam by many conservative American Christians. Contrary to Zwemer's predictions, political Islam was hardly disintegrating. To the contrary, by the 1970s political Islam seemed to take an ever-more prominent role on the global stage. The fear these developments generated made it difficult to keep popular American Christian notions of the eternal hostility between Muslims, Christians, and Jews at bay, even though some conservatives realized the damage those beliefs could do to missions among Muslims. Adding to their fears about Islam, by the 1960s American Christians perceived a new and unexpected domestic challenge coming from Muslims in America itself.

CHAPTER 6

Christians Respond to Muslims in Modern America

AT THE 1893 WORLD'S PARLIAMENT OF RELIGIONS in Chicago, Islam's chief representative was a white American, a former Presbyterian (re)named Mohammed Alexander Russell Webb (see Figure 6-1). Dressed in traditional Indian garb, including a white turban, he addressed the assembly about Islam's great merits. He lamented the widespread ignorance and misrepresentations regarding Islam among Americans. Webb proclaimed that the "Moslem system is designed to cultivate all that is purest and noblest and grandest in the human character." Specifically, he argued that Islam held within it the ideal of "perfect brotherhood," and dissolved social inequalities across the globe. Webb inaugurated an American Muslim critique of American Christian culture, which proposed that Islam offered the cure for the country's desperate inequalities. The brotherhood of Muslims would provide an alternative to racially divided Christianity and Western culture.[1]

American Christians had long recognized Islam as its chief global missionary competitor, and a possible player in end-times scenarios. Islam's increasingly public presence in America during the twentieth century also represented a source of concern to many American Christians. That concern could turn to irritation and alarm when American Muslims highlighted the race and class divisions within American society, and pointed to Islam as the solution. A scholar of Muslim law, G. H. Bousquet, warned in Samuel Zwemer's *Moslem World* in 1935 that Islam in America could "play here a magnificent trump: namely, the far greater *real* equality of races in Islam than that existing in Christian America." Although Bousquet only knew of some small Muslim efforts to recruit African Americans as of 1935, his analysis proved prescient.[2] Beginning in the 1930s, African-American advocates of Islam (or the Nation of Islam) used the ostensible race-blindness of Islam to criticize dominant white Christian society. After 1965, Muslim immigrants to America also became an increasingly visible phenomenon, raising anxieties about American Muslims' aggressive evangelism, lack of assimilation, or their possible association with terrorist plots. The fear of an American Muslim threat generated a new apologetic response from American Christians in which African-American leaders often played a critical

FIGURE 6-1. Mohammed Alexander Russell Webb (1893), The Newberry Library, Chicago.

role. American Christians argued variously for deeper understanding of the new "Muslim neighbors," or wariness concerning what trouble these native-born "cults" or immigrant Muslims might be planning.

Although he was one of the earliest American Muslims with a public profile, Mohammed Webb was not the typical American advocate for Islam. He had served as American consul to the Philippines, where he converted to Islam. Traveling through southern and southeastern Asia, he became familiar with a number of Indian and Arab Muslim leaders, who saw Webb as their chance to gain a foothold for Islam in elite American circles. Supplied with ample finances, Webb returned to the United States and founded the American Moslem Brotherhood and the Moslem World Publishing Company. He labored to clear up American misconceptions regarding Islam. Webb, sounding like a Muslim version of Samuel Zwemer, wrote that the "plainly apparent decay of Church Christianity and the defection from that system of many of the most intelligent and progressive people in nearly all large American cities seem to encourage the belief that the time has now arrived for the spread of the true faith from the Eastern to the Western Hemisphere." He anticipated Islam's adoption as the dominant American religion, but his missionary funds soon dried up. *The New York Times* printed an 1895 article ridiculing Webb and his lack of support, with the exaggerated title "Fall of Islam in America." Webb died in 1916, apparently having made very little progress in his recruitment of elite Americans to Islam.[3]

Although Webb helped pioneer the *da'wa*, or Muslim mission movement, to America, his vision of reaching the increasingly secularized urban elite for Islam did not come to pass. Instead, Muslims in America have enjoyed their greatest successes in winning native-born African-American converts. Most of the earliest Muslims in America came as slaves from West Africa. Although their formal devotion rarely survived the middle passage across the Atlantic and the crucible of plantation life, these early Muslims set an example by which many African-Americans came to identify Islam as a religion benefiting their oppressed race. Even though evangelical Christianity vastly outpaced Islam among African-Americans, a minority of blacks remained attracted to Islam. As seen most famously in the career of Malcolm X, African-American Islam could feed alternatively into a racial separatist mode (which Malcolm adopted while a key disciple of Elijah Muhammad in the Nation of Islam), or a multiracial mode (which Malcolm adopted after his transforming experience of the *hajj*, or pilgrimage to Mecca, and conversion to orthodox Islam). Like Malcolm, many African-Americans have found forms of Islam more politically, socially, and spiritually satisfying than Christianity.[4]

Because Christianity had become so pervasive within the African-American population by the time of the American Civil War, black apologists for Islam had to frame their religion as a suitable alternative to the Christian faith. The first such apologist was, ironically, a Presbyterian missionary, Edward Wilmot Blyden. Originally from the Caribbean island of St. Thomas, Blyden came to America to study at Rutgers Theological College, but was denied admission there because of his race. He arrived in the United States in 1850, the year that the Fugitive Slave Law passed, making it more dangerous for free blacks to remain in the North. Blyden jumped at a chance to go to West Africa with the American Colonization Society, and in 1851 he arrived in Liberia. Although the Colonization Society sought to bring Christian civilization to pagan Africa, Blyden's work in Liberia exposed him to African Muslims, with whom he was favorably impressed. Although he never seems publicly to have repudiated Christianity, Blyden became convinced that Islam held more promise as a unifying pan-African religion. He made these views known in his book *Christianity, Islam and the Negro Race*, published in London in 1887.[5]

Blyden's travels across the Atlantic world taught him that under Islamic rule, Africans tended to maintain autonomy and enhance their level of civilization, while white Christians held them in servility. "There is no Christian community of Negroes anywhere which is self-reliant and independent," and Africans in Christian societies tended to be "slow and unprogressive." By contrast, African Muslim communities often were "self-reliant, productive, independent and dominant." He explained that Islam had come to Africans through missionaries who had no colonizing agenda, while Christians viewed "the Negro as a slave." Islam fostered black empowerment, while Christianity provided only solace amidst the slaves' misery.[6]

Missionaries more conservative than Blyden, when faced with the challenge of non-Christian religions, insisted that only Christianity could save its adherents from eternal damnation, so that its effects were infinitely beneficial when compared to Islam or other faiths. Blyden, either out of remaining theological conviction, or out of a desire to retain American Christian support, still maintained that only Jesus's gospel could "regenerate humanity of all races, climes, and countries." Nevertheless, he lamented white Christians' racial exclusivity, and their faith's deleterious effects on non-Europeans. By contrast, Islam's influence in Central and West Africa revealed a "salutary character." While white Christian missionaries feared that Islam would supplant the religion of African animists, Blyden rejoiced that Muslim missionaries had converted so many African pagans, elevating their morality, culture, and learning. Islam proved to be the only faith that could unite the African tribes, as all Muslims, regardless of race, ancestry, or ethnicity were treated equally under Islam. No religion had so "overstepped the limits of race as the religion of Mohammed," he wrote.[7]

Blyden undoubtedly underestimated the realities of race-based slavery in Muslim Africa, because he was so enamored with the way many Africans seemed to maintain integrity and independence under Islam's canopy. He noted that if Christianity entered Africa with the same civilizing (but not colonizing) agenda, many Muslims would "become ready converts of a religion which brings with it the recommendation of a higher culture and a nobler civilization." Like many of his Western modernist counterparts, Blyden evaluated missionary work based on its civilizing effects. He expected godly religion to produce pan-African power and independence. Concern for individual salvation had faded almost entirely from his view. Even though Blyden occasionally spoke to black church groups in America in the 1890s, he seems to have largely abandoned traditional Christianity in favor of a pan-Africanist blend of Christianity and Islam.[8]

The extent of Blyden's direct influence on later African-American Muslims remains unclear, but he certainly established a pattern in which some African-American, or Afro-Atlantic Christians would come to see Islam as a superior religion for the aims of black nationalism and needs of their race. African-American Muslims tended to fashion novel forms of Islam which blended the concerns of pan-Africanism in ways difficult to reconcile with traditional Islam. The most important of these African-American Islamic movements was the Nation of Islam, but the Moorish Science Temple of America also represented an important precedent. Noble Drew Ali, born as Timothy Drew in North Carolina in 1886, founded the Moorish Science Temple movement. Rejecting not only Christianity but also key parts of Islam, Drew Ali proclaimed that he was a prophet of Allah, and produced *The Holy Koran of the Moorish Science Temple of America*. Despite its title, *The Holy Koran* has essentially no similarities with the Muslim Qur'an. Drew Ali taught that African-Americans should abandon their slave identities by changing their Anglophone names and accepting that they were actually "Asiatic" peoples by race. He preached black economic independence and separatism, and viewed Christianity as a degraded European religion. Islam (or his version of it) represented the true religion of Asiatics. Drew Ali founded the first Moorish temple in Newark, New Jersey, in 1913. He and his followers established many temples and attracted tens of thousands of members before Drew Ali's mysterious death in 1929.[9]

The Moorish Science Temple heralded many of the same themes as the more famous Nation of Islam, and may have directly influenced the Nation's founders W. D. Fard and Elijah Muhammad. Fard appeared in Detroit in 1930, presenting himself as an Arab peddler of silks. He instructed poor blacks about health and dietary restrictions, and slowly revealed to them that he was a prophet from Mecca sent to minister to African-Americans. American blacks, he taught, actually belonged to the lost ancient tribe of Shabazz. Fard built upon, but then rejected, the evangelical Christian heritage of most of his followers. Many of his converts had grown up as Baptists or Methodists in the South, and many of their families had only recently relocated to the urban North. Fard initially preached to them from the Bible, and he even encouraged them to listen to white Christian fundamentalist preacher J. Frank Norris's radio show. But then he began to denounce the teachings of the Bible and insisted that the "original people," African-Americans, "must retain their religion, which is Islam." One of Fard's early converts recalled hearing Fard point out errors in the Bible: "up to that day I always went to the Baptist church," the black Muslim said. "After I heard that sermon from the prophet, I was turned around completely." Fard wanted the Nation of Islam to challenge Christianity's dominance among poor African-Americans.[10]

When Fard mysteriously disappeared in 1934, Elijah Muhammad (see Figure 6-2) assumed leadership of the Nation of Islam. The son of an itinerant Baptist preacher in Georgia, Muhammad expanded and institutionalized the sect's ministry. The Nation of Islam, like the Moorish Science Temple, taught doctrines that made it incompatible with some basic principles of traditional Islam. Elijah Muhammad asserted that the departed Fard was the long-awaited Mahdi, a messianic figure who was in some sense divine. Traditional Muslims reject the notion that any human could share in the divine nature. The Nation of Islam also considered Elijah Muhammad the last prophet of Allah, which would imply that he had supplanted the Prophet Muhammad. Moreover, the Nation of Islam espoused exotic views regarding the origins of the races. According to Elijah Muhammad, six thousand years ago an evil scientist, Yacub, had developed the inferior devilish white race. Blacks were the original, and therefore the most innocent and noble race. The Nation of Islam's extreme pan-Africanism resonated with some African-Americans who had become embittered by white supremacy in America. Muhammad continued to pepper his teachings with Christian themes, especially those of Christian apocalypticism. One scholar has even called Muhammad's theology a form of "black Islamic dispensationalism." Muhammad told his followers, for instance, that the numbers of Franklin Roosevelt's new Social Security program represented the mark of the beast.[11]

FIGURE 6-2. Elijah Muhammad (1964), by Stanley Wolfson, *New York World-Telegram and the Sun* Newspaper Photograph Collection, Library of Congress.

Despite Elijah Muhammad's sometimes outlandish views, he slowly developed a following, especially in northern cities. Black newspapers like the *Amsterdam News* (New York) and the *Pittsburgh Courier* gave Muhammad editorial space in the 1950s. Readers of those papers expressed a range of responses to the Nation of Islam, from surprised delight to frowning criti-

cism. These reactions give an important glimpse of black Christian opinions of the Nation's beliefs. One reader, who signed as "A Negro Teenager,"
confessed that he found Elijah Muhammad's column compelling until he
realized that Muhammad advocated black segregation. "I had planned to
join that religion but now I am not so sure," he wrote. He noted that the
black Muslims did not seem to believe in Jesus, and reminded readers that
Jesus was the only way to heaven.[12]

In late 1957, the *Amsterdam News* featured competing columns by Elijah
Muhammad and George Violenes, the pastor of Christ Community Church
in Harlem. Violenes offered a less-than-robust response to Muhammad,
noting patronizingly that he could not "blame Mr. Muhammad for his
warped ideas of the white race because his education and knowledge of history and literature are limited." Violenes praised white people's contribu-
tions to science and learning, but acknowledged that the "white race has
made quite a few mistakes and has not always been fair to the darker peoples
of the world." He could not accept Muhammad's characterization of all
whites as devils because the Bible made clear that "out of one blood has God
created all people upon the earth." He also posited that blacks had pros-
pered under Christianity more than any other religion. Violenes suggested
that if Muhammad "would only pray, God through His only begotten son,
will forgive him of his infidel mind, and give him new spiritual birth." Violenes offered to baptize Muhammad himself.[13]

The *Pittsburgh Courier* received letters from readers across the country
expressing their views on Elijah Muhammad's columns in the late 1950s.
Reverend William Holmes of Marrero, Louisiana, wrote that Muhammad's
"wild ravings" were "anti-Christ," and that no one "who reads the Bible can
agree with this writer." But two letter-writers in the same edition saw
Muhammad differently. One from Chicago proclaimed that he himself was
a prophet and announced a vision of the millennial future when no whites
would remain on the earth to torment African-Americans. Another from
Inkster, Michigan, commended the editor for printing Muhammad's column, saying that he had found the true light in the Nation of Islam.[14]

Reverend Joseph P. King, conversely, wrote to the *Courier* from Chicago
and denounced Muhammad for his unenlightened beliefs: "fanatical adherence to the unknown is a throwback to early man," he averred. "The Negro
has enough self-sent messiahs, root-merchants and conjurers." Only those
committed to racial "uplift" should be accepted as African American leaders, King wrote. Unlike Violenes, King seemed unconcerned with Muhammad's Muslim beliefs, but disagreed with Muhammad's assertion that
"Islam is the only salvation for the Negro." King's negative views were coun-

tered with several letters praising Muhammad. One woman from New York City promised to save Muhammad's columns for "future reference."[15]

A year later, the discussion about Muhammad continued in the *Courier*, as a group of Chicago Pentecostals wrote that both Elijah Muhammad and the Prophet Muhammad suffered from demonic possession. A Los Angeles pastor warned Christian African-Americans that as someone who denied Christ's resurrection, Muhammad was "spiritually dead." This pastor, apparently a dispensationalist, believed that the Nation's members needed "enlightenment as to the conflicts of today's world affairs, the prophecies of the Middle East, and the teaching of the second coming of Christ." Finally, a Boston pastor wondered how anyone could preach such an "ideology of hate" as Elijah Muhammad. He insisted that blacks did share in the "foundation of America," so there was no sense in calling for a separate African-American nation. African-American Christians who criticized the Nation's theology generally characterized it as fanatical, unenlightened, ignorant, or the product of an unconverted mind.[16]

Although the Nation of Islam seems to have alarmed many Christian African-Americans in the cities, it did not come to most other Christian Americans' attention until 1959. That year, reporter Mike Wallace's television documentary *The Hate that Hate Produced* created a modest media sensation regarding the Nation. Within a month of the show's broadcast, civil rights leader and Baptist minister Martin Luther King, Jr., warned obliquely of "hate groups" in the African-American community that preached "black supremacy." King understood well the suffering of the black community, but he insisted that they should not substitute "one tyranny for another."[17] Many Christians, especially those concerned with the plight of African-Americans, saw the Nation of Islam as an understandable but fundamentally misguided reaction to racial injustice in America.

Some white Christians began to comment on the Nation, as well. In 1959, eminent religion professor and former Methodist missionary Charles Braden explained that the Muslim missionary presence in America reflected both the traditional Muslim immigrant religion and the new African-American movements. Blacks found Islam attractive for its message of equality. He lamented Elijah Muhammad's racist theology, but acknowledged that the "bad racial record of a large segment of Christianity in America" led some African-Americans to listen to it. In 1961, the *Christian Century* classed the rise of the Nation of Islam among episodes reflecting "erratic Negro behavior in predominantly white communities." The "pseudo-Islamic racists" wanted to set up a separate black nation, the magazine reported, and hoped to establish "Negro supremacy in world politics" by 1970. Like many politically or theologically liberal Christians, the *Christian Century*'s writers tended to present the Nation as a "social mirror" that reflected grievous racial problems in America. Their coverage hardly suggested that the Nation represented a legitimate religious alternative, however. A 1963 Southern Baptist Convention publication on world religions, similarly, explained that the Black Muslims had "reacted against discrimination toward the Negro and have replaced the myth of white supremacy with the opposite myth of black supremacy."[18]

Many American Christians also reflected on the dramatic rise of Malcolm X, his break with Elijah Muhammad, and Malcolm's assassination in 1965. Following Elijah Muhammad's lead, Malcolm condemned Christianity as the tool of white oppressors, even though Malcolm's own father had been a Christian lay preacher. Turning traditional Christian imagery on its head, Malcolm spoke of his time as a Christian as the days when he was spiritually lost: "I was then in total darkness. I was deaf, dumb, and blind. . . I was a dope-addict. I was a liar. I was a thief. I hated my own kind. I was a drunkard. But then I couldn't help being what I was. I WAS A CHRISTIAN!"[19] Malcolm continued his assault on the black Christianity of his youth in his *Autobiography*. Christianity represented the religion of the master class, who taught African Americans "to worship an alien God having the same blond hair, pale skin, and blue eyes as the slavemaster." It made the slaves complacent, forcing them to accept "whatever was dished out by the devilish white man; and to look for his pie in the sky, and for his heaven in the hereafter." Malcolm, not one to make fine distinctions, failed to commend white reformers like Christian abolitionists, or to see any value in the historic black church.[20]

Malcolm X's fusillades against Christianity provoked a variety of reactions from American Christians, ranging from sympathy to outrage. Newspaper columnist Albert B. Southwick interviewed Malcolm for the *Christian Century* in 1963 and labeled him a "charismatic demagogue." Southwick warned mainline Christian readers that the Nation claimed to have done better rehabilitation work among black prisoners than "all the social agencies, psychiatrists and Christian ministers and priests combined." He saw the Nation as capitalizing on deep black resentment and the crumbling of Christian authority among African-Americans in the cities. "One wonders if modern Christianity has the vigor needed to meet the new challenge of Black Islam," Southwick commented.[21]

Malcolm's violent death generated a similar variety of responses from American Christians. African-American Baptist pastor Richard Gleason of Chicago went so far as to liken Malcolm X to Christ: "As Christ reflected what the masses felt, reflected their needs, so did Malcolm." Both were killed because they offended the established powers. Conversely, evangelical *Christianity Today*, which had remained relatively silent regarding the black Muslims, quoted Malcolm criticizing white Christianity, and reminded readers of Malcolm's statement that President Kennedy's assassination represented "chickens coming home to roost." The "ultimate irony" in his death, according to the magazine, was that his funeral would be held at Harlem's Faith Temple, Church of God in Christ. *Christianity Today's* editors apparently saw the "Islamic Negro Nationalists" as relatively serious threats and lamented any Christian cooperation with the Nation's leaders.[22]

Sociologist C. Eric Lincoln, writing in the *Christian Century*, adopted the "social mirror" approach to Malcolm and his death. Clearly, Lincoln preferred the nonviolent philosophy of Martin Luther King, Jr., as the means to resist white oppression. But, Lincoln noted patronizingly, white racism created an understandable violent backlash in the "steaming ghetto," where "tens of thousands. . .simply have not reached the level of sophistication which would enable them to understand the value and the dignity of nonviolent resistance." Malcolm represented a demagogic manipulator of the abused and ostensibly unsophisticated black masses. "His spirit will rise again, phoenix-like—not so much because he is worthy to be remembered as because the perpetuation of the ghetto which spawned him will not let us forget." Liberal Catholic writer James O'Gara struck a similar tone in *Commonweal*, as he sympathized with the plight of American blacks, and found poor African-Americans' attraction to the Nation of Islam comprehensible. But the black Muslims and Malcolm X represented "an extreme reaction to a culture based on white superiority." However morally instructive its origins were, the Nation of Islam's philosophy of black power and separatism was not to be taken seriously by Christian observers.[23]

Pacifist Catholic writer Thomas Merton took among the most positive views of Malcolm X in a 1967 review of the *Autobiography*. To Merton, Malcolm's admirable qualities came to light not during his association with the "ghetto religion" of the Nation of Islam, but after his break with Elijah Muhammad. In his black Muslim phase, Malcolm preached an "impassioned, obsessive racist eschatology which, for all its sweeping ruthlessness, has so far not directly promoted any really significant political action." But upon his return from the *hajj*, Malcolm's real importance became clear. He had become a "world citizen" with "an extraordinary sense of community." Malcolm had first outgrown the "ghetto underworld" of crime and drugs, and then he outgrew the "religious underworld, the spiritual power structure that thrives on a ghetto mystique." Because Malcolm transcended two such profound immaturities, Merton found his struggles "understandable." Had not death cut his authentically Muslim phase short, he "might have become a genuine revolutionary leader." Unlike other Christian observers, Merton noted serious social reform potential in Malcolm's orthodox Muslim phase. Because of the Nation's strident racial views and unusual mythology, Merton and others did not see it as a legitimate religious movement.[24]

The Nation of Islam's growth increased Christian leaders' anxiety regarding African-Americans. Could Christianity hold the allegiance of urban blacks? Fear of the internal threat from Islam tended to elicit regret from many Christians that racism in America had helped create the Nation's black-supremacist theology. A 1967 tract titled *Black Muslim Encounter*, published by the Southern Baptist Convention's Home Mission Board, condemned both white and black forms of segregation. Its author postulated that only integrationist Christians could consistently reject the black Muslims' separationist message. White Christians who supported segregation, the tract wryly noted, had no better allies than the black Muslims.[25]

Other Christians used the Nation of Islam as evidence of a broader groundswell of secretive American cults challenging traditional Christianity's authority. Evangelical professor Walter Martin's frequently updated and reprinted manual *The Kingdom of the Cults* took notice of the Nation of Islam in its first edition in 1965, the year of Malcolm's death. Under Martin's definition, a cult differed significantly from the religion it claimed to espouse, and tended to follow a charismatic leader. Although most of Martin's cults came out of Christianity, the Nation fit because it was rejected theologically by many traditional Muslims, and because of the roles W. D. Fard, Elijah Muhammad, and Malcolm X played in its growth. Martin's article on the Nation used excerpts from Eric Lincoln and Louis Lomax, two of the top experts on the black Muslims. It also reprinted a lengthy interview with Malcolm X. Like earlier articles in the *Christian Century*, Martin expressed understanding of the motivations behind Elijah Muhammad's movement. "It has capitalized upon the Christian church's apparent reticence in some quarters to support vigorously the rights of Negroes guaranteed under the Constitution." Nevertheless, Martin showed no sympathy for the Nation itself, which he called "a black Ku Klux Klan." He feared that the black Muslims might present "the awesome spectacle of a growing black funnel engulfing potentially millions of Negroes." The threat was not simply spiritual, but challenged the entire American political system. By asking for a separate black state within America, they proved themselves to be "un-

American." He implored the average African-American to "trust the influential friends he has among white legislators," and to allow black Christian moderates like Martin Luther King to lead.[26]

Reflecting trends in the news, Martin's 1985 edition of *The Kingdom of the Cults* had dropped its chapter on the Nation of Islam, but included a chapter on traditional Islam (which he immediately acknowledged was not a cult), and the "unanticipated invasion" of Islam in the West. In his 2003 edition, the Nation was back in a combined chapter with traditional Islam. This chapter (revised by apologist James Beverley) noted the surging interest in Islam since September 2001, and presented the Nation as "a force to be reckoned with" that swayed great numbers of young African-Americans. Beverley particularly mentioned the Nation's influence on rap artists such as Public Enemy and Ice Cube. He explained that since Elijah Muhammad's death, his son Warith Muhammad had taken the group in a more orthodox Muslim direction. Beverley also commented on the splinter group led by Louis Farrakhan that retained the Nation's name and kept the movement in the news. Beverley assessed the growth of the Nation by noting that "racism and apartheid existed in America until the 1960s and 1970s civil rights legislation." Thus, the black Muslims' rage was understandable (at least until those civil rights reforms were passed). Nevertheless, "black Muslims are simply replacing one form of oppression with another; embracing slavery to a cult that binds them to a bigoted ideology and a heretical view of God." He expected that a Christian emphasis on salvation by grace alone would appeal to the "works-oriented" black Muslims.[27]

As indicated by the changes in Martin's *Kingdom of the Cults*, the Nation of Islam faded somewhat from popular view after Malcolm X's death. Boxer Muhammad Ali became the Nation's most visible spokesman after Malcolm, and was the subject of an incredulous 1968 article in the *Christian Century*. Its author, James Kidd, a Congregational pastor from Chicago, led a church "field trip into the black ghetto," highlighted by a stop at the Nation's restaurant, Salaam's. Ali "just happened" to be there during the group's visit, and they quizzed him for more than an hour about the Nation's beliefs. Ultimately, Kidd commended the "spirit" of the Nation, but found its theology (especially concerning UFOs that would soon pour out Allah's wrath on the white race) "incredible."[28]

Christian magazines kept tabs on the Nation of Islam during the 1970s and '80s, speculating on its status vis-à-vis America's social and religious "mainstream." A 1973 *Christianity Today* article, "Black Muslims: Moving into Mainstream?" noted increasing interfaith cooperation and respectability in the movement. The author, Pentecostal writer James S. Tinney, pointed to cultural affinities between conservative Christians and black Muslims, but ended his article with a recapitulation of black Muslim theological oddities. Three years later, Tinney reported optimistically on changes in the Nation led by Elijah Muhammad's son Wallace (later Warith Deen). He was "moving the group closer to orthodox Islam, [and] at the same time incorporating more Christian terminology into his teachings." Religion professor James Whitehurst amplified Tinney's themes in a 1980 *Christian Century* article titled "The Mainstreaming of the Black Muslims: Healing the Hate," which very positively assessed Wallace Muhammad's work in aligning the Nation (renamed the American Muslim Mission) with orthodox Islam.[29]

Ultimately, a "mainstreamed" black Muslim movement meant a less threatening one to Christian observers. Accordingly, the Christian media gave dwindling attention to Wallace Muhammad's American Muslim Mission in the 1970s and 1980s. Instead, occasionally outrageous statements made by Louis Farrakhan, who in 1978 broke away from Wallace Muhammad's organization, garnered the bulk of Christian attention and renewed warnings about the Nation as a cult. Farrakhan reestablished the Nation of Islam and returned to some of Elijah Muhammad's abandoned racial and theological teachings. Farrakhan rocketed into the national spotlight because of anti-Semitic comments in a 1984 speech, in which he called Zionism a "gutter religion" and Adolf Hitler a "great man." His sporadic fame culminated in the 1995 "Million Man March" in Washington D.C., which assembled hundreds of thousands of African-Americans, including many Christians, to call for black independence, dignity, and morality.[30]

Many black Christians found Farrakhan's strident message compelling. Benjamin Chavis, a United Church of Christ minister and former leader of the NAACP, formally joined the Nation of Islam in 1997 after helping Farrakhan organize the Million Man March. Other African-American church leaders saw Farrakhan as a fraud, or worse. African-American apologist and minister Elreta Dodds, for instance, decided to write her book *The Trouble with Farrakhan and the Nation of Islam: Another Message to the Black Man in America* (1997) in response to the Million Man March, as she perceived that many black Christians had unwittingly fallen under Farrakhan's spell. Like earlier African-American Christian attackers of Elijah Muhammad, she painted Farrakhan as an "antichrist and a false prophet." She argued that Islam, the Nation of Islam, and Christianity were all entirely incompatible, and did not worship the same God. Dodds conceded that America had a long record of racist oppression against African-Americans, but that did not justify putting faith in a man "guided by Satan" or placing "ethnicity above spirituality." "Demonic forces" summoned the hundreds of thousands of

African-American Christians who appeared at the Million Man March. Her disagreement with the Nation transcended the theological and philosophical: she saw it as a matter of spiritual warfare.[31]

Some white Christians' responses to Farrakhan's Nation of Islam returned to the theme of the Nation as a threatening cult. Evangelical author Richard Abanes's alarmingly titled *Cults, New Religious Movements, and Your Family: A Guide to Ten Non-Christian Groups Out to Convert Your Loved Ones* (1998) came armed with a bevy of bizarre racist quotes from Farrakhan and his followers. He concluded that although the Nation provided a needed sense of dignity to African-American men, "the belief system taught by the NOI is nothing but white supremacy in reverse." Popular evangelical pastor Rick Warren endorsed Abanes's book with the assurance that it could "cult-proof" one's family, but Abanes did not give much evidence that his typical readers were being targeted by Farrakhan and the Nation. The chapter seemed mostly to remind evangelicals of the old fears about aggressively separatist black Islam.[32]

Evangelist Moody Adams (a fringe figure among conservative American Christians, to be sure, although Dodds cited him in her bibliography) went much further than Abanes, much less tastefully, when he described Farrakhan as a terrorist and a "degenerate raping America's Lady Liberty." Unlike most Christian critics of the Nation of Islam (including Dodds), Adams made no distinction between the Nation of Islam's views and traditional Islam. "Islam," he wrote, "is the religion of the natural man who wishes to indulge in hatred, violence, murder, war, execute his justice now and be rewarded on earth." Adams's extreme anti-Islamic views were shown in a 2002 PBS documentary titled "Anti-Islam." Although he espoused views of Islam that were much less careful than the average American Christian critic's, his ideas foreshadowed the coming of a more virulent kind of anti-Muslim rhetoric among American Christians angered by the attacks of September 11, 2001.[33]

Despite the return of the standard anti-cult and anti-Muslim responses, the most fascinating rejoinders in the 1990s to the newly visible Nation of Islam came from African-American Christians like Dodds. African-American Christians had often offered theological counterpoints to the Nation of Islam such as those in the 1950s black newspapers, but never in such a public and well-organized way as in the 1990s. *Christianity Today* took notice of the African-American response to the Nation in a 1994 article which presented Farrakhan's movement as socially attractive but "spiritually empty" for converts. The article profiled several leaders of "Project Joseph," an evangelical apologetics ministry led by African-Americans. Carl Ellis, one of

Project Joseph's key leaders who had briefly followed Malcolm X in the 1960s, speculated that the black Muslims would have little success if the African-American churches would become more socially relevant and doctrinally precise. In particular, he argued that the black churches should offer more leadership opportunities for young men, and emphasize grace over works. Unless they renewed the theological focus on salvation by grace, the churches would "continue to hemorrhage young members." To these evangelicals, the success of the Nation of Islam primarily reflected the deficiencies of Christian churches.[34]

In his *Free at Last? The Gospel in the African-American Experience* (1996), Ellis presented Malcolm as an unwitting vessel of God's truth, despite his acceptance of black Islam and traditional Islam. Only by the grace of God had Malcolm risen from the ghetto to a position of such great influence. He "gave us a new meaning to being Black: we were human," Ellis explained. The failures of the black church blocked Malcolm's apprehension of full spiritual truth in Christ. Nevertheless, "without realizing it, Malcolm X reoriented the African-American collective consciousness toward a truer scriptural view." To Ellis, black Islam represented a flawed assertion of a great truth: the inherent dignity of African-Americans. This was a belief that had originated in Christianity, but had been lost in the racist milieu of the institutional church. As Ellis reiterated in a 2000 interview with *Christianity Today*, endemic racism in the church had frustrated efforts to deal with cultural or social issues beyond personal salvation. Islam, both black separatist and traditional, filled that void for many African-Americans. Ellis still believed in the efficacy of Christian apologetics, love, and prayer. Those were "three things that a Muslim, a Hindu, or anybody else has no resistance against." At its core, "Islam is nothing but a works-righteousness treadmill," he postulated. Black Muslims would eventually succumb to Christ's offer of grace.[35]

Haman Cross, pastor of Detroit's Rosedale Park Baptist Church, took an approach more like that of Dodds, presenting Malcolm X and Farrakhan as dangerous cult leaders in *Have You Got Good Religion? The Real Fruit of Islam* (1993) and *What's Up with Malcolm? The Real Failure of Islam* (1993). Like Moody Adams, Cross excoriated Islam as a "murderous, pagan, seventh-century moon cult," the Prophet Muhammad as a "liar" and a "crook," and the Qur'an as "one big fake." He saw black Muslims as "the illegitimate children of orthodox Islam." Unlike Ellis, he conceded no spiritual value to Malcolm's work, stating that Malcolm had led "thousands of oppressed souls not only into the darkness of Islam, but also into the bosom of hell." Cross also lampooned the requirements of Islam's five pillars, wondering what one should do if it was the fasting time of Ramadan and "your homeys take you out for baby back ribs"? Similarly, he warned that the Qur'an teaches that God would not hear the prayers of someone who had flatulence or bad breath: "Should you keep Pepto Bismol and Scope on hand at times of prayer?" he asked. Cross identified African-Americans' attraction to Islam as idolatrous rage against the true God of the Bible for his permitting racism and white oppression. Dodds, Ellis, and Cross represented an African-American evangelical response to black Muslims that conceded that racial injustice had generated understandable anger among African-Americans. Black Islam, or traditional Islam, only furthered a cycle of fury and violence, while authentic Christianity (different from the predominantly racist Christianity of American history) alone could bring healing and forgiveness. But Ellis could see the true God working in Malcolm's life, while Cross and Dodds saw only Satanic deception.[36]

Informed Christian observers have known that, despite all the attention given to the Nation of Islam and its various incarnations, the American Muslim community included much broader and more orthodox versions of Islam than the black Muslims. Indeed, of the millions of Muslims in America, roughly half to two-thirds of them are part of immigrant communities. The majority of American Muslims identify with the Sunni tradition, and a strong minority are Shi'is.[37] Relatively few belong to the Nation of Islam or any of its offshoots, but because of the news appeal of the Nation's sensational theology, and its leaders' inflammatory rhetoric, one might get the impression from the media and some Christian apologists that the Nation represents the majority of American Muslims. In this disproportionate emphasis, American Christian views of American Muslims have tended to follow the lead of the secular media.

But Christian observers have also increasingly noted the phenomenon of immigrant "Muslim neighbors" in America. Just as Muslims proved an alluring evangelistic target internationally, so also have many American Christians called for proselytization of Muslims living in America. One of the key signals of a new domestic Muslim presence in America was the opening of the elaborate Islamic Center in Washington, D.C. in 1957. President Dwight Eisenhower spoke at the dedication of the Center, assuring American Muslims that they were welcome in America because of the nation's commitment to freedom of religion. Newspapers buzzed that the Eisenhowers even removed their shoes before entering the Islamic Center's prayer room. The new Muslim community grew slowly in America before 1965, but after immigration reforms of that year many more Muslims began arriving from overseas. Christian observers soon began to focus on the evangelistic opportunities presented by this wave of non-Christian immigrants.[38]

As was often the case, the Southern Baptist Convention's well-organized missionary apparatus took the lead among American Christians in responding to domestic Islam. The Home Mission Board printed a pamphlet titled *A Baptist Look at Islam* in 1967, designed to survey the Muslim presence in America and basic traditional Muslim beliefs. The pamphlet's author, Joseph Estes, the Southern Baptist Convention's director of the Department of Work Related to Nonevangelicals, warned that the Nation of Islam was known for its "violent disposition and radical doctrines," and was aggressively recruiting in America's cities. He cautioned that the large body of traditional Muslims in America rejected the teachings of the black Muslims. After reviewing the major tenets of Islam, Estes concluded that "despite its rigid legalism and fervent religious practices, Islam offers its adherents nothing like the assurance of salvation which is in Christ." A similar 1975 article in the Southern Baptist publication *Home Missions* noted that "evidence that the crescent is present in the land of the stars and stripes mounts steadily."[39]

Southern Baptists' tentative calls for acknowledging and witnessing to American Muslims reflected a broader Christian awareness of the domestic Islamic presence in America. In the 1970s, many evangelical groups in America, including the Home Mission Board, began implementing specific evangelistic programs among Muslims. An obvious place to start was college campuses, where many evangelicals had preexisting student ministries that could reach out to non-Christian international students. For example, Southern Baptist missionary Ray Register started a ministry to Muslim students at North Carolina State University in 1975 as part of his doctoral work at Southeastern Baptist Theological Seminary. Register advocated a ministry of "dialogue" with Muslims, which featured a deeper understanding of Muslim beliefs and a commitment to befriending and engaging Muslim friends in conversations about faith. He pointedly recommended not getting "side-tracked by defending American foreign policy" in the Middle East, which presented one of the greatest barriers to Muslim-Christian dialogue. The goal of Muslim-Christian friendship, in Register's view, was mutual understanding as well as "interfaith witness." Understanding and amicable conversation could happen in the context of evangelism, a duty that both traditional Muslims and Christians were required by their faith to perform. Working with a local Baptist church, the Foreign and Home Mission Boards, and the local chapter of the evangelical parachurch ministry Inter-

Varsity Christian Fellowship, Register began attending Arab Club and Muslim Student Association meetings at N.C. State. During his two-year stint in Raleigh, he made contact with over two hundred Muslims from the university and the surrounding area, and spoke with many of them about the similarities and differences between Islam and Christianity.[40]

Major American parachurch organizations that focus on college campuses, including Campus Crusade for Christ, InterVarsity, and the Navigators, developed extensive international student ministries featuring outreaches to Muslims. The evangelical agency International Students, Inc., has worked exclusively with the foreign student population in America, including many Muslims. In a 1978 International Students pamphlet, *How to Share the Good News with Your Muslim Friend*, Max Kershaw posited that many American Christians had met Muslims but did not know how to respond to the "unique challenge and opportunity" they presented. Like Ray Register, Kershaw advocated a dialogic model of evangelism. He recommended Christy Wilson's *Introducing Islam* as a reliable source for in-depth information on Muslims. Kershaw also advised Christians to avoid the issue of the Palestinian crisis, warning that most Arab Muslims felt that the United States had unfairly supported Israel. This is a common refrain in manuals on Muslim evangelization. Edward Hoskins's *A Muslim's Heart* (2003) suggested that American Christians should not argue with Muslims about the Palestinian situation, and advised readers to pray that God would "give *us* a more balanced view" of world politics. Similarly, Kershaw cautioned against the use of dispensationalist eschatology in evangelism. He dryly commented that "trying to prove from the Bible that Israel has a right to Palestine may not be the most tactful way to develop good relations with an Arab, nor is it necessary to the sharing of the Gospel." Many American Christians active in domestic evangelism or overseas missions have realized that American foreign policy and dispensationalism created barriers between them and potential Muslim friends.[41]

The quickly growing Muslim community in America generated a craving for comprehension and coordination among activist American Christians, not unlike the urge that motivated Samuel Zwemer and his colleagues to systematize overseas missions to Muslims in the early twentieth century. Roy Oksnevad, director of the Billy Graham Center's Muslim ministries, explained that Christian workers among American Muslims had by the 1990s begun to grow frustrated over a lack of coordinated efforts. Thus, the Graham Center organized a 1999 conference on Christian evangelism of North American Muslims. There, an evangelical scholar of Islam, Larry Poston, warned participants that liberal theology and Christians' undisciplined lives threatened to squander the apologetic advantage that Christianity enjoyed over Islam. Conferees also noted that while hundreds of workers appeared to minister among North American Muslims, they suffered from feelings of isolation and futility.[42]

Participants at the Graham Center conference described ministries among all manner of American Muslims, including new immigrants, refugees, and international college students. David Philip, a campus minister at an un-named state university, described his work among the hundreds of Muslim students there. He responded to "felt needs," welcoming new students and helping them get acquainted with the community. Like Ray Register, he also attended Muslim Student Association functions. He held public debates about Islam and Christianity, but confessed that individual contacts worked best. So Philip simply went through the student phonebook looking for Muslim-sounding names "like Ali, Hasan, Khadijah, [and] Mohammad." He called them and asked if they would like to discuss issues of faith. He de-scribed his goal as seeing "that every Muslim student in the United States is prayed for by name and then has the opportunity to receive a Bible, Jesus video [an evangelistic film portrayal of Christ produced by Campus Cru-sade], a chance to study the Bible, and a chance to interact with the body of Christ and see Christians in action." While many Muslim students were un-derstandably wary of such overtures, the freedom of expression available on college campuses and the potential loneliness of international students made ideal scenarios for evangelical proselytizing.[43]

Evangelical Christians have always used cutting edge media technology to reach potential converts, and missionaries to American Muslims appear no different, especially with regard to the Internet. David Philip mentioned that he recommended the web site *answering-islam.org* to all his Muslim contacts, and Jochen Katz, the evangelical webmaster of *answering-islam .org*, attended the Graham Center conference, as well. Katz explained that he maintained the web site so interested Muslims could "research issues that they are not supposed to read about." Katz estimated that the site received about fifty thousand visitors a month, and perhaps half of them were Mus-lims. The site featured evangelistic material for Muslims, apologetics read-ings designed for Christians wishing to share their faith with Muslims, and testimonials of Muslim converts to Christianity.[44]

Further reflecting this growing interest in Muslims, American Christian readers have become increasingly fascinated by "insider's" books on Islam, often written by Muslim converts to Christianity. These kinds of publica-tions have come in starkly different forms. Some assumed that Christian readers would want to share their faith with Muslim neighbors in America, and gave advice on how to engage Muslims in conversation. Other books sought to "expose" or "unveil" the ostensibly hidden truth about Muslims' beliefs, and focused less on the practicalities of evangelism. These latter types of books proliferated after 2001.

Evangelical Iranian-American author Shirin Taber, a former Muslim, presented one of the most irenic "insider's views" of Islam published in America after 2001. Her *Muslims Next Door: Uncovering Myths and Creating Friendships* (2004) explained that "learning to empathize with Muslims and to understand the issues that trouble them can help smother the flames of suspicion and the fear of terrorism." Nevertheless, she also hoped that friendships with Christians would point American Muslims to faith in Christ, just as she had experienced an evangelical conversion in Seattle as a teenager. She gave many practical examples of how Christians could befriend Muslims on the basis of shared cultural values, including the importance of childrearing and moral qualms about Western pop culture. Taber had memories of having been harassed in American schools during the Iranian Revolution and American hostage crisis, and she pled with her Christian readers not to treat American Muslims similarly because of 2001's attacks. She insisted that Muslims and Christians had many cultural and moral similarities, although their theological differences were ultimately insurmountable. She suggested that American Christians' blind devotion to Israel prevented understanding of Muslim anger over the Arab-Israeli crisis, and that political support for Israel had become more important to many American Christians than a winsome Christian witness to Muslims. Her closing chapter recounted the story of Sarah, an Iranian Muslim friend, becoming a Christian after Taber counseled her about the forgiveness that Christ offered. She suggested that Christian sympathy would both make America a more welcoming place for its Muslim residents, and also lead to greater frequency of Muslim conversions to Christianity.[45]

Despite the prevalence of conservative Christian hostility toward Muslims, a number of evangelicals like Taber have emphasized understanding over suspicion, while maintaining a priority of converting Muslims. Presbyterian ministers Bruce McDowell and Anees Zaka, for example, deplored the stereotyping of Muslims by Americans, arguing that the negative images hurt the cause of evangelism. Muslims are "in many ways. . .just like each of us," they wrote. They are not "all militants seeking to destroy everything that Western civilization holds dear. . . .Our enemy is Satan, not Muslims." They urged conservative Christians to befriend and evangelize the neglected Muslim neighbor in North America. They especially recommended a ministry model they called "Meetings for Better Understanding." Having become wary of the liberal implications of the word "dialogue," they assured readers that the meetings involved no theological compromise. Instead, participants in the meetings would formally discuss and compare their religious beliefs. McDowell and Zaka believed this exchange could present a powerful form of evangelism, as "the gospel has its own power to change their minds and open their hearts to say yes to Jesus." McDowell and Zaka reported that such meetings were being held in major cities and on college campuses across the country as of 1999. While some might see an inherent kind of duplicity or cultural violence in attempts to convert through dialogue, all will agree that this model at least has the advantage of emphasizing voluntary peaceful conversation between believers. Traditional Christians and Muslims are unlikely to abandon the hope of converting the other, so realistic strategies for mutual understanding must proceed in that context.[46]

Not all American evangelicals have adopted such a welcoming or conversational perspective, of course, as some worried that domestic Muslims sought political hegemony, or represented the seeds of a radical terrorist presence within America. Egyptian-born evangelist Michael Youssef forecast in 1983 that the Islamic nations of OPEC planned an economic jihad against the West to bring it under submission to Allah, and accordingly advised the United States to pursue energy independence. Christian apologist Robert Morey's ominously titled *The Islamic Invasion* (1992) warned that the millions of Muslims in the United States would not assimilate into American culture. Morey viewed Islam as a particularly intolerant religion that essentially represented a "form of cultural imperialism." Prophecy writer Michael Fortner has stated bluntly that the "many millions of Muslims that have immigrated to Europe and the U.S. is [sic] part of a planned invasion." Southern Baptist missions expert William Wagner stated that Muslims planned to change the world by taking it over in *How Islam Plans to Change the World* (2004). "The continuing wars and acts of terrorism are a result of the unfolding conflict between Islam and the West," he wrote, reflecting a Christianized version of Harvard political scientist Samuel Huntington's "clash of civilizations" thesis, which posited in the 1990s that future global conflicts would center around religion and culture, instead of ideology or economics. Like Huntington, Wagner predicted inevitable conflict between Muslim culture and the West. "I see the situation being so acute that we could easily be living in the last days," he warned. He believed that America was being infiltrated by aggressive Saudi-funded Wahabbist Muslims who desired not to assimilate, but to evangelize and conquer.[47]

Wagner expressed disdain for the dialogic model of evangelism. Based on his missionary experiences, Wagner believed that dialogue with Muslims was largely futile because of their hegemonic agenda. Instead, Wagner argued that the most effective means of evangelizing Muslims was through "spiritual power encounters" in which Islam and Christianity clashed, and Christianity was shown to be the true faith. He especially pointed to factors largely out of the missionaries' control, such as dreams, visions, supernatural voices, and healings, as the most promising means to convert Muslims to Christianity. Although Wagner seemed to dismiss the specific end-times predictions of the dispensationalists, he expected the world to see growing Muslim violence, especially against Christians. "Ultimately," he wrote, "there will be one large conflict before Jesus Christ does return, not to proclaim the merits of Muhammad but rather to establish [Christ's] kingdom." Where Samuel Huntington had simply predicted an ongoing clash between Islam and the West, Wagner added that the battle would be settled eschatologically by the return of Christ.[48]

Adding to the perception of the threat of Islam in America, Wagner and other Christians have highlighted Muslims' successes in evangelizing America's prisoners. Conservative political writer and leading evangelical Charles Colson began informing his readers after 9/11 that Muslim clerics were making great inroads in prisons. He warned of a "huge, nationwide network of outreach programs" by radical Islamists, seeking to convert American and western European prisoners to Wahhabist Islam. Convicts are "taught that the more aggressive they are, the more favor they gain with Allah." The message of Muslim brotherhood and the opportunity to strike back against the United States might prove irresistible to thousands of angry black inmates. In a view that might strike non-Christians as ironic, Colson proposed that the solution to the Islamist threat was to convert prisoners to evangelical Christianity through ministries like his own, Prison Fellowship. When prisoners "embrace Christ, they eschew violence," he asserted. In 2006, Colson renewed his call to stop radical Muslim evangelization of American prisoners in response to a university study warning of a terrorist presence in the prison system. He lamented a recent court decision limiting Prison Fellowship's presence in the Iowa prisons, saying such verdicts left "jihadists and other radical groups as the only game in town."[49]

Colson and Taber, both evangelicals, would agree that Christians should share their faith with American Muslims and try to convince them to follow Jesus. Nevertheless, a comparison of their approaches shows the deeply conflicted feelings American Christians harbor toward Muslims in their presence, especially in the wake of the 2001 terrorist violence in America. Some like Wagner and Colson warned about the dire consequences of radical Muslim evangelism, while Taber and Register offered positive views of Muslim life and culture, suggesting that through conversation and understanding Christians could win Muslim friends and converts. Behind both views lies the traditional Christian emphasis on proselytism and conversion. No matter how irenic an approach (like Taber's) they might take, the fact remains that traditional Christians (like many traditional Muslims) believe they hold, and should share, exclusive religious truth. Pluralism and mutual understanding, then, will not likely be the ultimate priorities held by the millions of conservative Muslim and Christian believers in America. Nevertheless, a significant number of voices within popular American Christianity, even after September 2001, have pointed to mutual understanding and reasoned witnessing as their responsibility both as Christians, and as participants in American civil society. Eclectic and sometimes obscure as their views may be, Christian ministers and writers like Ray Register and Shirin Taber have demonstrated that American Christians need not resort to stereotypes or fear-mongering to maintain their traditional Christian witness to a "Muslim neighbor."

Beginning with figures like Mohammed Alexander Russell Webb, Edward Wilmot Blyden, and Noble Drew Ali, Muslims have exercised increasing influence in American culture and have provoked apologetic responses from American Christians. Islam's presence in America has primarily diverged between domestic novel versions of the faith (like the Nation of Islam) and more traditional forms practiced by immigrant Muslims and other native-born American converts. American Christians had long seen Islam as their great missionary competitor, but its growing visibility in America often elicited reactions of fear. Muslims in America, particularly African-American Muslims, adeptly used America's endemic racism as a tool for criticizing hegemonic Christianity. These criticisms, and Muslims' successes at attracting American converts, led American Christians to register a variety of responses to Islam. Domestic Islam (especially the Nation of Islam) appeared to many Americans as a regrettable social mirror, revealing the deep social problems in American race relations. To others, the Nation of Islam seemed to be a dangerous cult, while domestic traditional Muslims presented a possible vanguard of the global terrorist threat. Finally, even after September 11, 2001, some conservative Christians called for generosity toward American Muslims, while still pursuing the mandate to evangelize them.

CHAPTER 7

Maturing Evangelical Missions and War in the Middle East

IN THE MID-1960s, an evangelical revival broke out in Muslim-dominated Indonesia that some observers thought might herald a major rupture in Muslim resistance to the gospel. Reports on the numbers of converts from nominal Christianity, animism, or Islam on the Indonesian archipelago ran from the impressive to the implausible: the Indonesian Bible Society said that four hundred thousand people had experienced salvation between 1965 and 1967, while United Press International speculated that two-and-a-half million Muslims alone had converted to Christianity. Many missionaries on the ground supplied more modest statistics, but still characterized the revival as reminiscent of scenes from the book of Acts, featuring all manner of miracles, including healings and resurrections. German evangelical Kurt Koch told American readers that southern Sumatra in particular had "become the stage for the greatest revival ever known among Muslims." By 1970, he believed that fifteen hundred Muslims, including a number of imams, had converted to Christianity. The revival also precipitated Muslim violence against Christians, with news of murders and church burnings. Some Muslims tried to ruin the Christians' reputations by saying they were "on the side of Israel," a political position that played as poorly among Indonesian Muslims as those in the Middle East. Koch predicted that the violence would grow worse, even as conversions became more common. "This is but a part of the picture facing the world before its end," he believed. By the late 1970s, Indonesia had become a showcase for the hope that Muslims would soon convert in large numbers to Christianity.[1]

Despite the excitement generated by the Indonesian revival, missions to Muslims still seemed an overwhelming task made more difficult by its long-term neglect. After Samuel Zwemer died in 1952, the impetus for organizing Western missions to Muslims seemed to falter. The drive to organize was hindered by the decline of missions in the 1930s, the intervention of two world wars, the Great Depression, and the difficulties associated with the Arab-Israeli conflict. Heightened eschatological speculation related to the

Middle East did not help the cause of missions, and some missionary advocates argued that dispensationalism was hindering evangelization of Muslims. Dispensationalists' hope for Israel seemed also to imply pessimism for Muslim or Arab conversions. But the recurring theme of the neglect of missions to Muslims haunted many conservative American Protestants, including dispensationalists. By the 1960s and '70s, evangelical missionaries generally, and missionaries to Muslims in particular, seemed more prepared to renew Zwemer's quest for global systematization of missions.

Since the 1930s, more liberal Christians have continued to downplay the need for proselytizing non-Christians and pointed to the priority of interfaith dialogue instead. The mainline World Council of Churches began trending away from evangelism as even a secondary purpose of interfaith dialogue in the 1970s. For instance, they issued a 2001 document on Muslim-Christian relations that cast suspicion on manipulative missionary activities that targeted the vulnerable for proselytism. Although the World Council conceded that believers "enjoy the liberty to convince and be convinced," they averred that Muslims and Christians should ultimately "respect each other's religious integrity." Such views have elicited contempt from conservative interlocutors with Islam. When in 1977 Wade Coggins of the Evangelical Foreign Missions Association received an invitation to participate in a National Council of Churches dialogue with Muslims, evangelical colleagues advised him simply to ignore the letter and not dignify it with a response.[2] Liberal inclusivists simply have not generated much enthusiasm for overseas or domestic missions recently, when compared to conservatives.

Following the fundamentalist-modernist split, and the nearly wholesale transferal of American overseas missions to evangelicals, conservatives became ready by the 1960s to move beyond the piecemeal efforts of individual agencies into a concerted effort to reach "unreached" peoples, including Muslims, with the gospel. The desire to coordinate Muslim missions was a sign of institutional evangelicalism's maturation, and a continuing example of American Christians' belief that Muslim missions had been largely ignored. New evangelical missions also developed in tandem with an increasing eschatological fascination with Israel, Islam, and the last days. As evangelist Anis Shorrosh observed in 1981, in light of the Middle East crisis, "everywhere there is a sense of the apocalyptic." But some missions advocates wondered about dispensationalism's negative effects on the Christian witness to Muslims.[3]

In 1960, missionaries and missions scholars held one of the earliest neo-evangelical conferences on Muslim evangelization at Trinity Seminary (later Trinity Evangelical Divinity School) in Chicago, organized by representatives from schools and agencies like the Fellowship of Faith for Muslims (Canada), Denver's Conservative Baptist Seminary, InterVarsity Christian Fellowship, and the Interdenominational Foreign Mission Association. Illustrating the continuing lively connections between British and American evangelicals, the featured speaker at the conference was J.N.D. Anderson, an evangelical Orientalist at the University of London and a former missionary in Egypt. Anderson restated the common Western Christian belief that as targets of proselytism, Muslims were the "hardest nut we have to crack." Islam had proven the most resistant religion to Christian conversion, and missionaries everywhere had found that "it is harder to lead a Muslim to personal faith in Christ than it is to lead anyone else." Anderson saw Muslims as worshiping the same God as Christians, but he thought they badly misconceived God, and that they could not be saved through their religion. He offered an extremely sober view of global Muslim evangelization, because of the massive opposition to conversion, the strengths of Islam, and the enormous numbers of people unreached by an effective Christian witness. Anderson offered no easy answers, but insisted that through prayer Christianity could eventually triumph in the Muslim world.[4]

The greatest of the new evangelical missions conferences transpired in Lausanne, Switzerland, in 1974, where about 2,500 evangelicals from across the world gathered at the behest of the American evangelist Billy Graham. Graham and the organizers explicitly saw Lausanne as a return to the global evangelistic fervor represented at Edinburgh in 1910, as the Lausanne covenant called on all evangelicals to unite "for the evangelization of the whole world." Graham lamented how the world church had lost its way since 1910 by deemphasizing the need for personal salvation through Christ. He called on evangelicals to return to the militancy of the student missions movement of the late nineteenth century, but also to be cautious about attaching the gospel to any political or cultural agenda.[5]

The evangelization of Muslims was only a small part of the vast agenda at Lausanne, but the subject did command some attention. Evangelist F. S. Khair-Ullah of Lahore, Pakistan, gave an address at Lausanne on ministry among Muslims and called for more personal and accommodating witnessing techniques that were sensitive to the difficulties faced by Muslim converts to Christianity. He saw intellectual combat with Muslims as ineffective. An "evangelism among Muslims" strategy group concurred with Khair-Ullah's emphases, and especially focused on "the cultural disorientation of the convert." They recommended that as many forms of Muslim devotion as possible be allowed for Christian converts, including the five daily prayers and Friday worship. They raised the prospect that converts might defer public baptisms indefinitely. The strategy group drew the line at certain Muslim practices which they considered unacceptable for new Christians, including prayers for the dead, the "vain repetition" of prayers, and attendance at mosque meetings. Among evangelical missionaries, all signs pointed to efforts to abandon Western cultural baggage that missionaries might have formerly imposed on converts. Especially in difficult Muslim areas, evangelicals increasingly promoted a "contextualized" approach that borrowed as many indigenous manners and concepts as possible to communicate the gospel in culturally appropriate ways.[6]

The Lausanne Congress spawned a series of smaller, more focused conferences, including the 1978 North American Conference on Muslim Evangelization at Glen Eyrie Conference Center in Colorado Springs, Colorado. The themes of this conference included the failure of American Christian evangelization of Muslims, the need for a culturally relevant gospel for Muslims, and the urgency of further systematization of evangelical missionary work among Muslims. Don McCurry, a longtime Presbyterian missionary to Pakistan and the conference's director, highlighted several factors that made the interest in missions to Muslims particularly acute in the 1970s: the Arab-Israeli conflict, the Middle East's role in the global oil economy, and the new Christian efforts to evangelize the world, especially unreached people, among whom Muslims represented the largest single bloc. To missions experts, "unreached" meant those who had no effective gospel witness among them, and much of the Muslim world fell into that category. (American evangelicals often did not count liberal Protestant, Eastern Orthodox, or Catholic churches as effective Christian witnesses.) To make matters worse, as of 1978 only two percent of North American missionaries were laboring among Muslims.[7]

Aside from the fact that so few Christian missionaries were working among Muslims, McCurry argued that the greatest reason for the lack of Western success in evangelizing Muslims was the tradition of "cultural imperialism" in missions. He deplored the expectation of "double conversion, that is, first to Christ, and then to the culture of the missionary." He saw this historic mistake as particularly grievous in missions to Muslims, as Christian missionaries had so often assumed that "Islamic cultures are totally evil." The philosophy of contextualization required missionaries to contemplate the essentials of the gospel and biblical morality, and abandon superfluous expectations for new believers.[8]

The conference featured a great deal of reflection on the failures and imperialist mindset of previous American missionaries. "We Christians have loved so little, and have put forth such little effort to regard Muslims as people like ourselves," the conference report remarked. Christians had brought trouble on themselves, the conferees concluded, as many "tended to misrepresent and belittle the moral and religious stature of Muhammad and the Quran." They also noted the grave difficulties facing Muslim converts to Christianity in many Muslim areas where "apostates" could suffer extreme punishments. By 1978, missionary apologists like those at Glen Eyrie held great confidence that, in the future, American Christians could extricate themselves from their Western cultural milieu, and encounter Muslims with no agenda other than that mandated by the gospel.[9]

The evangelicals at the Glen Eyrie conference also expressed conflicted views about the Arab-Israeli crisis. Professor Charles Taber of Milligan College (a Church of Christ school in Tennessee) believed that a contextualized sympathetic gospel required Christians to distance themselves politically from Israel. He wondered how conferees could "escape the taint of a widespread hermeneutic among conservative Christians that identifies modern Israel with God's promises to Abraham and justifies all Israel's excesses as fulfillments of prophecy?" Taber called on Christians to repent for their historic relations with Muslims, including complicity in the Crusades and "Zionist terrorism against Palestinians." Conference notes revealed that conferees had a mixed response to Taber's political views, with some commending his boldness. Others called on Taber to get down from his "soap box," and to avoid the issue of the Arab-Israeli conflict altogether. His opinions, and this ambivalent response to them, reveal again the surprising range of views on Palestine among conservative American Christians.[10]

One of the most tangible outcomes of the Glen Eyrie Conference was the establishment of the tellingly named Samuel Zwemer Institute, to be housed at the U.S. Center for World Mission in Pasadena, California. The conference self-consciously emulated Zwemer's example, remembering his conferences in Cairo (1906) and Lucknow (1911) as direct precedents. McCurry, who was to be the institute's director, saw the Zwemer Institute as a "nerve center" for coordinating the global evangelization of Muslims. It would also conduct "Muslim Awareness Seminars" across the country to involve more Christians in missions to Muslims. Despite its ambitious beginnings, the Zwemer Institute struggled to maintain financial support. To survive, it relocated from Pasadena to Concordia Seminary in Fort Wayne, Indiana, and then in 2003 it merged with the Muslim Studies program at Columbia International University (South Carolina). Although the Zwemer Institute seems now to have entered a more stable phase of its existence, its financial troubles point to the difficulties American Christians have with giving sustained organized attention to Muslim missions.[11]

By the 1970s, many American Christians had come to believe that the philosophy of contextualization held the key to breaking through the long-standing Muslim resistance to Christianity. Among the most salient books calling for contextualization was Phil Parshall's *New Paths in Muslim Evangelism: Evangelical Approaches to Contextualization* (1980). Parshall, an evangelical missionary to Bangladesh, specifically endorsed Samuel Zwemer's studied approach to Muslim proselytization, yet warned that evangelicals also needed to open themselves to tactical innovations in the field. He insisted that such departures did not require theological compromise, as "proper usage of contextualization can maintain total fidelity to the Word of God." Parshall described his ideal view of a contextualized mission to Muslims in a case study of an actual small church of Muslim converts in a town, presumably in South Asia, that he called "Gaziville." There, Muslim converts took leadership in the church and in evangelism. The former Muslims placed a strong emphasis on the role of supernatural phenomena in their piety, including dreams, visions, and divine healings. Western missionaries played a support role to the church, and dressed and lived modestly. The Western Christian women wore the Muslim head covering, or *hijab*, as a sign of respect. Church services retained as many forms of mosque rituals as possible, including the removal of shoes and prostration during prayers. The believers called themselves "followers of *Isa* [Jesus]" rather than Christians.[12]

While patterns of conversion are difficult to translate into reliable statistics, anecdotal evidence like Parshall's would suggest that contextualized evangelism, along with improved organization, has led to greater success in Christian missions to Muslims in the past thirty years. In the 1970s and '80s, evangelical missionary agencies mixed acknowledgments of the past failures in Muslim evangelism with optimistic assessments of potential across the Muslim world. R. V. Davis of Sudan Interior Mission proclaimed that because of modernization's corrosive influence on Islam, "today is Africa's time of receptivity to the gospel." Raymond Joyce of the Fellowship of Faith for Muslims asked "Will Islam ever come to Christ? Are there any evidences that the granite wall of Islam is crumbling? The answer is yes! The Lord is using a number of earth-shaking events," especially in the Middle East, to make Muslims more receptive to the Christian message. By the 1980s, American interest in missions to Muslims had become more intense than ever. A 1986 article in *Evangelical Missions Quarterly* noted that missions to Muslims had become so popular among Christian college students that one remarked "I don't know whether God is calling me to the Muslim world or if it's peer pressure."[13] This new draw reflected increasing evangelical organization, advertising, and tactical sophistication, as well as the growing prominence of the Muslim world in American news.

Despite these changes, Christian experts still agreed that missions to Muslims lagged far behind Muslims' percentage of the world's non-Christian population. As usual, American Christians thought that the use of the latest trends in media technology might make up the evangelistic gap more quickly. In particular, during the 1960s many mission agencies began to contemplate using radio and/or television to proclaim the gospel to the un-reached millions of Muslims. In 1969, Lionel Gurney of the Red Sea Mission Team wrote excitedly to the director of the International Christian Broad-casters, telling him that he saw "wider open doors into Muslim hearts than we have ever known." Nevertheless, the immense numbers of Muslims, compared to the scarcity of Christian workers, made for an intimidating scenario. "We feel the coming of the Lord cannot be too far delayed and we are not ready for his appearing." Gurney believed that radio might be the answer: "Four hundred million Muslims have still to hear the gospel of the grace of God for the first time." Radio could help Christians "get the job done before the Lord returns."[14]

This enthusiasm for radio and literature distribution among Muslims came to a head in a 1974 conference on media in Islamic cultures conducted by the International Christian Broadcasters and Evangelical Literature Overseas, both American-based evangelical agencies. The conference was hosted by the North Africa Mission in Marseilles, France, from which the agency broadcast gospel programming into North African nations across the Mediterranean Sea. Following the missionary trajectory toward contex-tualization, the Marseilles conference agreed that communicating in cultur-ally appropriate ways to Muslims was more important than the media tech-nique chosen. One missionary, identified as "Christian Goforth," noted that effective evangelism among Muslims would need to be patient and cultur-ally sensitive, for "Muslim peoples today are usually bitterly opposed to the Gospel." Goforth warned the missionaries that in their broadcasts and liter-ature they should use no language that unnecessarily exacerbated hostilities between Muslims and Christians. Revealing the difficulties that the Arab-Israeli crisis caused for evangelical missions, he especially cautioned the conferees that Muslims had taken "great offense" at the Western nations' support for Zionism. One participant went so far as to recommend that the word "Israel" never be used in gospel communications to Muslims, and that phrases like the "children of Abraham" should be substituted. Carefully crafted Christian radio programs and literature could avoid typical bar-riers to evangelism by reaching inquisitive Muslims in the privacy of their homes. Goforth hoped that the Muslim world could be slowly converted through effective use of media, prayer, and validating miracles, such as healings. Participants covenanted together to use whatever technological means possible to reach Muslims, but also to "consider the cultural, as well as the spiritual nature of Islam," so as not to create useless offense.[15]

Despite increasing attention given to Muslim evangelization, American Christian efforts still hardly penetrated the vast numbers of unevangelized Muslims around the world, who remained generally resistant to Christian conversion even if actually confronted with Christian overtures. Nevertheless, images of Muslim converts to Christianity remained popular in American Christian literature. For the post–World War II evangelical community, the wildly popular autobiography *I Dared to Call Him Father* (1978) by Bilquis Sheikh embodied the hope of Muslim conversion. Sheikh, a Pakistani noblewoman, was converted from a nominal Islamic faith after receiving a series of dreams and visions about Jesus (similar to those reported by Parshall and others). Through the encouragement of American and British Pentecostal missionaries, Sheikh soon received the baptism of the Holy Spirit, writing that in the middle of the night she "saw [Jesus's] face. Something surged through me, wave after wave of purifying ocean breakers, flooding me to the tips of my fingers and toes, washing my soul." In 1968, Sheikh received an invitation to tell her story at a Billy Graham congress on evangelism in Singapore, and finally in 1972 she fled Pakistan after numerous threats against her life and came to America, sponsored by the Christian charity Samaritan's Purse. She became a regular church and conference speaker, but after a 1989 heart attack she decided to return to Pakistan, where she died in 1997. Her book remains a strong seller in America, and has been translated into many languages as an evangelistic and devotional text.[16]

Stories like *I Dared to Call Him Father* have given American Christians hope for Muslim evangelization, despite grim statistics reflecting overwhelming odds against reaching, much less converting, most Muslims. Christian missions experts have typically acknowledged the theological differences between Islam and Christianity, but have tended to downplay the serious theological responses that thoughtful Muslims mobilize against Christian overtures as primary reasons for the lack of missionary success. Muslims do believe in Jesus, whom they call *Isa*, as a prophet of God, born to the Virgin Mary, who worked many miracles to reveal God's truth. Most Muslims see Christian doctrine about Jesus as having degenerated into the corrupt and absurd doctrine of the Trinity, which confuses Jesus's identity with Allah's. To Muslims, this conflation represents sinful idolatry. As a recent column in the *Manila Times* put it, Muslims believe that Jesus was a "holy human prophet" sent by God to "guide all of us onto the Straight Path." This widely shared perspective gives Muslims a ready rebuttal against Christian arguments for their conversion.[17]

Christian missions experts have increasingly realized that many of the world's Muslims are never even confronted with Christians' claims about the divinity of Jesus, because they remain untouched by any direct proclamation of the Christian gospel. Recent global missions trends among Western and non-Western Christians alike have centered around the prospect of reaching unreached people groups, especially those in the "10/40 window." The 10/40 window is a concept developed and popularized by Argentinean evangelist Luis Bush, and refers to a group of countries lying between 10° and 40° latitude (north of the equator), from the west coast of Africa to Japan. This area of the globe contains the greatest concentration of the world's unevangelized people, according to missions demographers. Within the 10/40 window, the greatest number of unevangelized people are Muslims. A key 10/40 brochure noted that just as Muslims were moving out from the 10/40 window to evangelize the world, so also "we must penetrate the heart of Islam with the liberating truth of the gospel." Doing so would require overcoming Satanic strongholds, the brochure stated.[18]

In the 1990s, conservative Protestants like those in the 10/40 movement became fascinated with the concept of spiritual warfare, believing that malevolent spiritual forces often prevented missionary progress in specific geographic regions. Spiritual warfare expert George Otis, Jr., explained that "two powerful demonic forces, with great biblical significance, stand at the epicenter of the unreached world—the [demonic] prince of Persia (Iran) and the spirit of Babylon (Iraq)." The "prince of Persia" referred to a demonic power mentioned in Daniel 10:13. Another book on the 10/40 window held that "timeless spirits" ruled Iraq "with a blood lust since the dawn of history," and that Saddam Hussein's government was "energized by the demonic forces of yesteryear."[19]

Otis developed the theme of the demonic strongholds behind Islam most fully in his book *The Last of the Giants*, written during the Persian Gulf War. In it, he posited that the fall of Soviet Marxism left a spiritual void that had been filled by several key powers, including especially Islam. "Of all the spiritual superpowers facing the Church at the end of the twentieth century, the strongest, and certainly the most visible, of these is Islam." Otis held that from its beginnings, Islam had dallied with demonic occult spirits. He suggested that the Prophet Muhammad had received his revelations from demons, and argued that historic Islam was "intertwined with an elaborate web of demons, saints, omens, and amulets." Otis explained the horrific brutality of Iraq and Iran's governments as a manifestation of demonic forces at work in those lands. To Otis, there was "mounting evidence to suggest that the powerful demonic prince of Persia has recently been loosed from his cosmic struggle with the archangel Michael and is once again prowling the neighborhoods of the Middle East." Otis reflected a tendency among conservative American Christians to associate the often vicious actions of Middle East despots not only with the evil behavior of men, but with the agency of malevolent unseen spirits. This logic represented a form of theodicy, trying to explain the wicked actions of people against people in a world ostensibly ruled by a good all-powerful God. As Islamic fundamentalism grew, Otis predicted, "the hatred of millions of terminally sentenced demons will give way to a level of violence the world has not yet known."[20]

Despite this bleak forecast, as the year 2000 approached, evangelical missions leaders called for prayer for the key cities of the 10/40 window, suggesting that focusing on the window held the key to bringing the gospel to every people. Otis remained optimistic about that goal, as "the soldiers of the Lord of hosts have now encircled the final strongholds of the serpent—the nations and spiritual principalities of the 10/40 window." Once the gospel had been fully proclaimed there, perhaps by the year 2000, the stage would be set for the return of Christ. The ambition of this "AD 2000" movement reminds one of the Student Volunteer Movement's "evangelization of the world in this generation" ideal. There are also signs that the efforts to evangelize the 10/40 window, like the SVM's work before it, may have fallen considerably short of the goal. The sheer magnitude of the task of making the Christian gospel available to billions of people—while the population within the 10/40 window is swelling—may mean that the number of unevangelized people there is actually growing, not shrinking.[21]

The new evangelical missions to Muslims proceeded against the background of the increasing turmoil and periodic wars in the Middle East. News from the Middle East no doubt influenced the interest in missions to Muslims, but it also fueled dispensational readings of the times that focused on the inevitable hostility between the chosen Jews and the "Ishmaelite" Arab Muslims. Direct political links between American evangelicals and Israeli leaders grew stronger, as evidenced by the 1971 Jerusalem Conference on Biblical Prophecy, which gathered an all-star cast of conservative leaders in Jerusalem, including W. A. Criswell of First Baptist Church, Dallas, Carl Henry of *Christianity Today*, and British evangelical luminary John Stott (who later repudiated Christian Zionism). Israeli Prime Minister David Ben-Gurion welcomed conferees. Participants struck a breathless tone of expectancy regarding the end of the "time of the Gentiles," and the second coming of Christ. Evangelical leader Harold John Ockenga, president of Gordon College and Gordon-Conwell Divinity School, explained that a correct interpretation of the "times of the Gentiles" revealed that it was to last precisely 2556.6954 years. When counted backwards from the Israeli occupation of Jerusalem on June 6, 1967, 2556.6954 years led to March 7, 588 B.C., the date when King Nebuchadnezzar began his siege of Jerusalem. This represented a "remarkable manifestation of the fulfillment of God's Word," Ockenga said. Although the majority of speakers seemed to believe that the founding of the state of Israel fulfilled Bible prophecy, Carl Henry also noted that God's "purpose in the reestablishment of Israel as a national entity does not exempt Israel any more than her neighbors from full answerability to justice and judgment." Political ethics restrained an unequivocal endorsement of Israel's actions, but most of the focus remained on the divine mandate behind Israel's claim to Palestine.[22]

News events in the Middle East continued to give American Christians plenty of grist for the prophetic mill. As one prophecy expert incautiously wrote in 1980, "biblical prophecy dealing with the end times should relate very closely to what is happening in the news today." Ratcheting up eschatological speculations, Syria and Egypt launched a surprise attack on Israel on the Jewish holy day of Yom Kippur, October 6, 1973. Although the Israelis eventually reversed Arab gains, the war proved costly and did not end on the same note of Israeli confidence as had the Six-Day War. The Yom Kippur War elicited even more prophetic speculations from conservative American Christians, including one of the most influential prophecy books of the late twentieth century, John Walvoord's *Armageddon, Oil, and the Middle East Crisis: What the Bible Says about the Future of the Middle East and the End of Western Civilization* (1974). (See Figure 7-1.) Walvoord, a dispensational stalwart at Dallas Theological Seminary, believed that prophetic signs pointed to the imminent rapture of true Christians from the earth. "As today's headlines report current developments in the Middle East, serious students of prophecy expect the next dramatic and important event to be the rapture," he wrote. Soon after the rapture, the seven-year Tribulation would begin, in which the Antichrist would make, and then break, a peace treaty with Israel.[23]

Although Walvoord painted a fairly conventional dispensational picture of the end in *Armageddon, Oil, and the Middle East Crisis*, his emphasis on the power of Arab oil cartels represented a new centrality for Muslim states in conservative American eschatology. His accounting for the connection between "Armageddon and oil" helped make the book fabulously popular in both the 1970s and in its reprinted version of the 1990s. Political Islam

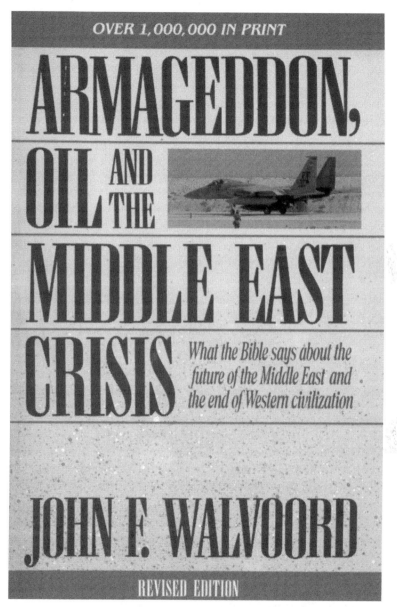

FIGURE 7-1. John F. Walvoord's *Armageddon, Oil, and the Middle East Crisis: What the Bible Says about the Future of the Middle East and the End of Western Civilization* rev. ed. (Grand Rapids, MI, 1990). Author's collection.

played its newly important role in Walvoord's scenario because of what he called the "Arab oil blackmail," a tactic felt keenly by Americans after the 1973 OPEC oil embargo. If not for oil, Walvoord speculated, the Arab-Israeli conflict would remain a sideshow to Cold War affairs. But because of OPEC's increasing power, world attention had begun to focus on the Middle East, making a diplomatic union between European and Middle Eastern nations more likely. The "Mediterranean leader" who could broker peace between Israel and the Muslim Arabs, and who would rule the new ten-nation "Mediterranean Confederacy," would subsequently proclaim himself the divine world dictator. As Hal Lindsey predicted, the Antichrist would then desecrate the rebuilt Jewish temple in Jerusalem. Walvoord noted that the Dome of the Rock stood as a "major obstacle to the rebuilding of a new temple." After the Antichrist secured the peace treaty with Israel, political Islam faded from Walvoord's last days narrative, presumably meeting its fate in the tremendous carnage at Armageddon.[24]

Messianic Jewish Christian Zola Levitt, who studied at Walvoord's Dallas Seminary at the same time as Hal Lindsey, stated bluntly in 1975 that the "Yom Kippur War was the beginning of the end." He thought that the Arabs' deceptions toward Israel represented the beginnings of the lies of the Antichrist. Levitt did not pretend to know the identity of the Antichrist, but he did leave open the possibility that he was U.S. Secretary of State Henry Kissinger, who brokered the peace deal ending the Yom Kippur War. Levitt was not alone in raising this possibility: Christian writer George Otis, Sr., noted that Kissinger's meteoric rise exemplified the type of ascent one might expect from the coming Antichrist. Moreover, Levitt believed that the Arab attack on Israel represented "mere preparation" for an imminent Soviet invasion, in which Middle Eastern Muslims would ally with the Russians. But Levitt remained fairly sanguine about the prospects for evangelizing Muslims, because he saw the Russian-Arab alliance as "false." The "sons of Ishmael" were "capable of being saved by the grace of God," Levitt reminded readers. Nevertheless, the Soviet-Arab alliance would precipitate the Russian invasion of Israel (the Gog and Magog attack), which would go down to miraculous defeat. For Levitt, Walvoord, and other dispensationalists, the centrality of the Arab states to the Middle East crisis gave a place for Arabs and Muslims in eschatological speculation, but the strictures of futurist eschatology still held them back from giving Muslims quite the same prominence as Israel, Russia, or the European/Mediterranean Confederacy led by the coming Antichrist.[25]

Liberal Christians viewed the dispensationalists' schemes with puzzlement and skepticism, of course, but some conservative Protestants criticized the premillennial dominance in popular Christian views of the Middle East crisis, too. Pentecostal minister Louis DeCaro, for instance, found no support for evangelical Zionism in Scripture. His *Israel Today: Fulfillment of Prophecy?* (1974), lamented how the dispensationalists, "overwhelmed with emotions, think they see in the continuing Arab-Israeli conflict some divine mysterious predestinating force compelling Israel to eventually possess all territory from the Nile to the Euphrates." These prophecy writers neglected "prophetic justice and true prophetic redemption." The meaning of Israel's founding and expansion in Palestine was strictly political, not spiritual. The promised redemption of Israel in the Old Testament would be fulfilled in the spiritual salvation offered to all people through Christ, not through delivery of Palestine to the Jews, according to DeCaro.[26]

The tension between varying Christian views of the Middle East situation became more evident during the presidency of Jimmy Carter, who was publicly known as a born-again Christian, but who did not accept the dispensationalists' views of Israel. Nevertheless, Carter did express a religiously-based fascination with the Arab-Israeli crisis, and once described the national survival of Israel as a "significant moral principle." He believed that to understand the "roots" of the current conflict it was "helpful to go back to the holy scriptures of ancient times." But Carter remained sympathetic toward the grievances of the Palestinians, and employed his Christian faith in pleas for peace between those who shared "the blood of Abraham." Carter's support for a Palestinian state, despite his apparently religious reasons for doing so, caused evangelical Christians influenced by dispensationalism to oppose his Middle East policies. His ambivalent view of the Palestinian question accounted in part for widespread evangelical support for Ronald Reagan in the 1980 presidential election. Reagan's personal credentials as a Christian were more tenuous than Carter's, but his support for Israel against the Palestinians was comparatively stronger. Reagan also occasionally noted personal interest in Biblical prophecy, commenting in 1983, for instance, that Old Testament prophets "certainly describe the times we're going through." Reagan was also willing to play Israel off its Arab neighbors to maintain the best possible situation for American oil interests.[27]

Some conservative Christians criticized Carter for his promotion of land-for-peace deals in the Middle East, but it remained an open question to many evangelicals whether prophecy mandated that Christians should give unquestioned support for Israel's land claims. As had become its common practice, *Christianity Today* hosted a debate over Israel in 1978, featuring columns by two conservatives, one supportive of Israel, and one critical.

The pro-Israel writer, G. Douglas Young, whom one historian has called "the pioneer of renewed Christian Zionism," was the president of the Institute of Holy Land Studies in Jerusalem. He offered a temperate but firm dispensational view when he argued that "God still has a part for ethnic Israel to play in the drama of redemption, *and* the modern political state of Israel *could* be act one in the fulfillment of the ancient prophecies." Young believed that Christ would return to a world with a regathered political Israel, but he cautioned against claiming that 1948 represented a sure sign of the end. Celebrated evangelical missionary writer Elisabeth Elliot countered Young with a denunciation of dispensational eschatology, which represented a "farrago of superficially interpreted Old Testament prophecy, glibly accepted propaganda, and uncritically indulged sentimentality." American Christians remained insensitive to the plight of the Arabs because of their "chauvinistic and fanatical interpretation of the state of Israel as a literal fulfillment of Old Testament prophecies," she wrote.[28]

Alternative conservative voices like Elliot's or DeCaro's might easily be forgotten, given the great dispensationalist furor regarding the Middle East in the 1970s and '80s. News events and global economic trends continued to push Islam to the center of popular eschatology. The Moody Bible Institute's Edgar James noted that while dispensationalists had long focused on Israel, "recent events. . .remind us that Arabs, too, have a prophetic future." Although James saw the Arab nations' oil wealth as a fulfillment of various prophecies, he also believed that Israel would eventually occupy all the land from the Nile to the Euphrates. He expected that the Arab nations, led by Egypt, the "king of the south" (Daniel 11), would attack Israel because of the Arabs' "continuing hatred of the Jew." James implied that the final conflict would not come until the gospel had been preached to all people, including Muslims. Thus, Christians should become more active in missions. "Some say the reason for meager missionary effort in Muslim lands is because many doors are closed. Perhaps a better assessment would be our degree of concerns for these nations" was lacking, he wrote. Unlike dispensationalism's critics who lamented its fatalistic effects on Arab missions, James believed that the coming eschatological war between Muslims and Israel should spur more missionary activity. "Maybe one day you will be able to share your faith with an Arab," he told his readers.[29]

Texas evangelist Paul Aaron's *Middle East in Bible Prophecy* (1979) similarly speculated that growing instability in Iran had begun to set the stage for a Russian invasion of the Middle East generally, not just Israel. Russia would seek to control Middle East oil reserves, but God would "supernaturally" foil their attack, as prophesied in Ezekiel 38 and 39. Like Levitt, Aaron took an ambivalent view of Muslims, conceding that the "seed" of Ishmael would be blessed because of his association with Abraham. But Ishmael's blessings were inferior to Isaac's: a "particular kind of blessing, partly good and partly not so good," was Ishmael's guarantee. Aaron characterized "Mohammedans" as "devout worshippers of God in their own way." But, he cautioned, they were not "saved, for this can only be accomplished through Christ." Aaron speculated that Jews and Muslims would both become unwitting followers of the Antichrist during the Tribulation. "Is it not ironic that the two greatest enemies of history, the Arabs and Jews, will come together under one false Messiah after worshiping the same God for so many centuries?" In Aaron's view, Jews and Muslims worshipped the God of Abraham, but refused to recognize the true Messiah. Thus, they would be left after the rapture to contend with the rising power of the Antichrist.[30]

As Aaron indicated, the Iranian Revolution of 1979, and the subsequent taking of American hostages from the U.S. embassy in Tehran, introduced a substantially new dimension to the news from the Middle East. Since American dispensationalists assumed that the events of the last days would revolve around Israel and its enemies, the Islamic Revolution in Iran definitely demanded scrutiny. The turmoil in Iran inspired influential Pentecostal evangelist Lester Sumrall to write *The Holy War Jihad: The Destiny of Iran and the Moslem World* (1980). He took a viciously negative view of Muslims, in contrast to the mixed opinions of conservatives like Paul Aaron and Zola Levitt. Sumrall claimed bluntly that the Qur'an "encourages Moslems to wage a war (JIHAD) against non-Moslems in the name of Islam." This supposed Muslim hatred for all non-Muslims, which was "satanic in origin," motivated "the Moslem to destroy Christianity and Judaism off the face of the earth." The Ayatollah Khomeini's overthrow of the Shah and the subsequent taking of American hostages was a fulfillment of that mandate, but more than that, Sumrall assured readers, "It was spiritual! It was prophetical!" The Islamic Revolution began a process by which Iran and other Muslim states would ally with Russia (as prophesied in Ezekiel), invade Israel, and be miraculously destroyed. Sumrall hinted that this represented the battle of Armageddon, but then noted that the rise of the Antichrist would only follow the destruction of Russia and the Muslim nations.[31]

The Iranian Revolution signaled a new moment in conservative Christians' evaluation of global politics, when Islam itself, and not just political Islam as it related to Israel, took a central role in some eschatological speculations. Sumrall's book was joined by other works like German evangelical Marius Baar's *The Unholy War: Oil, Islam, and Armageddon*, published in

America in 1980. This intensely anti-Islamic book broke through several barriers that had previously limited Islam's centrality in dispensational eschatology. Baar posited that the Antichrist would actually rise up out of Islam, because only political Islam combined the economic power and religious hostility toward Israel needed to fulfill the "spirit" of Antichrist spoken of in the book of 1st John. Like others, Baar pointed to the importance of the Arabs' ostensible descent from Ishmael, who represented an "anti-Isaac" perpetually at war with the Jews. Ishmael's blessings only "reflected" Isaac's, and "Satan exploited this blessing" to produce the religion of Islam. The ancient hatred explained why the Ishmaelites claimed a right to Palestine, not any recent historical or political developments.[32]

Baar thought it unlikely, contrary to the opinion of many earlier Protestant observers, that the Antichrist would emerge from Roman Catholicism. It was more certain that "the Antichrist will arise out of Islam." Jesus had emerged from the line of Isaac, but the Antichrist would probably come from Ishmael's line. The Jews "will be led by the Spirit of Christ" when they convert en masse to Christianity, while the Arabs were "led by Satan." While many had assumed that Muslim powers would align themselves with the Antichrist in the last days, Baar took a new step in predicting that the Antichrist would be a Muslim and lead the Muslim states against Israel in Armageddon. Only after 2001 did such views become common among some conservative American Christians. Baar also broke with Hal Lindsey and others by predicting that the Jewish temple would not be rebuilt in the last days. "There is no power on earth capable of dislodging the Muslims from the Temple Square," he wrote. Baar only anticipated that Muslim economic and political power would grow as the end approached. He believed that the Antichrist would hail from Iraq, and with Russian support would lead a ten-nation Arab confederacy against Israel. Baar apparently did not anticipate a separate Russian attack against Israel that would precede Armageddon. Although Baar exercised less caution in his predictions than most other dispensational writers, he did illuminate a trend in prophecy writing that increasingly posited a major role for "Ishmaelite" Islam.[33]

Similarly, Hal Lindsey followed up *The Late Great Planet Earth* with *The 1980s: Countdown to Armageddon*, and spent a chapter detailing the "Islamic peril" and its eschatological importance. Lindsey argued that the hostility between the Arabs and Israelis came from the ancient Isaac-Ishmael rivalry, but that oil had centered world attention on the Middle East crisis and would soon lead to the apocalypse. He anticipated that the Arab oil states would use their economic leverage to persuade the world's powers, including the United States, to abandon Israel to destruction. He predicted that

Arab nations would agree to, and then break, a peace deal with Israel brokered by the Antichrist. Arab political power, enhanced by oil and fueled by
anti-Jewish hatred, would unify for the attack, supported by Soviet backers.
"There is a religious fervor that a charismatic Moslem leader could spark
into a full-fledged 'Jahid' [sic] or holy war. . . .It is a matter of Arab racial
pride to regain Palestine for the Arab Palestinians. But it's a matter of sacred
Islamic honor to once again control Jerusalem," Lindsey explained. Soviet
hostility to Israel remained a key feature of this scenario, but Muslim anger
and oil power were becoming ever-more essential to the prophesied attack
on Israel.[34]

Although dispensationalists universally called for American diplomatic
support for Israel, they also taught that conflict between political Islam and
Israel was inevitable, regardless of diplomacy. Radio Bible teacher Derek
Prince's *The Last Word on the Middle East* (1982) explained that God had already spoken the "last word" through prophecy, so that the final great attack
on Israel was predetermined and imminent. Muslim Arabs would try to destroy Israel, as prophetically mandated. Prince framed the Middle East
crisis as a spiritual war between authentic and false prophecy. "The strongest
spiritual force that opposes God's purposes and God's people [the Jews] in
the Middle East today is Islam, the Mohammedan religion. Yet Mohammed,
the founder of Islam, was a false prophet" because he denied Christ's divinity and resurrection. "Thus," Prince concluded, "the conflict in the Middle
East has its real origin in opposing spiritual forces, not in nationalistic or
economic factors." Evangelical journalist David Dolan concurred, writing
that "there are strong supernatural forces at work behind the Arab/Israeli
dispute. . .there may *not* be a man-made solution." Prophecy expert Dave
Hunt wrote that the "real battle is not between Arabs and Jews but between
Allah and Yahweh." Such thinking offered little opportunity for evaluations
of the temporal policies of Israel toward the Palestinians, or prospect for
successful compromise and negotiation between the warring sides.[35]

One did occasionally see notes of caution about Israeli behavior from
dispensationalists. Prominent prophecy writer Tim LaHaye commented
obliquely in 1984 that if the Israelis were ever "to become inhumane in their
treatment of the Arabs, the United States would have to reevaluate her policies toward Israel." The Moody Bible Institute's Charles Dyer called for
America to support Israel's right to exist, but renounced some evangelicals'
calls for the Arabs' expulsion from Israel, and warned that "we don't necessarily approve of everything the Israeli government does." Such hypotheti-
cal warnings of contingent support made little impact on dispensationalist
opinion. Derek Prince anticipated that Armageddon would commence

when Arab nations called for the internationalization of Jerusalem. When Israel refused to comply, the United Nations would raise up a great international army to attack Jerusalem, setting the stage for the last great battle, and the return of Christ.[36]

Middle East prophecy expert Mike Evans, who has sported friendships with, and endorsements from, conservative Israeli leaders such as former Prime Ministers Menachem Begin and Benjamin Netanyahu, also assessed the growing global prominence of political Islam as "one of the great, but overlooked signs that the return [of Christ] is near." Evans wrote in 1986 that the Temple Mount would become the focus of fulfilled prophecy, and a "Temple of Doom" to Arabs who tried to wrest it from Israeli control (borrowing a phrase from the 1984 movie *Indiana Jones and the Temple of Doom*). Unlike some other prophecy watchers, Evans did not believe that the destruction of the Dome of the Rock was inevitable, for the temple's original location appeared to be on undeveloped land elsewhere on the Mount. He not only attributed the Middle East crisis to the ancient Ishmael-Isaac rivalry, but he simply addressed Muslim Arabs as "Ishmael," writing that "Ishmael was destined to rise with enormous power as the great clock of history ticks its way closer to the midnight hour." As for Islam, Evans considered it "a religion of violence, a thing hated by the God of the Bible." Nothing could be done to solve the Middle East crisis except the return of Jesus, Evans assured his readers.[37]

Continuing to follow the course of the news, prophecy writers pounced on the opportunity presented by Saddam Hussein's invasion of Kuwait in 1990. Jews for Jesus founder Moishe Rosen wrote that the events of the Gulf War "may be signs of more biblical prophecy being fulfilled before our eyes, the beginning of the end, the overture to Armageddon." Religious publishing houses maximized the opportunity: John Walvoord saw his updated *Armageddon, Oil, and the Middle East Crisis* reprinted by the hundreds of thousands, and Lindsey's *The Late Great Planet Earth* soared in sales. Prophecy expert Grant Jeffrey's *Armageddon: Appointment with Destiny* became Bantam Books' most popular religious title of 1990. That book, like others, asserted that the prophecy of Gog and Magog forecast a combined Russian-Arab invasion of Israel that would be miraculously foiled. In addition to Ezekiel 38 and 39, Jeffrey pointed to Psalm 83's declaration that Israel's neighbors would rise up as a confederacy to destroy the Jews, and argued that all the peoples listed referred to Israel's present-day Muslim Arab enemies, the descendants of Ishmael.[38]

Jeffrey also raised the prospect that the ancient Iraqi city of Babylon would be rebuilt and then destroyed in the last days. Earlier prophecy writers had interpreted passages that spoke of the future destruction of Babylon as referring to the idolatrous world system generally, but with the growing prominence of Saddam Hussein and Iraq, experts like Jeffrey advocated a more literal reading of those scriptures. Jeffrey noted that Saddam had spent "over one billion dollars rebuilding the ancient city of Babylon." Charles Dyer and Oklahoma pastor Mark Hitchcock (both graduates of Dallas Seminary), joined Jeffrey with entire books devoted to the rebuilding and future destruction of Babylon. Other end-times books made connections between the Antichrist and the city of Babylon, too. "Brother Bartholomew," the Antichrist in Salem Kirban's *666*, was born in a manger in Babylon, and (implausibly) given the name 666 because he was born on June 6 at 6 o'clock. Bartholomew kept his Arab, and presumably former Muslim, identity a secret. In Tim LaHaye and Jerry Jenkins' phenomenally popular *Left Behind* series of the 1990s, the Antichrist, a Romanian named Nicholas Carpathia, rules from a rebuilt Babylon. In that series, the Antichrist's "Muslim brothers" also agree to move the Dome of the Rock to New Babylon, freeing Jews to rebuild the temple on the Temple Mount. Mark Hitchcock averred that Israel's neighboring Muslim nations—except for Iraq— would join in the ill-fated Gog and Magog invasion prior to the rise of the Antichrist. Ezekiel did not list Iraq, according to Hitchcock, because Babylon was destined to become the economic capital of the Antichrist's last-days' kingdom.[39]

Feeding the eschatological frenzy, Harvest House Publishers arranged for the 1991 English translation and publication of Messianic Jewish writer Elishua Davidson's *Islam, Israel, and the Last Days*, which in its survey of Islamic history implied that the Prophet Muhammad had been demon-possessed at the time of his Qur'anic revelations. She too saw the conflict over Palestine and Jerusalem as prophetically determined, and referred to the presence of the Dome of the Rock and the Al-Aqsa mosque on the Temple Mount as a "continuing blasphemy." Like most other dispensationalists, she predicted that the Muslim nations would ally with Russia in the Gog and Magog invasion of Israel, a development that was "inevitable." Remarkably, Davidson posited that the Muslims remaining alive after the Gog and Magog disaster would realize the error of their ways. "The combination of the founding of a Jewish state, the safekeeping of Israel through five major wars, and the victory in the Gog-Magog war will be powerful lessons indeed." Defeated and humiliated, "throughout the Islamic world, hundreds of thousands of men and women will be seeking for an answer. They will turn to the Word of God and come to understand the prophetic Scriptures—and they will discover who God really is." Davidson did not cite any verses to back up this optimistic prediction.[40]

These kinds of dispensational scenarios dominated the field of popular American Christian eschatology and its relationship to Islam in the late twentieth century. That dominance generated a backlash among some evangelicals. Certain conservative Christians continued to warn that dispensationalist views of the Middle East crisis created unnecessary problems for the cause of Muslim/Arab evangelization. Soon after the Yom Kippur War of 1973, Harry Genet of the Evangelical Alliance Mission wrote in the newsletter *Muslim World Pulse* that conservatives had "perverted a commendable interest in the Lord's return. . . . We excuse a callous disinclination to take the gospel to some ethnic groups by assuming they will be on the wrong side of the Armageddon battle lines!" He exhorted his readers to "make sure that your view of eschatology is not diluting your compassion for men and women for whom Christ died." Similarly, Church of Christ missions writer Tim Matheny lamented widespread misunderstandings between Christians and Muslims that were only exacerbated by pro-Israeli dispensationalism. "An evangelist does not stand on good ground at all with the Arab," he warned, "when he claims that Israel's activity in reclaiming the land of Palestine is all part of God's plan." How could homeless Arabs conceive of Israel's appropriation of the land as God-ordained? "The open advocacy of premillennialism is highly detrimental to evangelistic efforts in the Middle East," Matheny concluded. Evangelical sociologist and pastor Anthony Campolo concurred, asking how conservative Christians could "tell our Arab brothers and sisters that Jesus loves them and has a wonderful plan for their lives when we believe that the plan necessitates removing them from their homeland and destroying their dignity?" Campolo, too, warned that the American Christian witness among Arabs was hindered by dispensational Zionism.[41]

Other conservatives, including some dispensationalists, agreed. Samir Massouh, an instructor at Trinity Evangelical Divinity School in Illinois, argued that the politicization of prophecy jeopardized the fulfillment of the "great commission," Christ's command in Matthew 28 to take the gospel to all nations. "By identifying itself too closely with Zionism without denouncing the evils on both sides, the Church will unnecessarily alienate millions of Arabs," Massouh asserted. Mark Hanna of evangelical Talbot Theological Seminary, who identified himself as a moderate dispensationalist, contended that dispensationalism did not require a pro-Israeli political stance. "The pro-Israeli bias of evangelicals. . .has driven countless

Arabs, Muslims, and other 'Third World' peoples from the Savior." Jerry Falwell of the Moral Majority, a leading evangelical supporter of Israel whom Hanna debated in *Christianity Today*, conceded that this dispensational alienation of Arabs and Muslims "was probably true." But, he wondered, "how is it relevant to what God's Word teaches about his program for Israel?" A few dispensationalists apparently tried to use prophecies concerning Israel to witness to Muslims. Raymond Joyce recalled speaking privately with a number of distraught Muslims who visited him after the Six-Day War. "When I showed them the prophecies concerning Israel and their future, they were amazed and left shaken and dumbfounded," he wrote. But such attempts to use dispensational eschatology in direct evangelism of Muslims were probably rare.[42]

Some Middle Eastern converts to Christianity also expressed anger over dispensational hostility to Arabs and Muslims. Lebanese-American evangelist Louis Bahjat Hamada, a Druze who converted to Christianity after coming to America, lambasted dispensationalists in his *Understanding the Arab World* (1990). "The Arabs have been perceived by most Christian fundamentalists and others as the enemies of God. . .thus, more than one billion Arabs and Muslims have been cheated and deprived of hearing and believing a balanced biblical view of God's universal love." Hamada argued against a negative view of Hagar and Ishmael, stating that God intended to bless them, and that both had become true followers of God, according to Genesis. He advocated an even-handed mediating role for America's Middle East policy. He warned conservative Christians to occupy themselves with evangelism, not political theology. While some skeptical observers might accuse Hamada and other evangelicals of exchanging one kind of cultural violence for another by their advocacy of proselytism, the critics of dispensationalism believed that a faithful proclamation of God's love in Christ could avoid the pitfalls of politicized theology.[43]

Other Middle Easterners who became evangelicals, like Palestinian immigrant Anis Shorrosh, accepted dispensational eschatology, but still maintained a relatively positive view of Arabs and Muslim culture. Like Hamada, Shorrosh emphasized God's promised blessings to Ishmael, especially that God would make him "a great nation." He pointed to the Arabs' great numbers and increasing oil wealth as fulfillment of that prophecy. Nevertheless, Shorrosh also highlighted the prophecy that Ishmael would be a "wild man" to explain the ostensible combativeness of the Arabs. "The wars, uprisings, and rebellions that have plagued the Arabs are definitely a fulfillment of God's word," he concluded. As a dispensationalist, Shorrosh endorsed the Israelis' prophetic right to Palestine, thinking it "strange that the

Arabs control three million square miles of land but cannot allow Israel, their kinfolk, to have ten thousand square miles." Even though Shorrosh's Arab family had to flee Palestine in 1948, he still believed that Israel's establishment reflected God's plan, and a sign of Christ's imminent return.[44]

Even though dissident voices against dispensationalism had been heard for years, in the 1980s small groups of conservative American Protestants began to organize formally against Christian Zionism. For instance, Donald Wagner of North Park University (an Evangelical Covenant college in Chicago) helped organize Evangelicals for Middle East Understanding in 1986. Wagner had grown up in dispensationalist churches, and even experienced conversion at a meeting where the evangelist's topic was the last days and Armageddon. Another key leader of Evangelicals for Middle East Understanding, Gary Burge of Wheaton College (an influential evangelical college in suburban Chicago), also came from a dispensationalist background, and recalled the great impact that Hal Lindsey's writings once made on him. Burge and Wagner had abandoned the pro-Israeli eschatology of their youth and became convinced that dispensationalists were unduly "anxious for Armageddon" (the title of Wagner's 1995 book). Wagner co-founded Evangelicals for Middle East Understanding to promote the interests of the "Arab churches, the Arab peoples in general, and a just peace for the Israeli-Palestinian conflict." Like other critics, Wagner argued that dispensationalism hindered evangelism among Muslims, although he also criticized exclusively conversionist proselytism of any kind. Recalling nineteenth-century missionary debates regarding the status of Middle Eastern Christians vis-à-vis evangelical outreach, Wagner argued that any evangelical missionary strategies, such as AD 2000 and the 10/40 window, would fail in the Middle East unless conducted in conversation with, and in deference to, indigenous Middle Eastern liturgical Christians. While groups like Evangelicals for Middle East Understanding formed a notable alternative to the dominant pro-Israeli stance of conservative American Protestants, it seems unlikely that their work has wrought a substantial transformation in many conservative Protestants' views of Arabs and Palestinians, either Christian or Muslim. Twenty years after its founding, Evangelicals for Middle East Understanding has ceased independent operations, having been folded into the Christian relief organization Venture International.[45]

By the end of the twentieth century, two features clearly dominated conservative American Protestants' views of Islam. First, evangelicals had largely taken over the business of American Protestant missions to Muslims, and they continued to dream of Muslim conversions on a massive global scale. This led to a new level of organization, spearheaded by the Lausanne and

10/40 window movements, that helped coordinate worldwide evangelical outreach to Muslims and other non-Christians. The evangelical missionary community believed that the world's Muslims were spiritually ready for conversion to Christianity, but that missionaries needed to become ever-more savvy and culturally contextualized in order to effectively proselytize in Muslim countries. Sometimes in tension with the missionary impulse, conservative Protestants, and many Americans generally, also increasingly fell under the influence of popular dispensational theology. That theology tended to paint Muslims, especially Arab Muslims, as being on the wrong side of the global eschatological conflict. As Muslims fought against Israel, they appeared to fulfill two biblical inevitabilities: the ancient hatred of Ishmael for the blessed Isaac, and the coming apocalyptic war against the state of Israel. Popular American Christian views of eschatology, Israel, and Islam set the stage for an explosion of new Christian literature on Islam after the terrorist attacks of September 11, 2001. Given the historical background of American Christian views of Islam, it comes as no surprise that the horrifying events of September 11 generated fresh speculations among Americans about the "real" nature of the Muslim faith, the prospects for Muslim conversions, the ancient roots of the Arab-Israeli conflict, and the place of Muslims in last-days scenarios.

CHAPTER 8

American Christians and Islam
After September 11, 2001

ONE OF THE MOST COMPELLING STORIES emerging from the days surrounding the terrorist attacks of September 11, 2001, concerned the imprisonment of American Christian missionaries Dayna Curry and Heather Mercer in Afghanistan. Curry and Mercer, inspired by the zeal of their evangelical congregation in Waco, Texas, had become relief workers in Kabul with the German-based relief agency Shelter Now International. They were detained for proselytizing by the ruling Taliban shortly before September 11, evacuated from Kabul when Northern Alliance and American forces occupied the city, and finally liberated in November 2001. The missionaries briefly became media celebrities, and visited with another evangelical from Texas, President George W. Bush, at the White House. Curry and Mercer's book *Prisoners of Hope* (2002) presented Afghan Muslims as spiritually empty and full of questions about Christianity that the Taliban desperately tried to keep them from asking. The women did commend Muslims for "their devotion to prayer and desire to be fully submitted to God," but the Afghans did not have saving faith. This compelled Mercer and Curry to go and witness to them, the dangers posed by the Taliban regime notwithstanding.[1]

Despite attempts by Bush administration officials to downplay the theme of religious conflict, Mercer and Curry's story serves as one memorable example of how American Christians have understood the vast matrix of events related to the terrorist attacks of 2001 as, in part, a clash between Christianity and Islam. The mass killings in New York and Washington loosed a flood of Christian publishing on Islam and terrorism. While 2001 is too recent to make any definitive conclusions, it appears that the post-September 11 Christian literature on Islam is new in its abundance, but not its essential topics, including the "real" nature of Islam (in contrast to the views given by pundits and politicians), the prospects for Muslim conversion to Christianity (including some celebrated cases of actual converts), and the place of Islam in the last days. But the American Christian view of Islam has also continued to be contested, even among conservatives, as some call for charity and understanding amidst the din of apocalyptic warnings and denunciations of Islam.

The shocking indiscriminate violence of the September 11 attacks precipitated exceedingly incautious remarks about Islam and the Prophet Muhammad by some leading American Christians. The *700 Club*'s Pat Robertson exclaimed "Somehow I wish the Jews in America would wake up, open their eyes and read what is being said about them. This is worse than the Nazis. Adolf Hitler was bad, but what the Muslims want to do to the Jews is worse." Samaritan Purse's Franklin Graham, the son of evangelist Billy Graham, called Islam a "very evil and wicked religion." Liberty University's Jerry Falwell said on *60 Minutes* that "Muhammad was a terrorist." His comments spurred riots among Muslims in Asia, and elicited a fatwa from an Iranian cleric calling for Falwell's assassination. Falwell subsequently apologized.[2]

President George W. Bush has actually moderated the direction of conservative American Christians' conversations about Islam since 2001, even to the point of alienating some evangelicals. Given his outspoken Christian beliefs, Bush's language about Islam has been closely scrutinized. On a visit to Washington, D.C.'s Islamic Center on September 17, 2001, Bush struck a conciliatory tone, stating clumsily that "Islam is peace." In his September 20, 2001 speech to a joint session of Congress, he made a clear distinction between Muslims generally and the terrorists. To Muslims, he said "We respect your faith. It's practiced freely by many millions of Americans, and by millions more in countries that America counts as friends. Its teachings are good and peaceful, and those who commit evil in the name of Allah blaspheme the name of Allah. The terrorists are traitors to their own faith, trying, in effect, to hijack Islam itself. The enemy of America is not our many Muslim friends; it is not our many Arab friends. Our enemy is a radical network of terrorists, and every government that supports them." Later in the speech, however, Bush spoke in a language of spiritual warfare that may have blurred his earlier distinctions. "The course of this conflict is not known, yet its outcome is certain. Freedom and fear, justice and cruelty, have always been at war, and we know that God is not neutral between them." President Bush sought to mobilize support against terrorists, and particularly against the Taliban in Afghanistan, by framing the new war in transcendent spiritual categories. But the use of that rhetoric made it more difficult to distinguish the religious from the political meaning of the war. In any case, some conservative Christians scoffed at Bush's distinction between Islam and terrorism. Randall Price of World of the Bible Ministries asked in 2001: "Is the United States waging a war with Islam?" He answered, "if it isn't, it should be!"[3]

The Bush administration has maintained a relatively consistent refrain in saying that Islam, as a religion, is not America's enemy. This tactic has driven a wedge between Bush and some of his most conservative Christian supporters. Fundamentalist apologist Dave Hunt commended Bush's vigilance against terrorism, but lamented his naiveté "in calling Islam a religion of peace. . . . How could President Bush, a professing Christian, honor Muhammad as a prophet of God"? Hunt thought Bush was caving in to "political correctness." Bush took his conciliatory stance even further when in November 2003 he asserted that Christians and Muslims worshipped the same God. This brought a quick response from key conservative Protestant leaders. Richard Land of the Southern Baptist Convention said that Bush was "simply mistaken," while Ted Haggard of the National Association of Evangelicals wrote that "the Christian God encourages freedom, love, forgiveness, prosperity and health. The Muslim God appears to value the opposite." Hunt angrily called it a "blasphemous insult to the God of the Bible to equate him with the pagan deity Allah."[4] Conversely, Dudley Woodberry, a specialist on Islam at evangelical Fuller Theological Seminary, argued that Christians, Muslims, and Jews did "refer to the same Being when they refer to God—the Creator God of Abraham, Ishmael, Isaac and Jacob." But, Woodberry cautioned, the religions disagreed profoundly about the attributes of God and Jesus.[5]

Despite the criticisms directed toward him by some evangelicals, President Bush has carefully cultivated a new image of American religious pluralism that theoretically includes Muslims. At a dinner celebrating Id al-Fitr (the end of the fast of Ramadan) in December 2001, Bush remarked that the convergence of Hanukkah, Advent, and Id al-Fitr should spur Americans of three "great faiths, Islam, Judaism, and Christianity, to remember how much we have in common: devotion to family, a commitment to care for those in need, a belief in God and His justice, and the hope for peace on earth." The concept of "Judeo-Christian" civilization, forged in the antifascist and anticommunist mood of post–World War II America, has given way to symbols of a new Abrahamic heritage that proposes the possibility of civic peace between authentic Muslims, Jews, and Christians.[6]

As indicated by the controversy over Bush's remarks, September 11 generated unprecedented interest among American Christians in understanding and revealing the "true" nature of Islam. Across the Christian spectrum, responses to Islam after September 11 ranged from calls for sympathy to denunciations of Islam and the Prophet Muhammad as demonic. Mainline Episcopal priest Barbara Brown Taylor wrote in the *Christian Century* that the church's first task in light of the attacks was to foster peacemaking between Christians and Muslims, for we were all "children of one God, with one soul called humanity." The U.S. Conference of Catholic Bishops, likewise, denounced "those who would attribute the extremism of a few to Islam as a whole or who suggest that religion, by its nature, is a source of conflict." They called for "deeper understanding of and engagement with Islam" by Catholics. An editorial in the Catholic journal *Commonweal* commended the bishops' statement, but cautioned that yet another call for mutual understanding "flirts with the Pollyannaish." "Dialogue," it warned, "may confront us with irreconcilable differences as much as unsuspected affinities." The conservative Catholic and anti-Islamic apologist Robert Spencer, however, argued that "violence and terror are fundamentals of Islam." Like Protestant conservatives, Spencer rebuked President Bush for his naive view of Islam.[7]

Many conservative Protestants expressed views like Spencer's. Among the denunciations of Islam, no comments created as much of a sensation as former Southern Baptist Convention President Jerry Vines's 2002 assertion that Muhammad was a "demon-possessed pedophile." His statement precipitated outrage among a number of Christians, including a group of Southern Baptist missionaries in Muslim countries, who anonymously pleaded with American leaders to "concentrate on sharing Christ in love. . . instead of speaking in a degrading manner about [Islam or the] prophet."[8] Vines cited one of the new "Muslim insiders" books, Ergun and Emir Caner's *Unveiling Islam: An Insider's Look at Muslim Life and Beliefs*, as the basis for his comments.

Showing their continuing fascination with Muslim converts to Christianity, conservative American Protestants such as Vines have commonly relied on former Muslims for their information on the nature of Islam. Angered by the perceived deceptions of their former religion, and by the rough treatment received from Muslims following their conversion, Christian converts have often supplied the conservative American Protestant with inflammatory characterizations of Islam. The Caner brothers have become two of the key former Muslim apologists for Christianity since September 2001. Their family had emigrated from Turkey to Ohio, where the Caners converted to Christianity through a local Baptist church. After receiving graduate degrees at conservative seminaries, both attained senior positions at Baptist theological schools: Emir is Dean of the College at Southwestern Baptist Theological Seminary (Fort Worth, Texas), and Ergun is the Dean of Liberty Baptist Theological Seminary (Lynchburg, Virginia). Both have written extensively on Islam, but their *Unveiling Islam*, released soon after the attacks, has become their most influential book, with more than one hundred thousand copies printed. In the book, the Caners described their conversion to Christianity and subsequent disownment by their Muslim father. They offered a survey of Muslim beliefs and history, depicting Islam as an aggressive religion of violence. Citing surah 60 of the Qur'an, they asserted that "the Muslim is called to hate enemies of Islam in order to achieve more hope of Paradise." Similarly, they argued that Muslim tradition made clear that "jihad has as its primary characteristic a bloody struggle involving military battles."[9]

Vines chiefly appropriated the Caners' evaluation of the Prophet Muhammad. The Caners hardly used as sensational language as Vines, but they reported as fact the disputed tradition that Muhammad's youngest wife, Aisha, was nine years old when their marriage was consummated. Although many Muslims believe this tradition, others have argued that she was significantly older when they first had sex. For many Christians, the possibility that Muhammad had sexual relations with a nine-year-old girl has provided salacious evidence used to denigrate the Prophet's character. The Caners also suggested that Muhammad may have received his revelations from demonic sources, pointing to Muhammad's own concern that he might have encountered a *jinn* (evil spirit), not an angel, when his revelations began. Interestingly, given Vines's comment, the Caners recommended that Christians not insist in debates that Muhammad was demon-possessed, as doing so did "little to advance the gospel witness." Liberty and Southwestern seminaries' decisions to promote the Caners to their respective Dean's offices heralds the brothers' growing sway in conservative Protestantism. Two Turkish former Muslims holding senior administrative positions at conservative Baptist seminaries speaks simultaneously to the growing ethnic diversity of American Protestantism, and to the power of the Muslim conversion story in American Christian thought.[10]

The Caners' post-2001 celebrity as Muslim converts is not unique. Reza Safa, the founder of Harvesters World Outreach ministries, is a former Shi'i Muslim from Iran. Safa presented the clash between Islam and Christianity as a battle of spirits in his *Inside Islam: Exposing and Reaching the World of Islam* (originally published in 1996, with an updated version after September 2001). To him, Islam represented an "antichrist force, a spiritual principality that would resist and oppose freedom and truth." Countering Islam required a demonstration of spiritual power from the Christian church: "Islam is growling and roaring throughout the world, and there is only one force that can put a stop to that spirit—the church of Jesus Christ. Let's roar back with the power and fire of the Holy Spirit of God. . . . Let's believe God for the fall of Islam." He also criticized American Christians' historic lack of effort in bringing the gospel to Muslim nations.[11]

Another former Muslim, who goes by the name Mark A. Gabriel (he changed his name after his conversion), wrote in his book *Islam and Terrorism* (2002) that he had reached positions of high religious influence in Egypt before abandoning Islam. Gabriel explained that he completed a doctorate in Islamic history at Al-Azhar University in Cairo, and served as imam of a mosque in Giza, but became troubled by perceived contradictions in the Qur'an. Soon he no longer believed that Islam was a religion of peace, and began publicly questioning the authority of the Qur'an. The university fired him, and the Egyptian secret police seized and tortured him. The experience ultimately led him to abandon Islam, and through the influence of an Egyptian Christian, he decided to convert. This led Gabriel's father to attempt to kill him, but he fled the country, going first to South Africa, and then America.

Assuming that Gabriel's story is true—and there have been questions raised about his real identity—one can understand the anger with which he described Islam and its devotees. Like the Caners, he painted Islam as an inherently violent religion. Gabriel asserted that dying in the cause of jihad was the only way that a Muslim could be sure to enter heaven. This represented the fundamental motivation behind suicide bombings. Those who engaged in violent jihad were "practicing true Islam." He warned that jihadists "want nothing less than to control the world and submit it to Islam." He remained sanguine about the prospects for Muslim conversion, however: "When Muslims meet with Jesus and receive His gift of forgiveness and eternal life, they are not going to need to commit suicide or kill others." A key claim of insider's exposés of Islam like Gabriel's and the Caners' is that, contrary to George Bush's assertions, violent jihad represents not a perversion of Islam, but an essential feature. On this matter, many conservative Christians have rejected the Bush administration's view of Islam.[12]

Taking a somewhat more charitable approach than Gabriel, former Sufi Muslim Abdul Saleeb (another pseudonym) teamed with influential Reformed Christian theology professor R. C. Sproul to produce *The Dark Side of Islam* (2003). Despite the book's sinister-sounding title, Saleeb called on Christians to "take Islam seriously as a coherent, systematic faith that presents strong challenges against the Christian faith." He and Sproul argued that Islam and Christianity differed fundamentally on major doctrinal issues, such as the nature of God, sin, and salvation. For instance, Muslims do not view sin as a radical problem, while Christians believe it is a damnable disease of the heart. Islam's "dark side" was revealed in its relationship to jihadist violence. All Christians who had ever committed violence in the name of their religion were betraying Christ's peaceful teachings, but "when Muslims engage in violence, murder, and other acts of terrorism, they can legitimately claim that they are following the commands of God as found in the Qur'an," the authors believed. Elsewhere Saleeb wrote that a "religious foundation for violence [is] deeply embedded within the very worldview of Islam." Saleeb and Sproul explicitly denied the claim by President Bush and others that Islam was a religion of peace. Many Muslims were peace-loving, but many other "Muslims believe they are justified in using violence to spread their message," they concluded.[13]

Popular Christian writer and California pastor John MacArthur took an even more hostile approach to Islam than Gabriel or the Caners in his *Terrorism, Jihad, and the Bible*, published soon after the 2001 attacks. MacArthur touched on many of the same themes as the Caners—including pedophilia and demon-possession—but used more incendiary language to present Islam and its history in a most negative light. He rooted the Arab-Israeli conflict in the ancient hostility between Isaac and Ishmael, and believed that Arab Muslims hated Jews because God had eternally promised them the land of Canaan. "In Israel today, untold numbers of terrorists, claiming descent from Ishmael, have declared war against the rest of the world," he wrote. Like Gabriel and Saleeb, MacArthur believed that the terrorists found explicit justification for religious violence within the sources of traditional Islam. While the Caners had only speculated that the Prophet Muhammad's revelations might have been demonic, MacArthur stated that "it seems certain" that the Qur'an came from satanic spiritual forces. Muhammad went into trances, suffered seizures, and produced a text that contradicted the Bible. These experiences had "all the characteristics of demonic possession." MacArthur asserted that Islam indulged a twisted sensuality that led Muslim men to become suicide bombers. This perversity emerged in Muhammad's relationship with Aisha, who, according to MacArthur, may have been as young as six when they married. This was simply "an act of pedophilia," he concluded. Imams promised young Muslim men that if they experienced martyrdom in jihad, they could enter Paradise where they would enjoy a "perpetual orgy" with devoted virgins. In sum, the Muslim faith was "a perverse and evil lie that invariably produces perverted and diabolical deeds." Islam itself caused the terrorist attacks. While extreme in tone, MacArthur's book represented a kind of conservative American Christian polemic that, in light of the horrors of September 11, 2001, excoriated Islam as satanic, demented, and inexorably violent.[14]

Similarly, popular prophecy writer Hal Lindsey warned Americans that "Islam represents the single greatest threat to the continued survival of the planet the world has ever seen." In his book *The Everlasting Hatred: The Roots of Jihad* (2002), Lindsey reiterated the point that Islamic rage against Israel and America did not result from geopolitical policy, but from the ancient hatred of Ishmael for Isaac. Thus, that anger predated 1948, and was "eternal." Hatred for Jews lay at the heart of Islam as a religious system: "Islam literally resurrected the ancient enmities and jealousies of the sons of Ishmael...toward Jews and enshrined them as religious doctrine." Prophecy specialist Grant Jeffrey concurred, writing in 2006 that from ancient times, "Satan has stirred Ishmael's descendants to bitterly hate and to kill the Jews." MacArthur, Jeffrey, and Lindsey's essentialist views of Islam created a sense of political futility: regardless of what negotiations transpired in the Middle East, violent conflict between Muslims, Jews, and Christians was inevitable. Ironically, this fatalist belief in predestined conflict mirrors a similar rhetorical tactic by Muslim jihadists, who assume unavoidable spiritual conflict between true Muslims and the infidels who would always hate them. Lindsey believed that the Middle East crisis was only setting the stage for the return of Christ.[15]

Lindsey's provocative and hostile views of Islam precipitated a revealing dust-up with Trinity Broadcasting Network (TBN), which pulled Lindsey's prophecy program in December 2005 over concerns that Lindsey's polemics would hinder the network's efforts to evangelize Muslims globally. TBN founder and president Paul Crouch commented that he knew of no case in which "making inflammatory, derogatory anti-Muslim statements has led a single follower of Islam to Christ." Crouch warned that Muslim-dominated governments monitored the content of TBN's satellite broadcasts for any anti-Muslim sentiments. The network put Lindsey back on the air in January 2007 only after they installed technology that could block individual programs from its Middle East satellite feed. The conflict between Lindsey and TBN reflected again the tension between dispensational views of Islam and Israel, and the actual evangelism of Muslims.[16]

From the fringes of Christian fundamentalism, some followed the logic of inexorable spiritual conflict and called openly for preemptive American war against Islam itself. Among the most explicit proposals came from apologist Robert Morey, whose plan to defeat Islamic terrorism featured military strikes against the holy sites of Islam, including Mecca, Medina, and the Dome of the Rock. "What if Mecca and the Kabah were only blackened holes in the ground?" Morey wondered. He speculated that Islam would collapse within a generation if it lost its holy sites. "Once Muslim governments took their foot off the neck of their people, millions of Muslims would convert to Christianity," he believed. Domestically, he called for a crackdown on illegal immigrants, and for American law enforcement to be given full authority to "infiltrate" Muslim groups in America to smoke out terrorists.[17]

As we have seen, other Christians, including a number of conservatives, called for a more sober approach to Islam than MacArthur's, Morey's, or Lindsey's, despite the widespread anger created by the murderous attacks of 2001. *Christianity Today*, for instance, published "Is Islam a Religion of Peace?," a 2002 feature article by evangelical writer James Beverly, who depicted Islam as torn between moderates and jihadists. The article cautioned readers to remember that "the vast majority of Muslims believe that nothing in Muhammad's life or in the Qur'an or Islamic law justifies terrorism." To Beverly, the doctrine of jihad did not necessarily require Muslim violence, and he hoped that the forces of moderation would win the battle for Islam's soul.[18]

Similarly, evangelical Baptist theologian Timothy George's *Is the Father of Jesus the God of Muhammad? Understanding the Differences Between Christianity and Islam* (2002) modeled a measured Christian conservatism regarding Islam. George maintained that serious irreconcilable theological differences separated traditional Christians and Muslims, yet he called on Christians to promote charity and seek understanding with Muslims, even in light of terrorism. "We must avoid angry condemnations of all Muslims on the one hand and a facile minimizing of Christian truth-claims on the other," he cautioned. George explicitly denied the belief that Muhammad's revelations came from demons, and instead affirmed that Muhammad's establishment of monotheism was "in keeping with biblical faith." He would not countenance sensational denunciations of Islam, but neither would he accept an approach that relativized differences between the religions. He specifically cited the 1932 "Laymen's Report" on missions, which called for an end to missionary proselytizing, as a moment when mainline Protestantism began to go astray regarding Islam and other non-Christian religions. George reminded his readers that while Islam and Christianity had much in common theologically and historically, "there are nonetheless certain irreducible differences that cannot be easily plastered over in the name of a superficial niceness." To George, the mutually exclusive claims of Christianity and Islam had to be recognized before Muslim and Christian dialogue could proceed honestly.[19]

Anticipating President Bush's 2003 claim that Christians and Muslims worshiped the same God, George asked whether the father of Jesus was the

God of Muhammad, and answered both "yes" and "no." He was the same God, in the sense that there really was only one God, the Creator God that both religions acknowledged. They were not the same God, however, in the sense that Muslims and Christians held fundamentally divergent views about God's characteristics. George placed the doctrine of the Trinity (God is one in three persons: the Father, the Son, and the Holy Spirit) squarely at the center of the impasse. "Apart from the revelation of the Trinity and the Incarnation [God became a man in the person of Jesus], it is possible to know *that* God is but not *who* God is," George asserted. In other words, Muslims acknowledged the existence of the one true God, but badly misunderstood his characteristics. They especially failed to recognize the true identity of God's only son, Jesus. Traditional Muslims would counter that if God was one, then the Trinity made no sense. Jesus was a great prophet, but was not God. Similarly, while traditional Christians believe that Christ won salvation for sinners by his death on the cross, Muslims do not believe that Jesus actually died on the cross, but that someone (perhaps Judas) took his place.[20]

Conservatives like George thought that September 11 represented a wake-up call for Christians to appreciate the theological differences between Christians and Muslims, without trading recriminations and rhetorical violence with the jihadists. Similarly, although calls for missions to Muslims became more muted after 2001, some evangelical missions experts saw the attacks as an opportunity for evaluation and reflection, if not new missionary gains. Dudley Woodberry wanted Christians to revisit their view of Muslims and America's role in the Muslim world, particularly with regard to the Arab-Israeli conflict. Instead of "mutual demonization," he called for Muslims to clarify whether violence was an appropriate means to accomplishing their goals. He summoned Christians to consider, perhaps for the first time, the legitimate reasons why so many Muslims hated America. Woodberry also believed that with a sympathetic understanding approach, Christians might find new opportunities for evangelism in the wake of the Afghan war, as "disillusionment with fundamentalist rigidity under Taliban rule will create a hunger for grace and fertile ground for the seed of the Gospel."[21]

Robert Sayer of the evangelical agency Arab World Ministries agreed with this perspective, noting that his ministry stood against any retributive attacks on Muslims in North America. Sayer saw the days following September 11 as a "crucial window of opportunity," and he prayed for the "God of redemption to bring good from the ashes of this [terrorist] evil." Arab World Ministries found the Iraq war that began in 2003 more difficult to present positively to its supporters, acknowledging that among the organization's international constituency there were widely varying opinions about the conflict. Its leaders cautioned that Christians "should be careful about interpreting how God works or should work in human history."[22]

The temptation to interpret how God was working in the terrorist attacks and the Iraq war, and the impulse to present America and Israel as exclusively representing God's interests, proved irresistible to many conservative American Christians. The years following 2001 produced an abundance of new Christian eschatological literature, including many reflections about the possible roles for Islam and terrorism in the apocalypse. Shortly after September 11, prominent Pentecostal pastor John Hagee produced *Attack on America: New York, Jerusalem, and the Role of Terrorism in the Last Days*, which offered a fairly conventional reading of Islam and the Arabs' place in the end times, despite the consternation caused by the terrorists' violence. Hagee is pastor of Cornerstone Church in San Antonio, which boasts 18,000 active members, and the CEO of Global Evangelism Television which broadcasts his sermons across much of the globe. He suggested that the Arab/Israeli rivalry went back to the children of Abraham. "The root of the problem" is that "the Jews are descended from Isaac; the Arabs are descended from Ishmael."[23]

Hagee also taught that Islam is an unusually aggressive religion: "no matter what the Arabs [meaning Muslims] say about peace, their religion demands that they defeat Christians and Jews. Islam proclaims a theology of triumphalism. Simply translated, Muslims believe that it is the will of Allah for Islam to rule the world." In the end, Muslims still played only a secondary role in Hagee's scenarios. While other experts like John Walvoord had argued that the coming Antichrist would broker an ill-fated peace deal between Israel and the Arab nations, Hagee contended that the Arab nations would ally with Russia and attack Israel with nuclear weapons in the Gog and Magog attack. "With gratefulness to Allah. . .they will embark on their plan of plunder and genocide," he proclaimed. The invasion would miraculously fail, and the Antichrist would emerge from the states of the former Roman Empire. He would broker a seven-year peace treaty that would inaugurate the Tribulation. Hagee was not sure whether the rapture would come before or after the destruction of Russia and the Muslim nations, but he did believe it would occur before the Antichrist came to power. As was so often the case with prophecy writers, Hagee blended political opinion with his eschatology. He has become one of the most active evangelical supporters of Israel, and George W. Bush's foreign policy. In December 2002, at Cornerstone Church's annual "Night to Honor Israel," Hagee reportedly addressed Saddam Hussein directly in light of the impending war with Iraq, by saying "Listen Saddam. There is a Texan in the White House, and he's going to take you down."[24]

Popular prophecy writer Grant Jeffrey concurred with Hagee's expectation that the attacks were setting the stage for the joint Russian-Arab foray against Israel. His *War on Terror: Unfolding Bible Prophecy* (2002) blended analysis of the global war on terror with predictions of the inevitable progress toward a one-world government headed by the Antichrist. Jeffrey insisted that Saddam Hussein was behind the September 11 attacks, so that the American government needed to depose Saddam as soon as it finished the war in Afghanistan. "Fortunately," he wrote, "America is now led by President George W. Bush, a man who believes in Jesus Christ as his Savior, and who understands the true nature of the evil threat posed by thousands of terrorists." Jeffrey accepted Bush's assertion that the war on terror was "not a war against Islam," however. While encouraging Americans to take the war to Iraq, Jeffrey also reminded them that the course of events in the last days was eternally set, and the late troubles were "unmistakable signs of the soon coming of our Messiah to set up His kingdom."[25]

Books like Jeffrey's can be difficult to interpret because they offer specific policy advice (such as invading Iraq) while asserting that nothing men may do could ultimately change the future. Jeffrey and other prophecy writers such as Mark Hitchcock positively cite Harvard political scientist Samuel Huntington's "clash of civilizations" thesis, which posited an inevitable conflict between the world's great civilizations because of their religious and cultural differences. Hitchcock wrote that Huntington's thesis was "precisely the situation" described in the Bible's prophecies of the end, as the powers of the West, Middle East, and Far East would duel for world supremacy. In his scenario, Jeffrey anticipated that before the return of Christ, the ancient city of Babylon would be rebuilt, the Arabs and Russians would invade Israel in the Gog and Magog attack, and the Antichrist would rule through a worldwide totalitarian government. He speculated that growing United Nations power might generate Security Council resolutions against Israel, which would serve "as the legal pretext for the coming Russian-Arab invasion of Israel." That incursion would be miraculously destroyed by earthquakes, fire, and brimstone. Although Jeffrey advocated the American invasion of Iraq, he also posited that rebuilt Babylon would survive the destruction of Gog and Magog "to become one of the leading centers of satanic pagan worship in the last days." Similarly, while he advocated a vigorous prosecution of the war on terrorists, he also cautioned that the growing emphasis on national security was "moving us relentlessly toward the surveillance society of the coming Antichrist." Nothing would stop these eventualities.[26]

Once the Bush administration decided to invade Iraq, prophecy experts began folding that new war into their end-times scenarios. Mike Evans, who in 2002 had founded the "Jerusalem Prayer Team" with Pat Robertson, Tim LaHaye, Jerry Falwell, and others, wrote in 2003 that the Iraq war was "a struggle between good and evil" and perhaps "the setting up of a chessboard dividing the players for an apocalyptic battle prophesied" in the Bible. Evans went so far as to find the Iraq war directly predicted in Scripture, especially in Jeremiah 50:9, which spoke of an "assembly of great nations from the north country" rising up against Babylon. As in his earlier work, Evans pointed to the Isaac-Ishmael rivalry as the reason for the Arab-Israeli conflict, and like Gabriel and Saleeb, he saw violent *jihad* as an integral part of Islam, not an aberration. The violence perpetrated by regimes in Iran and Iraq "testify of a malevolent manifestation of a religion conceived in the pit of hell," Evans declared.[27]

Again, Evans's analysis of Iraq and the Palestinian controversy gave the Middle East situation a prophetic gloss of inexorable conflict that would result in apocalypse. Dark spiritual forces lay behind terrorism, as Evans asserted that "demon spirits" were "orchestrating the terrorist threat" and that a demon was "resident in Saddam Hussein." Only Christian prayer could stop these threats, but even prayer could not forestall the coming events of the last days. Evans worried that George W. Bush, whom he knew to be a "man of faith who believes the Bible," might be led astray by less devout advisors such as Secretary of State Colin Powell, who were trying to convince Bush to allow the Palestinians to have their own state within Israel. A correct reading of prophecy required opposition to the Palestinian state. "How will Bush reconcile his faith in the Bible" with a "Road Map" to peace that offered the Palestinians land that God had given to Israel forever? "The only Road Map for peace is the Bible," he wrote. Jesus would only return to an undivided Jerusalem. Earthly powers might scheme against Israel, but "God still has the deciding vote," Evans proclaimed. Unlike Evans, other evangelicals enthusiastically supported the Bush administration's "Road Map," including *Christianity Today* editor David Neff, who appeared at a December 2003 interfaith meeting promoting the peace plan. Neff asserted that most American evangelicals, dispensationalist or otherwise, would be willing to support the Road Map if it brought peace between Israelis and Palestinians without jeopardizing Israel's security.[28]

The Moody Bible Institute's Charles Dyer took an approach to the

Middle East crisis more like Evans's than Neff's. Dyer, who earlier had predicted the rebuilding of Babylon in the last days, forecast in his 2004 book *What's Next? God, Israel and the Future of Iraq* that eventually the Antichrist would make a peace treaty with Israel, temporarily settling the Middle East crisis. This peace would precipitate the Gog and Magog attack. Making a change that reflected the ever-more central place of Islam in eschatology, Dyer eliminated Russia's role in that invasion and saw Gog and Magog as composed exclusively of fundamentalist Islamic countries like Iran and the Sudan, who would be angry because the peace treaty endorsed Israel's right to exist. Dyer predicted that the Muslim invaders would be miraculously destroyed by God. The humiliation of the Gog and Magog defeat would subsequently lead other Muslims to abandon Muhammad and turn to the Antichrist as "a new prophet." But the Antichrist would become enraged at the rebuilt Babylon, destroy it, and then turn his sights on Israel, where the last war would be fought. Echoing Mike Evans's quip, Dyer wrote that "God's 'road map for peace' goes right through the Mount of Olives," where Christ's feet would stand at his return.[29]

Many other conservative Christian prophecy writers have not withdrawn Russia from the Gog and Magog invasion, even in light of September 11 and a growing nuclear threat from Iran. In *Iran: The Coming Crisis* (2006), Mark Hitchcock followed his mentor John Walvoord in maintaining that all the countries composing Gog and Magog were Islamic, except for Russia. He defended the long-held dispensational belief that Ezekiel 38's "Rosh" represented Russia. To Hitchcock, Ezekiel 38–39 represented the "final jihad." Grant Jeffrey proposed a very similar scenario in *The Next World War* (2006) in which Russia and the Muslim nations would unite around their shared anti-Semitism and attack Israel. But Charles Dyer's colleague at the Moody Bible Institute, Jewish studies professor Michael Rydelnik, withdrew Russia from Gog and Magog in his *Understanding the Arab-Israeli Conflict: What the Headlines Haven't Told You* (2004). Rydelnik explicitly repudiated those like Hitchcock who identified "Rosh," "Meshech," and the armies of the "far north" as Russia. He commented that "this approach seems to take its interpretation more from Cold War headlines than the biblical text." Instead, Rydelnik interpreted the list of nations as including several former Soviet republics, as well as Turkey, Iran, Libya, and the Sudan. "The hatred of Israel among militant Muslims will increase to the point of all-out war with the Jewish state," he concluded. He predicted that the Islamic invasion would occur after the Antichrist brokered the Middle East peace, in the middle of the Tribulation. Once the Islamic nations had been destroyed, the Antichrist would "turn on Israel and unleash a horrific period of anti-Semitism."[30]

Rydelnik realized that Ezekiel's list of nations left out most of Israel's Arab neighbors, so he also surveyed a variety of prophetic passages accounting for those countries' role in the last days. He adopted Charles Dyer's argument that literal Babylon would be rebuilt and destroyed, and Lebanon and parts of Syria would be annexed by Israel in the millennial kingdom. While the southern part of Jordan would be destroyed and left desolate, the people of the northern sections, the descendants of the Moabites and Ammonites, would convert en masse to Christianity in the end. So would the Egyptians and the "Assyrians" of Syria and Iraq. As for the Middle East conflict itself, Rydelnik acknowledged that political solutions should be pursued, but he expected they would fail. He seemed to reject the idea of the Ishmael-Isaac rivalry as the cause of the conflict, implying that the Arab Muslims who saw themselves as descendants of Ishmael were mistaken. He similarly conceded that the world of Islam included both moderates and militants, but he asserted that "jihad, even violent jihad, is the obligation of every adherent of Islam." Islam drove the insoluble Middle East crisis. Peace would only arrive "when the Peacemaker comes."[31]

Many Christian conservatives in America have sought to spiritualize the meaning of the Middle East conflict and Iraq war, seeing them as evidence of heavenly battles that might set the stage for the return of Christ. Perhaps no text since 2001 took a more spiritualized view of the Iraq war than Prophet Glenn Miller's *The Prophetic Fall of the Islamic Regime* (2004). Miller, a charismatic minister who believes that he has the God-given gift of prophetic truth-telling for the interpretation of world events, argued that God had orchestrated the Iraq war through his chosen instrument, George W. Bush. The Iraq war, according to Miller, was not primarily "about Saddam Hussein or his regime." He prophesied that God intended the war to destroy the evil spiritual force behind Islam itself. The war "was about the lying and masquerading Islamic Allah, who is a demon prince, and this false god's stranglehold over that portion of the world." Obviously, Miller did not agree with Bush's assertion that Muslims and Christians worship the same God, despite the fact that Miller called Bush "God's choice." Bush came to power to fulfill the prophetic mandate to remove Saddam that his father, George H. W. Bush, had failed to obey in the first Gulf War. Miller argued that Allah was not God, but a "false god, who cannot save anyone from anything. Rather, through his false prophet, Mohammed, he continues to lead hundreds of millions into eternal darkness." He contended that as a result of the Iraq war, Islam's historic resistance to the gospel would be broken, and hundreds of millions of Muslims would soon become Christians. He called on Christians to "sharpen your sword of truth and be prepared to do battle against the Islamic lies." Miller reflected an exaggeration of the conservative tendency to see political events in the Middle East as epiphenomenal, masking the real spiritual war over Israel. God would use correct policy decisions to advance spiritual goals.[32]

Perhaps the most distinctive change in Christian eschatology since 2001 has been the rise of speculation in some circles that the Antichrist would come from Islam, and particularly that he would be (mis-)identified by Muslims as the messianic Mahdi. As some American Christians have learned more about the basics of Muslim theology, they have found in the Muslim hope for the Mahdi's return an eschatological narrative easily inverted and employed for Christian uses. More knowledge about Muslim theology has not lessened these Christians' hostility toward Islam. Ralph Stice, a professor at Nyack College, D.C., began his *From 9/11 to 666* (2005) with a speculative account of how America and the world might be taken over by the Mahdi Antichrist by 2017. In Stice's scenario, the Iraq war faltered badly and led to a collapse of American state and economic power. The Muslim states of the world united under the authority of the charismatic Mahdi, who was supported by a false prophet, *Isa*, who claimed to be the resurrected Christ, and who advised people to adopt Islam. This latter idea also played off a common Muslim eschatological belief about the return of Jesus, who would point his followers to Muhammad as the final prophet. The Mahdi assumed power of a one-world government that forced people to take a laser-burned mark of the Muslim creed. Only real Christians refused to take the mark, and the totalitarian Muslim government began beheading Christians in the streets. Stice rejected the view that the rapture of the church would occur at the beginning of the Tribulation. Christians would have to face the fury of the Muslim Antichrist.[33]

Among prophecy writers, Stice took an unusually negative view of other conservative American Christians. He placed himself explicitly in opposition to prominent post–World War II prophecy writers, who had too often "neglected. . .the undeniable presence of Islamic countries throughout apocalyptic literature." Stice presented himself as a "reasonable" interpreter of end-times prophecies, while others like Tim LaHaye and Hal Lindsey had focused too much on America's latest enemy (typically the Soviet Union, until the 1990s). He scoffed at LaHaye's Nicholas Carpathia, the "Romanian smoothie" who became the Antichrist in *Left Behind*. Stice thought it much more likely that Islamic prophecy revealed the true Antichrist in the Mahdi, because of the ancient hostility between Arabs and Jews (Ishmael and Isaac), and because of the strong resemblances between Islam's concept of the Mahdi and the Bible's descriptions of the Antichrist. Many American

Christians, including some dispensational preachers unprepared for the difficulties of the Tribulation, would eagerly follow the Mahdi and the false Jesus because of their promises of peace, safety, and Qur'anic moral order, he predicted. Stice condemned Americans' insatiable consumption of oil as the vice that bred Islamic fundamentalism and that would facilitate the rise of the Antichrist. This sin would "power the push towards Armageddon, as the Beast uses his great riches to bankroll his movement." Although his formulation of Antichrist, Tribulation, and Armageddon are typical of dispensational exegetes, Stice made a substantially new contribution to popular American political-eschatological literature with his criticisms of American Christians, American consumerism, and especially his insertion of the Mahdi as the Antichrist.[34]

In his disturbing insertion of the Mahdi into the eschatological mix, Stice was not alone. During 2005 and 2006, several books appeared that asserted either that the Antichrist would rise out of Islam, or specifically that the Muslim Mahdi was the Antichrist. Although we cannot yet discern whether this represents a temporary departure or a permanent change, at first glance this seems to signal a significant new anti-Muslim trend in some conservative Christians' eschatology. Unlike in most previous dispensational schemes, this new literature gives Islam center stage above all competitors. The author of *Antichrist: Islam's Awaited Messiah* (2006), writing under the pen name Joel Richardson because of death threats against him, claimed that "Islam is indeed the primary vehicle that will be used by Satan to fulfill the prophecies of the Bible about the future political/religious/military system of the Antichrist." Like Stice, Richardson believed that the messianic Mahdi and the Antichrist were one and the same. The Muslim *Isa* represented the False Prophet, who Muslims believed would return in the end to abolish Christianity. Moreover, the Antichrist's future empire would be almost entirely Muslim. Prophecy writer J. C. Alexander agreed in his *The Kingdom of the Beast and the End of the World* (2005), writing that "Muslims are prepared right now to follow the Antichrist under the banner of Islam." He envisioned a ten-nation Muslim Antichrist confederacy, since "Islam is a totally Antichrist religion." Unlike Stice and Richardson, Alexander suggested that the returning *Isa* would actually be the Antichrist, not the Mahdi.[35]

Joel Richardson abandoned long-time dispensationalist interpretations not only by interpreting the Gog and Magog attack of Ezekiel as exclusively Islamic, but especially by identifying Gog himself as the Antichrist (most dispensationalists have seen Gog and Magog as a military force separate from the Antichrist's). Richardson thought it predictable that the Antichrist would emerge from Islam, because he saw that religion as fatally compromised by a demonic and antichristian spirit. Echoing the Caners, Richardson asserted that Muhammad had received his revelations from demonic forces. "Islam, more than any other religion, philosophy, or belief system," Richardson concluded, "fulfills the description of the antichrist spirit [I John 4]." Missionary and prophecy writer Robert Livingston concurred in his *Christianity and Islam: The Final Clash* (2004), writing that "no faith on the planet. . .commands the undying, fanatical and violent devotion of so many adherents to its violently anti-Christ message as Islam." In Richardson's opinion, the two groups with the strongest resistance to the Christian gospel were Satanists and Muslims (he clarified that he was not trying to liken Muslims to Satanists generally). Like other anti-Muslim apologists, Richardson presented Islam as an inherently violent religion, and implicitly repudiated President Bush's assertions to the contrary. "While it is often said that the terrorists have 'hijacked' Islam, . . .it is in reality the so-called moderate Muslims who are trying to change the true teachings of Islam," he wrote. The terrorists were being faithful to core Islamic teachings. Theirs served as the perfect religion to produce the Antichrist's world domination: "Satan has already prepared a fifth of the world to receive his coming Antichrist with arms wide open," Richardson wrote. Robert Livingston similarly believed that Islam was "ready-made for the Beast and the False Prophet."[36]

While most modern prophecy writers have given up the nineteenth-century fashion of prophetic numerology, at least one student of the last days has seen in Bible numbers signs of the coming Islamic beast. Like Richardson and Alexander, Michael Fortner's *The Scarlet Beast: Islam and the Beast of Revelation* (2006) held that the Antichrist's base of power would be wholly Muslim, representing a revived Ottoman Empire. Fortner's study of Scripture revealed previously obscured hints at the Antichrist's Muslim identity, too, in the number 666. For instance, he showed that in Ezekiel 40, the prophet described the east gate of the Temple as containing six alcoves, each six cubits square. Everyone entering that gate was surrounded by a representation, then, of 666. "The people of 666, those who follow the beast and false prophet, will surround Israel," Fortner extrapolated. "The enemies that surround Israel, and have for the past 1,400 years, are Islamic. Could it be any clearer?" he asked. Fortner also reminded readers that the Six-Day War "lasted 6 days; 6th month, 1967, (666) that ended on the 6th." Moreover, he pointed to the 1998 Al-Qaeda bombings of U.S. embassies in Africa, the moment when the United States became aware of the terrorist campaign against it. "There are three sixes in 666; if you take 666 and multiply it by 3, you get 1998."[37] Again, we should note that Fortner's calculations are not typical of most dispensational writers, but they do illustrate the urgency with which some exegetes wished to find Islam in Bible prophecy.

It is difficult to say how widely views like Miller's, Stice's, and Richardson's are held among American Christians. Many self-identifying American Christians, including many evangelicals, would find these eschatological speculations troubling, or simply bizarre, and have taken a very different approach to the Middle East situation. Mainline Protestant church leaders, often disdainful of the dispensationalists' speculations, have tended to support the Palestinian side of the Middle East conflict. The Presbyterian Church (U.S.A.), for instance, has repeatedly called on Israel to "end the [Palestinian] occupation now" as an essential step in building a lasting Middle East peace. Even some conservative Protestants have denounced dispensational prophetic interpretations as biblically suspect and too dependent on the latest news. Biblical studies professors Marvin Pate and Daniel Hays of Ouachita Baptist University (Arkansas) deplored the changing views of Gog and Magog in prophecy books by Lindsey and others as "overly literalistic readings of the Bible and current events." They cited a number of evangelical scholars who interpreted Gog and Magog as a general future attack on God's people, not a showdown between Russia, her Muslim allies, and Israel. To these Bible scholars, Ezekiel 38 and 39 could not be keyed to any current political entities, including the state of Israel. Pate and Hays also echoed the long-term concern of some conservatives that dispensational prophecy could hinder Muslim evangelization: Christians should support "efforts to reach the Muslim world for Christ [instead of] trying to prove with questionable evidence that these Muslims are part of an evil end-time coalition intent on defying God."[38] Nevertheless, books reflecting the views of Islam as central to the fulfillment of Christian prophecy do sell reasonably well (better, usually, than books expressing doubts like Pate's and Hays's), and represent a new twist on an old Christian tendency to read the newspaper and the Bible side-by-side, a practice that some prophecy experts have recommended unreservedly. The news and the Bible "align by the day," Ralph Stice reminded readers on his web site's "Mahdi Watch."[39]

Polls have indicated, likewise, that conservative American Christians hold more sharply negative views of Islam than average Americans. Americans overall, according to a 2005 Pew Research Center poll, had a split favorable/unfavorable opinion of Islam. White Catholics had slightly more positive than negative views of Muslims, while white Protestants had slightly more negative views than positive. Practicing, or high-commitment, evangelicals held by far the most negative estimation of Islam among those surveyed, with 54 percent negative and only 24 percent positive. While such poll results are almost necessarily ambiguous in their meaning, it seems certain that evangelicals do have a disproportionately negative opinion of Islam and its followers, compared to other Americans, including other Christians. Whether conservative eschatological literature and Muslim exposés have formed—or mostly just reflect—those views, is unclear.[40]

Scholars and journalists have noted for some time the role of dispensational beliefs on American foreign policy, although much of that influence has remained "subterranean and indirect," as historian Paul Boyer put it. Popular Christian eschatology continues to shape some American leaders' views of the Middle East crisis and terrorism, too. Conservative American Christians remain among Israel's most enthusiastic supporters because of the perceived theological requirement for Christians to support Israel. Sometimes these views appear in the highest forums of American political power. Evangelical Senator James Inhofe of Oklahoma argued in a 2002 speech in the Senate that America should support Israel "because God said so." Citing God's promise to give the land of Canaan to Israel, Inhofe reminded his audience that this "is God talking." Therefore, Israel had an incontrovertible right to the land. The political struggles and violence masked the real spiritual battle being waged. According to Inhofe, "this is not a political battle at all. It is a contest over whether or not the word of God is true." Apologist Dave Hunt printed the text of Inhofe's speech in an appendix to his book *Judgment Day*, while Pat Robertson has posted the speech on his Christian Broadcasting Network web site. Inhofe highlighted the American conservative Christian tendency to downplay the desirability or efficacy of political negotiations, and to see a transcendent Manichean conflict being played out behind the scenes of the Middle East crisis.[41]

Some conservative American Christians have indulged the temptation to essentialize Muslims, terrorism, the Middle East conflict, and the Iraq war into an inevitable spiritual clash hurtling toward Judgment Day. In doing so, they have unwittingly aped the rhetoric of the Muslim jihadists they demonize, and also contributed to a sense among some Christian Americans that there is no point in trying to mediate or forestall conflict between America, Israel, and the Muslim world. They have also found themselves sometimes at odds with the Bush administration, which they otherwise enthusiastically supported. Contrary to the popular image of religious conservatives following lockstep behind Bush, it seems that on questions related to Israel, Islam, and the Middle East crisis, a significant rift opened between Bush and some of his conservative Christian supporters, who have seen

Bush as a naive, politically correct dupe who has failed to appreciate the true nature of Islam. Bush has undoubtedly sought to soften the anti-Muslim tone of the debate since 2001 in order to maintain friendly relations with Muslim allies in Pakistan, Saudi Arabia, and elsewhere. The conservative Christian purveyors of inexorable conflict with Islam have scoffed at attempts to placate Muslims, and have lamented as foolish more complex views of the global Muslim cohort.

But the prophets of apocalyptic war between Islam on one hand, and Christianity and Judaism on the other, have not totally dominated discourse among Christian conservatives. Some like Timothy George and Dudley Woodberry have chosen to call for deeper appreciation of Islam's positive characteristics, and have embraced a nuanced, this-worldly understanding of the often discouraging conflicts involving Islam, Judaism, and the Middle East. While many Christians cannot paper over the significant theological differences between their faith and Islam, some have matched their warnings against religious relativism with similar cautions against demonization of the Prophet and the Muslim faithful.

The years since 2001 have seen a great increase of fascination in America about Islam, and nowhere more so than among conservative American Protestants. Strikingly, much of the popular Christian literature on Islam has replayed old familiar themes: the appeal of converted Muslims, apologetic attacks on Muslim's "real" beliefs, the blending of political and theological opinions, and Islam's place in the last days. The terrorist attacks of 2001 provided new focus and intensity, but these rhetorical tactics have long delivered assuring messages to traditional American Christians confronting the perceived threat of Islam.

Epilogue

ALMOST WEEKLY we see evidence of the difficulties traditional Christians face in relating civilly to Muslims in the public sphere, while maintaining fidelity to their theological beliefs (and lest we forget, many Muslims face the same sorts of problems in relating to Christians). In September 2006, in an address nearly coinciding with the fifth anniversary of the 2001 attacks, Pope Benedict XVI favorably quoted a fourteenth-century Byzantine emperor who said "Show me just what Muhammad brought that was new, and there you will find things only evil and inhuman." The comments precipitated protests and rioting across the Muslim world, and heightened tensions between Catholics and Muslims that had lessened somewhat during the tenure of Pope John Paul II. Although Benedict subsequently apologized for offending Muslims, his remarks reveal the continuing allure of demonizing Islam in retaliation for horrifying jihadist violence. The controversy also demonstrates the challenges across Christian traditions in preserving peace in the civic arena with devotees of other religions.[1]

This book has shown how American Christian (particularly conservative Protestant) discussions of Islam have historically revolved around several key themes: the desire to see Muslims convert to Christianity, the fascination with missionary work among Muslims, the mixing of political policy and theology as it relates to the Muslim world (and Israel), and the insertion of Islam into eschatological schemes. Although American Christians have written and said proportionately more about Islam since 2001 than ever before, the evidence presented here shows that American Christian thinking about Islam has deep historical roots. The story of conservative American Christians' ideas about Muslims is characterized by continuity more than change. As Edward Said demonstrated in *Orientalism*, Westerners have often trafficked in "knowledge" of the Middle East that unconsciously masked a host of political and religious purposes. Certainly this has been the case with conservative American Christians, whose views of Islam generally tell us more about American Christians than any Muslims in particular.

In certain forms, the matrix of concepts comprising conservative American Christian views of Islam—conversionism, missions, religion and politics, and eschatology—serve understandable and even essential roles in traditional monotheistic exclusive religions. Many Christians and Muslims alike practice evangelism and seek conversion of those outside their religious communities, simply because they believe in the truth of their faith. Christian traditionalists, in particular, think that no one can enter heaven outside their belief system, and they desire to convince as many others as possible that no one can be saved except through faith in Christ.

Likewise, Christians and Muslims both believe that their faith has political implications. Whether or not this includes any blending of church and state is an open question in both traditions, especially in Islam. But presumably most religious traditionalists would argue that their faith informs their thinking about questions such as the public moral order, war and peace, and so on. Finally, many Christians and Muslims hold beliefs about the direction of history and the triumph of their exclusive faith at the end of the world. This age will not last forever, they believe, and one day their religion will be unequivocally demonstrated by God to be the truth. Secular or relativist critics may see exclusive religion itself as the problem that creates so much tension, ill will, and even violence between competing religionists. Why not accept and practice one's own beliefs, and allow others to do likewise in peace?

The difficulty with the secular or relativist critique of traditional religion is that it makes sense only to those not holding exclusive religious beliefs. Moreover, the global force of exclusive religion seems not to be waning. To the contrary, across the world exclusive faith is gaining adherents. While the advocacy of religious relativism, or a "live and let live" philosophy of religion, as a path to religious and civic peace may seem eminently sensible to some, it is not winning the allegiance of many people globally. Traditional Catholicism and Protestant evangelicalism and Pentecostalism are the Christian denominational forms growing across the world, especially in Latin America, Africa, and Southeast Asia.[2]

As a historian, my programmatic aims for this book are modest. Mainly, I have sought to tell a story of how conservative American Protestants have thought about Muslims, and let the readers draw their own conclusions about what we should think or do going forward. But it seems there is little point in calling for an end to exclusive religion, as many secular critics have done since 2001. Others have done that in the past. Thomas Jefferson predicted that all young men living in 1822 would die as Unitarians.[3] The forecast was laughably incorrect, as America by the Civil War had become an evangelical behemoth. Contrary to classical secularization theory, the end of exclusive religion does not appear to be in sight.

I do believe, however, that there is much room for improvement in the public discourse and behavior of religious traditionalists. It seems that one of conservative American Christians' main problems is an inability to appreciate their dual citizenships in the city of God and the earthly city, to use Saint Augustine's terminology. While the Christian's true citizenship is in heaven, she or he also has an important, albeit subordinate and temporary, residency in the earthly city. Christians have to live out their years in the earthly city, where they must pursue common earthly goods with those who, in the Christians' view, do not belong to the city of God. Among the most important of those goals is public peace and cooperation. Peace cannot compromise one's religious duties, but it is an important spiritual and civic responsibility in Christian Scripture (Romans 12:18, for instance, commands "If possible, so far as it depends on you, be at peace with all men"). Many traditional American Christians may yet be unaccustomed to the idea that their earthly cities now include many Muslims and other non-Christians, but this is the reality facing them in a religiously diverse and globalized society. (Any Christian efforts to seek amity in the public sphere will need to be matched by Muslim efforts, as well, in order to make serious changes.)

Traditional believers should maintain a separation between exclusive religious views and religion-based exclusive politics. Instead of distinguishing between the city of God and the earthly city, many conservative American Christians have implicitly or explicitly conflated America with the Christian Kingdom of God, routinely signaling to American Muslims and other Muslims around the world that "America" views them as a threat, or even a demonic menace to be destroyed by the American and Israeli forces of God. By portraying Islam as essentially evil and forecasting the inexorable clash of Muslims with American Christian military power, some conservative American Christian writers adopt the rhetorical style of those jihadists they claim God is fighting against.

The clumsy conflation of the kingdom of God and America was vividly revealed in the controversy over Keith Ellison, the first Muslim congressperson, using Thomas Jefferson's Qur'an to swear his official oath of allegiance on January 4, 2007. To be fair, relatively few prominent Christian conservatives protested Ellison's use of the Qur'an, but Representative Virgil Goode (Republican of Virginia) did comment that Ellison's election re-emphasized the need to end illegal immigration (regardless of the fact that Ellison, an

African-American, traced his ancestors' roots in America to the eighteenth century). If Americans did not stop unauthorized immigrants, Goode wrote in *USA Today*, "we are leaving ourselves open to infiltration by those who want to mold the United States into the image of their religion, rather than working within the Judeo-Christian principles" that made America great. The implication of such views is that an exclusively Christian morality undergirds American government and garners God's approval, so that the presence of non-Christian and non-Jewish immigrants, especially in government, threatened the American political-religious order. "Judeo-Christian" values had a unique role in American politics that Christians must defend against outsiders and immigrants, especially those practicing ostensibly un-American religions such as Islam, according to observers like Goode.[4]

Even though other traditional Protestants have made a clearer distinction than Ellison's critics about the relationship between the city of God and the city of man, their exclusive theological beliefs can still offend those outside the conservative Christian camp. Conflict often comes when the goods of the city of God clash with the goods of the earthly city. Non-Christians do not want to be told they are going to hell. That generates civic discord. But traditional Christians feel bound to tell others the truth about salvation, as they perceive it. That is their responsibility before God. Hopefully the two imperatives of civic peace and religious duty are not incompatible for traditionalists. Throughout the nineteenth and twentieth centuries, certain voices within the conservative Protestant community have called for generous study and sympathetic witness to Muslims. Examples such as James Merrick's advocacy of patient missions to Persians, Samuel Zwemer's commitment to understanding the Muslim cultures within which he lived, Kenneth Cragg's charitable explanation of his Muslim interlocutors' beliefs to the broader Christian community, and Timothy George and Dudley Woodberry's refusal to demonize Muslims even after September 2001, all give hope that conservative Protestants can maintain a peaceable but faithful witness to Muslims. Obviously, this book has offered a host of examples of Christian writers who have eagerly indulged anti-Muslim fantasies, manipulated knowledge of Islam for political purposes, and transformed actual Muslims into puppet-like figures in morose last-days predictions. As far as they have influenced their followers and readers, these Christians have made the continuation of violent conflict that much more likely. They have also made American Christians that much less capable of assessing the political and military wisdom of decisions like whether or not to invade Saddam Hussein's Iraq. Their work gives a less hopeful aspect to conservative

Christians' role in producing good relations between Christians and Muslims in American civic society, or on the global stage.

I do not believe the Christian impulse toward evangelism of non-Christians, including Muslims, will or should go away. Instead, I would only suggest that Christians take Muslims seriously, minimize or eliminate unnecessarily offensive language, highlight cultural commonalities, and refuse to indulge in sensational stories about the ostensibly evil and demonic character of Islam. They should refuse to baptize any political party or nation as exclusively "Christian," or to use any party or nation to advance spiritual goals. Ironically, if Christians focused both on maintaining civic peace and testifying to the truth of their religion, they probably would achieve better results in evangelism. Bluster, bombast, and excited forecasts of inexorable destruction do not make for good witnessing, but courtesy and understanding do. The history of American Christian thought about Islam, sadly, has demonstrated precious little courtesy and understanding.

Notes

Preface

1. Jonathan Edwards, *History of the Work of Redemption* (New York, 1793), 436–39, 504–5.

2. Edward Said, *Orientalism* (New York, 1978), 5. Robert Irwin's *Dangerous Knowledge: Orientalism and Its Discontents* (Woodstock, NY, 2006) has effectively illuminated many problems in Said's argument and evidence.

Chapter 1
Early American Christians and Islam

1. Reprinted in "Benjamin Franklin and Freedom," *Journal of Negro History* 4, no. 1 (Jan. 1919): 48–50; see also Joseph Ellis, *Founding Brothers: The Revolutionary Generation* (New York, 2000), 111–12; Robert J. Allison, *The Crescent Obscured: The United States and the Muslim World, 1776–1815* (New York, 1995), 104–6; David Waldstreicher, *Runaway America: Benjamin Franklin, Slavery, and the American Revolution* (New York, 2004), 238.

2. Cotton Mather, *American Tears upon the Ruines of the Greek Churches* (Boston, 1701), 38; Michael A. Gomez, "Muslims in Early America," *Journal of Southern History* 60, no. 4 (1994): 671–72; Albert Raboteau, *Slave Religion: The "Invisible Institution" in the Antebellum South* (New York, 1978), 5–7.

3. Linda Colley, *Captives* (New York, 2002), 43–72; Fuad Sha'ban, *Islam and Arabs in Early American Thought: The Roots of Orientalism in America* (Durham, NC, 1991), i; Ellen Friedman, "Christian Captives at 'Hard Labor' in Algiers, 16th–18th Centuries," *The International Journal of African Historical Studies* 13, no. 4 (1980): 616–18; Stephen Clissold, *The Barbary Slaves* (Totowa, NJ, 1977).

4. Paul Baepler, ed., *White Slaves, African Masters: An Anthology of American Barbary Captivity Narratives* (Chicago, 1999), 2–3; Nabil Matar, *Turks, Moors, and Englishmen in the Age of Discovery* (New York, 1999), 14–15; Colley, *Captives*, 4.

5. William Okeley, *Eben-Ezer or a Small Monument of Great Mercy* 2d ed. (London, 1676), 13, 26–27.

6. Cotton Mather, *Decennium Luctuosum* (Boston, 1699), 231.

7. Increase Mather, *A Relation of the Troubles* (Boston, 1677), 8–9; Baepler, *White Slaves, African Masters*, 7; Matar, *Turks, Moors, and Englishmen*, 83–107.

8. *Narrative of Joshua Gee* (Hartford, CT, 1943), 29.

9. Diary of Joseph Bean, Aug. 17, 1742, Bryn Mawr College Library, Special Collections.

10. Francis Brooks, *Barbarian Cruelty* (London, 1693), ix–x, 12, 32–34.

11. Ibid., 36–38.

12. Ibid., 58, 61, 67.

13. Muslim intellectuals, of course, have a long history of critical responses to Christianity, though none of those were written for a European audience in the early modern period. Matar, *Islam in Britain*, 182; Nabil Matar, ed., *In the Lands of the Christians: Arabic Travel Writing in the Seventeenth Century* (New York, 2003), xxxiii. For an overview of Muslim responses to Christianity, see William Montgomery Watt, *Muslim-Christian Encounters: Perceptions and Misperceptions* (New York, 1991). English translations of the Qur'an, such as Alexander Ross's and George Sale's, were available in England and the colonies, but both included prefatory comments hostile to Islam. Matar, *Islam in Britain*, 73–83; Sha'ban, *Islam and Arabs*, 30–33; Mukhtar Ali Isani, "Cotton Mather and the Orient," *New England Quarterly* 43, no. 1 (March 1970): 48. On Christian converts to Islam, see Nabil Matar, *Islam in Britain, 1558–1685* (New York, 1998), 18–20.

14. Matar, *Turks, Moors, and Englishmen*, 71–77.

15. Cotton Mather, *Magnalia Christi Americana* (Hartford, CT, 1853), 2: 671, quoted in Isani, "Cotton Mather and the Orient," 51–52.

16. Cotton Mather, *A Pastoral Letter* (Boston, 1698), 8, 12; Isani, "Mather and the Orient," 52–53.

17. Cotton Mather, *The Goodness of God* (Boston, 1703), preface and 32–33; Virginia, *A Collection of All the Acts of the Assembly* (Williamsburg, 1733), 220.

18. Mather, *The Goodness of God*, 39, 45, 46, 50; Matar, *Islam in Britain*, 27.

19. Robert Irwin, *Dangerous Knowledge: Orientalism and Its Discontents* (Woodstock, NY, 2006), 100; Clissold, *Barbary Slaves*, 149; Allison, *Crescent Obscured*, 39–41; Roger Emerson, "Peter Gay and the Heavenly City," *Journal of the History of Ideas* 28, no. 3 (July-Sept. 1967): 391; Stephen Stein, "Editor's Introduction," in Jonathan Edwards, *Apocalyptic Writings*, ed. Stephen Stein, vol. 5 of *The Works of Jonathan Edwards* (New Haven, CT, 1977), 63–64; Edward Said, *Orientalism* rev. ed. (New York, 1994), 72. Said points out the near-simultaneous publication of d'Herbelot's *Bibliothèque Orientale* (1697), which called Muhammad "le fameux imposteur," 65–66.

20. *Humphrey Prideaux, The True Nature of Imposture Displayed in the Life of Mahomet* 3d ed. (London, 1698), iv–v, viii–ix. On the claim of pure knowledge as opposed to political knowledge, Said, *Orientalism*, 9.

21. Prideaux, *True Nature of Imposture*, 13, 16; Allison, *Crescent Obscured*, 38.

22. Isani, "Cotton Mather and the Orient," 50; Robert Fuller, *Naming the Antichrist: The History of an American Obsession* (New York, 1995), 54; Eric Tobias Bjorck, *A Little Olive Leaf* (New York, 1704), 21; Prideaux, *True Nature of Imposture*, 27–28.

23. Humphrey Prideaux, *A Discourse for the Vindicating of Christianity* 3d ed. (London, 1698), 7.

24. Library Company of Philadelphia, *Books Added to the Library Since the Year 1741* (Philadelphia, 1746), 14; New-York Society Library, *A Catalogue of the Books Belonging to the New-York Society Library* (New York, 1758), 14; Union Library Society of Wethersfield, *The Constitution and By-Laws of the Union Library Society of Wethersfield* (Hartford, CT,

1784), 17; John Caldwell, *An Impartial Trial of the Spirit* (Boston, 1742), 11; Thomas Wells Bray, *A Dissertation on the Sixth Vial* (Hartford, CT, 1780), 29–30; Charles Leslie, *The Religion of Jesus Christ the Only True Religion, or, A Short and Easie Method with the Deists* (Boston, 1719), 24–25.

25. Jonathan Dickinson, *The Reasonableness of Christianity* (Boston, 1732), 60–61.

26. Henri de Boulainvilliers, *The Life of Mahomet*, English translation (London, 1731), 219; Vincent Buranelli, "The Historical and Political Thought of Boulainvilliers," *Journal of the History of Ideas* 18, no. 4 (Oct. 1957): 475–76; Kenneth M. Setton, *Western Hostility to Islam and Prophecies of Turkish Doom* (Philadelphia, 1992), 55; Colley, *Captives*, 107; Irwin, *Dangerous Knowledge*, 116–17.

27. Library Company of Philadelphia, *A Catalogue of Books* (Philadelphia, 1741), D2; "A Catalogue of Books: In the Library of 'Councillor' Robert Carter, at Nomini Hall, Westmoreland County, Va.," *William and Mary College Quarterly Historical Magazine* 10, no. 4 (Apr. 1902): 239; David Pailin, *Attitudes to Other Religions: Comparative Religion in Seventeenth- and Eighteenth-Century Britain* (Manchester, England, 1984), 104.

28. Roger Williams, *G. Fox Digg'd out of His Burrowes* (Boston, 1676), A3, A6, 158; Prideaux, *True Nature of Imposture*, 49–50.

29. Matar, *Islam in Britain*, 153–83; Timothy Marr, *The Cultural Roots of American Islamicism* (New York, 2006), 91; Richard Cogley, "The Fall of the Ottoman Empire and the Restoration of Israel in the 'Judeo-centric' Strand of Puritan Millenarianism," *Church History* 72, no. 2 (June 2003): 304–32; Cotton Mather, *The Wonderful Works of God Commemorated* (Boston, 1690), 38–41.

30. Nicholas Noyes, *New-England's Duty and Interest* (Boston, 1698), 32–33; Judah Monis, *The Whole Truth* (Boston, 1722), 7.

31. George Gillespie, *A Treatise against the Deists or Free-Thinkers* (Philadelphia, 1735), 40, 53; Samuel Davies, *The Mediatorial Kingdom and Glories of Jesus Christ*, in *Sermons on the Most Useful and Important Subjects* (London, 1756), in Ellis Sandoz, *Political Sermons of the American Founding Era* 2d ed. (Indianapolis, 1998), 1: 205.

32. Aaron Burr, *The Watchman's Answer* (Boston, 1757), 17–20, 34; Nathan Hatch, "The Origins of Civil Millennialism in America: New England Clergymen, War with France, and the Revolution," *William and Mary Quarterly* 3d ser., 31, no. 3 (July 1974): 415–16.

33. Thomas Paine, *Of the Evidence of Christ's Death, Burial, and Resurrection* (Boston, 1732), 15–16; Pailin, *Attitudes to Other Religions*, 103; John Walton, *The Religion of Jesus Vindicated* (Boston, 1736), 7.

34. *The Sad Estate of the Unconverted* (Boston, 1736), 22–23; Gilbert Tennent, *Twenty-three Sermons upon the Chief End of Man* (Philadelphia, 1744), 24–25.

35. Luke Tyerman, *The Life and Times of the Rev. George Whitefield* (London, 1876), 1: 360–61, 466.

36. Alexander Garden, *Take Heed How Ye Hear* (Charles-Town, SC, 1741), 12, 26.

37. *The Wonderful Narrative* (Boston, 1742), pp. 6, 65–71; Meric Casaubon, *A Treatise Concerning Enthusiasme* 3d ed. (London, 1656), 175–76.

38. *The Conversion of a Mehometan* 6th ed. (New London, 1773), 5; Matar, *Turks, Moors, and Englishmen*, 229, n.20. The 1757 tract has been attributed to John Edwards.

39. *Conversion of a Mehometan*, 12, 22.

40. Jonathan Edwards, "Notes on the Apocalypse," in Jonathan Edwards, *Apocalyptic Writings*, ed. Stephen Stein, vol. 5 of *The Works of Jonathan Edwards* (New Haven, CT: Yale University Press, 1977), pp. 173–76, quotes on 173, 176.

41. Jonathan Edwards, "Events of an Hopeful Aspect on the State of Religion," in Edwards, *Apocalyptic Writings*, 294; Jonathan Edwards, *An Humble Attempt to Promote Explicit Agreement and Visible Union* (Boston, 1748), 150; Gerald McDermott, *Jonathan Edwards Confronts the Gods: Christian Theology, Enlightenment Religion, and Non-Christian Faiths* (New York, 2000), 169–71; Edwards, *Apocalyptic Writings*, 45.

42. Jonathan Edwards, "Mahometanism Compared with Christianity—Particularly with Respect to their Propagation," in Edward Hickman, ed., *The Works of Jonathan Edwards*, reprint (Carlisle, PA, 1974), 2: 491–92; McDermott, *Edwards Confronts the Gods*, 167–69.

43. Edwards, "Mahometanism," 493; McDermott, *Edwards Confronts the Gods*, 171–74; Pailin, *Attitudes to Other Religions*, 101.

44. *Poor Richard, 1741* (Philadelphia, 1740), May; Marr, *American Islamicism*, 20–21.

45. Nathanael Emmons, *The Dignity of Man* (Providence, RI, 1787), in Sandoz, *Political Sermons*, 1: 893; Henry May, *The Enlightenment in America* (New York, 1976), 154.

46. John Leland, *The Rights of Conscience Inalienable* (New London, CT, 1791), in Sandoz, *Political Sermons*, 2: 1090–93; Allison, *Crescent Obscured*, 47.

47. Timothy Hilliard, *A Sermon Delivered September 3, 1788* (Boston, 1788), 19; Enos Hitchcock, *An Oration, in Commemoration of the Independence of the United States of America* (Providence, RI, 1793), in Sandoz, *Political Sermons*, 2: 1176–77. On Montesquieu's influence see May, *Enlightenment in America*, 40–41.

48. Diary of Joseph Bean, Oct. 23, 1741, Bryn Mawr College Library Special Collections.

CHAPTER 2
THE BARBARY WARS, THE LAST DAYS,
AND ISLAM IN EARLY NATIONAL AMERICA

1. Thomas P. Slaughter, ed., *Common Sense and Related Writings* (Boston, 2001), 82–83.

2. Allison, *Crescent Obscured*, 40–41.

3. *The Life of Mahomet; or, The History of that Imposture Which was Begun, Carried on, and Finally Established by Him in Arabia* (Worcester, MA, 1802), 37, 60, 83–84, 93.

4. Allison, *Crescent Obscured*, xv; Paul Baepler, ed., *White Slaves, African Masters: An Anthology of American Barbary Captivity Narratives* (Chicago, 1999), 8–9; Frank Lambert, *The Barbary Wars: American Independence in the Atlantic World* (New York, 2005), 198–202; Martha Elena Rojas, "'Insults Unpunished': Barbary Captives, American Slaves, and the Negotiation of Liberty," *Early American Studies* 1 (Fall 2003): 161.

5. John Foss, *A Journal, of the Captivity and Sufferings of John Foss* 2d ed. (Newburyport, MA, [1798]), 10–12; Baepler, *White Slaves*, 71–72.

6. Foss, *Journal*, 32–33, 122.

7. Ibid., 141, 182–83; James Wilson Stevens, *An Historical and Geographical Account of Algiers* 2d ed. (Brooklyn, NY, 1800), 170, 176; Lambert, *Barbary Wars*, 118.

8. Joseph Pitts, *Narrative of the Captivity of Joseph Pitts* (Frederick-Town, MD, 1815), 12.

9. Maria Martin, *History of the Captivity and Sufferings of Mrs. Maria Martin* (Boston, 1807), 48–49; Baepler, *White Slaves*, 147.

10. Martin, *History of the Captivity*, 59, 63–64, 70; Allison, *Crescent Obscured*, 80–82.

11. Eliza Bradley, *An Authentic Narrative of the Shipwreck and Sufferings of Mrs. Eliza Bradley* (Boston, 1823), iv, 20; Baepler, *White Slaves*, 11.

12. Bradley, *Authentic Narrative*, 61, 63, 76.

13. Benilde Montgomery, "White Captives, African Slaves: A Drama of Abolition," *Eighteenth-Century Studies* 27, no. 4 (Summer 1994): 629–30; Baepler, *White Slaves, African Masters*, 30–31, 47.

14. *The American in Algiers* (New York, 1797), 14–16, 23–24; Lambert, *Barbary Wars*, 114.

15. Royall Tyler, *The Algerine Captive* (London, 1802), 1: 136–39.

16. Ibid., 2:37–53, quote on 53.

17. Cathy Davidson, *Revolution and the Word: The Rise of the Novel in America* (New York, 1986), 208–09; Timothy Marr, *The Cultural Roots of American Islamicism* (New York, 2006), 57–58; Baepler, *White Slaves, African Masters*, 46–47; Montgomery, "White Captives, African Slaves," 616–17.

18. "The Yankee Mahomet," *The American Whig Review* 13 (June 1851): 559; George Seibel, *The Mormon Saints: The Story of Joseph Smith, His Golden Bible, and the Church He Founded* (Pittsburgh, 1919), 10; Arnold H. Green, "Mormonism and Islam: From Polemics to Mutual Respect and Cooperation," *BYU Studies* 40, no. 4 (2001): 200–01, 203–04; Marr, *American Islamicism*, 186–89.

19. Timothy Dwight, *The Duty of Americans, at the Present Crisis* (New Haven, CT, 1798), in Sandoz, *Political Sermons*, 1392–93.

20. Marr, *American Islamicism*, 94–114.

21. Charles Crawford, *Observations upon the Fall of Antichrist and the Concomitant Events* (Philadelphia, 1786), 17–21; Ruth Bloch, *Visionary Republic: Millennial Themes in American Thought, 1756–1800* (New York, 1985), 120, 144–45.

22. Samuel Langdon, *Observations on the Revelation of Jesus Christ to St. John* (Worcester, MA, [1791]), 120–21, 127; Benjamin Farnham, *Dissertations on the Prophecies* (East Windsor, CT, 1800), 39; Bloch, *Visionary Republic*, 121.

23. Eliphaz Chapman, *A Discourse on the Prophecies* (Portland, ME, 1797), 13–15, 26.

24. Benjamin Gale, *A Brief Essay, or An Attempt to Prove* (New Haven, CT, [1788]), 16, 20, 53, 61; Bloch, *Visionary Republic*, 120.

25. Thomas Wells Bray, *A Dissertation on the Sixth Vial* (Hartford, CT, [1780]), viii–ix, xi, 18–19, 50, 59; Jonathan Edwards, "Notes on the Apocalypse," in Jonathan Edwards, *Apocalyptic Writings*, ed. Stephen J. Stein, vol. 5 of *The Works of Jonathan Edwards* (New Haven, CT, 1977), 185; James West Davidson, *The Logic of Millennial Thought: Eighteenth-Century New England* (New Haven, CT, 1977), 246–47.

26. David Austin, *The Millennium* (Elizabeth Town, NJ, 1794), 272, 297; Timothy

Dwight, *A Discourse in Two Parts: Delivered July 23, 1812* (New Haven, CT, 1812), 11; Timothy Allen to Eleazar Wheelock, April 24, 1762, in Gratz American Clergy Collection, 9/2, Historical Society of Pennsylvania.

27. George Stanley Faber, *A Dissertation on the Prophecies* (Boston, 1808), 1: 34, 172; Ernest R. Sandeen, *The Roots of Fundamentalism: British and American Millenarianism, 1800–1930* (Chicago, 1970), 6–8.

28. Faber, *Dissertation*, 1: 195.

29. Ethan Smith, *A Dissertation on the Prophecies Relative to Antichrist and the Last Times* (Boston, 1814), 26; Elijah Parish, *A Sermon Preached before the Massachusetts Missionary Society* (Newburyport, MA, 1807), 17–18, compare Faber, *Dissertation*, 1: 172; Jedidiah Morse, *Signs of the Times* (Charlestown, MA, 1810), 22; Oliver W. Elsbree, *The Rise of the Missionary Spirit in America, 1790–1815* (Williamsport, PA, 1928), 125.

30. Enoch Shepard, *Thoughts on the Prophecies* (Marietta, OH, 1812), 6, 36–38, 106.

31. On the Millerites, see Edwin S. Gaustad, ed., *The Rise of Adventism: Religion and Society in Mid-Nineteenth-Century America* (New York, 1974); David L. Rowe, *Thunder and Trumpets: Millerites and Dissenting Religion in Upstate New York, 1800–1850* (Chico, CA, 1985); Ronald L. Numbers and Jonathan M. Butler, eds., *The Disappointed: Millerism and Millenarianism in the Nineteenth Century* (Bloomington, IN, 1987); Ruth Alden Doan, *The Miller Heresy, Millennialism, and American Culture* (Philadelphia, 1987); Everett Newfon Dick, *William Miller and the Advent Crisis, 1831–1844* (Berrien Springs, MI, 1994).

32. Josiah Litch, *The Probability of the Second Coming of Christ about A.D. 1843* (Boston, 1838), 150, 157; Josiah Litch, *Prophetic Expositions* (Boston, 1842), 2: 161, 198–99; Eric Anderson, "The Millerite Use of Prophecy: A Case Study of a 'Striking Fulfilment,'" in Numbers and Butler, *The Disappointed*, 80, 84–86; Marr, *American Islamicism*, 115–16.

33. Joshua Himes, ed., *Miller's Works: Views of the Prophecies and Prophetic Chronology, Selected from the Manuscripts of William Miller* (Boston, 1841), 1: 251-52, 2: 225-26, 295; William Miller, *Evidence from Scripture and History of the Second Coming of Christ, about the Year 1843* (Troy, NY, 1838), 114–18.

34. Himes, *Miller's Works*, 1: 173, 176–77; Smith, *Dissertation on the Prophecies*, 456–57.

35. George Duffield, *Dissertations on the Prophecies Relative to the Second Coming of Jesus Christ* (New York, 1842), 389–90; George B. Stacy, *The Dragon: That Old Serpent, the Devil* (Richmond, VA, 1860), 113–14; Pleasant E. Royse, *The Predictions of the Prophets* (Cincinnati, 1864), 567.

36. C. I. Scofield, *Scofield Reference Bible* (New York, 1909), 1330, 1337 n.1; Salem Kirban, *666* (Huntingdon Valley, PA, 1970), 230–31; James H. Moorhead, "Between Progress and Apocalypse: A Reassessment of Millennialism in American Religious Thought, 1800–1880," *Journal of American History* 71, no. 3 (Dec. 1984): 541.

37. Edward Bickersteth, *The Restoration of the Jews to Their Own Land* 2d ed. (London, 1841), 79–80; George Bush, *The Valley of Vision; or, The Dry Bones of Israel Revived* (New York, 1844), 40; Sandeen, *Roots of Fundamentalism*, 21; Michael B. Oren, *Power, Faith, and Fantasy: America in the Middle East, 1776 to the Present* (New York, 2007), 141–42.

38. A. J. Gordon, *Ecce Venit: Behold He Cometh* (New York, 1889), in Joel A. Carpen-

ter, ed., *The Premillennial Second Coming: Two Early Champions* (New York, 1988), 105; H. Grattan Guinness, *The Approaching End of the Age* (London, 1879), 474; T. B. Baines, *The Revelation of Jesus Christ* (London, 1901), 119–21; Timothy P. Weber, *Living in the Shadow of the Second Coming: American Premillennialism, 1875–1982* rev. ed. (Chicago, 1987) 16–17. Thanks to David Bebbington for the reference on Guinness, and biographical information on Baines.

39. Susan Juster, *Doomsayers: Anglo-American Prophecy in the Age of Revolution* (Philadelphia, 2003), 14–15, 263–64.

CHAPTER 3
FOREIGN MISSIONS TO MUSLIMS IN NINETEENTH-CENTURY AMERICA

1. Rufus Anderson, *History of the Missions of the American Board of Commissioners for Foreign Missions to the Oriental Churches* (Boston, 1872), 1: ix–x; Pliny Fisk, *The Holy Land an Interesting Field of Missionary Enterprise* (Boston, 1819), in *Holy Land Missions and Missionaries* (New York, 1977), 26–27.

2. ABCFM second annual appeal quoted in A. L. Tibawi, *American Interests in Syria, 1800–1901: A Study of Educational, Literary and Religious Work* (Oxford, England, 1966), 11. Levi Parsons, *The Dereliction and Restoration of the Jews* (Boston, 1819), in *Holy Land Missions*, 12, 19; Timothy Marr, *The Cultural Roots of American Islamicism* (New York, 2006), 83; Michael B. Oren, *Power, Faith, and Fantasy: America in the Middle East, 1776 to the Present* (New York, 2007), 80–83. On parallel developments in Britain, see Andrew Porter, "Evangelicalism, Islam, and Millennial Expectation in the Nineteenth Century," position paper no. 76, North Atlantic Missiology Project, 1998. On the early nineteenth-century missions movement, see Wilbert R. Shenk, ed., *North American Foreign Missions, 1810–1914* (Grand Rapids, MI, 2004); William R. Hutchison, *Errand to the World: American Protestant Thought and Foreign Missions* (Chicago, 1987); John A. Andrew III, *Rebuilding the Christian Commonwealth: New England Congregationalists & Foreign Missions, 1800–1830* (Lexington, KY, 1976); Clifton J. Phillips, *Protestant America and the Pagan World: The First Half Century of the American Board of Commissioners for Foreign Missions, 1810–1860* (Cambridge, MA, 1969).

3. Anderson, *History of the Missions*, 1; Tibawi, *American Interests*, 172–73; Ussama Makdisi, "Reclaiming the Land of the Bible: Missionaries, Secularism, and Evangelical Modernity," *American Historical Review* 102, no. 3 (June 1997): 690–91; Lester I. Vogel, *To See a Promised Land: Americans and the Holy Land in the Nineteenth Century* (University Park, PA, 1993), 100.

4. Anderson, *History of the Missions*, 1–2, 6.

5. Phillips, *Protestant America*, 137–38; elegy quoted in David H. Finnie, *Pioneers East: The Early American Experience in the Middle East* (Cambridge, MA, 1967), 152.

6. Sereno E. Dwight, *The Greek Revolution* (Boston, 1824), 27, quoted in Phillips, *Protestant America*, 141; Tibawi, *American Interests*, 79; Marr, *American Islamicism*, 70.

7. "Constantinople," *Missionary Herald* 37, no. 4 (Apr. 1841), 162; Josiah Litch, *Prophetic Expositions* (Boston, 1842), 2: 189–90.

8. [James Barclay], in D. S. Burnet, ed., *The Jerusalem Mission* (Cincinnati, 1853), in Robert T. Handy, ed., *The Holy Land in American Protestant Life, 1800–1948: A Documentary History* (New York, 1981), 85–87.

9. Josiah Harlan, *A Memoir of India and Avghanistaun* (Philadelphia, 1842), 189, 192, 194. Thanks to John Brooke for sharing this reference with me. On Harlan's religious beliefs, see Ben Macintyre, *The Man Who Would Be King: The First American in Afghanistan* (New York, 2004), 12–13, 41–42.

10. Merrick diary, Amherst College Library, quoted in Marr, *American Islamicism*, 121; Prudential Committee of the ABCFM, "Instructions of the Prudential Committee to the Rev. James Lyman Merrick," *Missionary Herald* 30 (Nov. 1834): 402–3; James Merrick, "Extracts from Letters of Mr. Merrick," *Missionary Herald* 31 (Oct. 1835): 366–68; James Merrick, "Extracts from Letters of Mr. Merrick," *Missionary Herald* 32 (May 1836): 165; Phillips, *Protestant America*, 147–48. For a negative assessment of Merrick, see Finnie, *Pioneers East*, 221–24.

11. James Merrick to Rufus Anderson, May 20, 1836, Papers of the American Board of Commissioners for Foreign Missions (ABCFM), Reel 553, doc. 63.

12. James Merrick, "Letter from Mr. Merrick," *Missionary Herald* 34 (Feb. 1838): 64, 66; Phillips, *Protestant America* 148; James Merrick to Rufus Anderson, Nov. 8, 1835, Papers of the ABCFM, Reel 553, doc. 58; Rufus Anderson to James Merrick, Nov. 5, 1839, in James Merrick, *An Appeal to the American Board of Commissioners for Foreign Missions* (Springfield, MA, 1847), 33; Marr, *American Islamicism*, 123–24.

13. James Merrick to Rufus Anderson, June 9, 1835, in Papers of the ABCFM, Reel 553, doc. 54; James Merrick to Rufus Anderson, July 19, 1845, in Merrick, *An Appeal*, 86–87; Merrick, *An Appeal*, 111.

14. Horatio Southgate, *Encouragement to Missionary Effort among Mohamedans* (New York, 1836), 3, 7; Marr, *American Islamicism*, 126–27.

15. Southgate, *Encouragement to Missionary Effort*, 9–10, 15, 24–25, 32.

16. Charles T. Bridgeman, "Mediterranean Missions of the Episcopal Church from 1828–1898," *Historical Magazine of the Protestant Episcopal Church* 31, no. 2 (June 1962): 104–13, quote on 109; P. E. Shaw, *American Contacts with the Eastern Churches, 1820–1870* (Chicago, 1937), 35–70; Paul William Harris, *Nothing but Christ: Rufus Anderson and the Ideology of Protestant Foreign Missions* (New York, 1999), 86–88; Finnie, *Pioneers East*, 224–27.

17. J. Hawes, *The Religion of the East* (Hartford, CT, 1845), 114–17.

18. Cyrus Hamlin, *The Oriental Churches and Mohammedans* (Boston, 1851), 2–3.

19. Hamlin, *Oriental Churches*, 13, 18–20; Cyrus Hamlin in Margarette W. Lawrence, *Light on the Dark River* (Boston, 1854), 144; Cyrus Hamlin, "Work among Moslems," *Missionary Herald* 74, no. 4 (Apr. 1878): 113.

20. Isaac Bird, *Bible Work in Bible Lands* (Philadelphia, 1872), 16; Dodge quoted in ibid., 430; Finnie, *Pioneers East*, 134.

21. William Bird to Rufus Anderson, Dec. 31, 1858, in Papers of the ABCFM, reel 542, doc. 196; Makdisi, "Reclaiming the Land," 692.

22. Joseph Warren, *A Glance Backward at Fifteen Years of Missionary Life* (Philadel-

phia, 1856), 223, 254; "Work among Moslems," *Missionary Herald* 74, no. 4 (Apr. 1878): 114; Arthur J. Brown, *One Hundred Years: A History of the Foreign Missionary Work of the Presbyterian Church in the U.S.A.* (New York, 1936), 549, 560.

23. Francis Mason, "Burman Mission," *American Baptist Magazine* 11, no. 8 (Aug. 1831): 245; Henry C. Vedder, *A Short History of Baptist Missions* (Philadelphia, 1927), 111–12.

24. G. Winfred Hervey, *The Story of Baptist Missions in Foreign Lands* (St. Louis, MO, 1886), 570–71, 578, 580.

25. Henry H. Jessup, "Mohammedanism," *Missionary Herald* 56, no. 3 (March 1860): 86.

26. William Eddy to Rufus Anderson, June 5, 1860, Papers of the ABCFM, reel 546, doc. 3; Henry H. Jessup, *The Mohammedan Missionary Problem* (Philadelphia, 1879), 45; Jessup, *The Women of the Arabs* (New York, 1873); Tibawi, *American Interests in Syria*, 256; Makdisi, "Reclaiming the Land," 703, 705.

27. Helen Barrett Montgomery, *Western Women in Eastern Lands* (New York, 1910), 52–53; Ruth Frances Woodsmall, *Moslem Women Enter a New World* (New York, 1936), 402.

28. Jessup, *Mohammedan Missionary Problem*, 78, 94, 135; Makdisi, "Reclaiming the Land," 707.

29. Henry H. Jessup, *Fifty-Three Years in Syria* (New York, 1910), 2: 546–48, 616; "'Matthew X' Mission," *Baptist Missionary Magazine* 70, no. 11 (Nov. 1890): 446.

30. Lisa Joy Pruitt, *"A Looking Glass for Ladies": American Protestant Women and the Orient in the Nineteenth Century* (Macon, GA, 2005), 44.

31. Claudius Buchanan, "The Star in the East," *Massachusetts Baptist Missionary Magazine* (Sept. 1809): 202–06; "Death of Sabat," *Christian Observer* 17 (Feb. 1818): 130–31.

32. Benjamin Allen, *The Death of Abdallah* (New York, 1814); "Abdallah and Sabat," in James Montgomery, *The Poetical Works of James Montgomery* (Boston, 1860), 3: 164–70; "Lady," *The Power of Christianity, or, Abdallah and Sabat* (Charleston, SC, 1814), 13; Thomas F. Barham and James Montgomery, *Abdallah; or, The Christian Martyr: A Christian Drama in Three Acts* ([England?], 1821); Courtney Anderson, *To the Golden Shore: The Life of Adoniram Judson* (Grand Rapids, MI, 1956), 52; John Campbell, *Alfred and Galba: Or, The History of Two Brothers* (Boston, 1812).

33. *A Brief Memoir of the Life and Conversion of Mahomed Ali Bey, A Learned Persian of Derbent* (Philadelphia, 1827), 24, 32; A.D.H. Bivar, "The Portraits and Career of Mohammed Ali, Son of Kazem-Beg: Scottish Missionaries and Russian Orientalism," *Bulletin of the School of Oriental and African Studies, University of London* 57, no. 2 (1994): 286–88.

34. *Brief Memoir*, 41–42; Bivar, "Mohammed Ali," 283–85; M. V. Jones, "The Sad and Curious Story of Karass, 1802–35," in Robert Auty, et al., eds., *Oxford Slavonic Papers* 8 (New York, 1975), 78–79.

35. Henry H. Jessup, *The Setting of the Crescent and the Rising of the Cross* (Philadelphia, 1898), 17, 144–45; Tibawi, *American Interests in Syria*, 292; J. Christy Wilson, *Apostle to Islam: A Biography of Samuel M. Zwemer* (Grand Rapids, MI, 1952), 41–45.

36. E.D.G. Prime, *Forty Years in the Turkish Empire* (New York, 1876), 425–26, 470.

37. Cyrus Hamlin, *Among the Turks* (New York, 1878), 349–51, 354, 378; Hutchison, *Errand to the World*, 98; Harris, *Nothing but Christ*, 128–32, 147–48.

38. James Bassett, *Persia: The Land of the Imams* (New York, 1886), 296–97, 338–39; John L. Esposito, *Islam: The Straight Path* 3d ed. (New York, 1998), 44–45.

39. Hilton Obenzinger, *American Palestine: Melville, Twain, and the Holy Land Mania* (Princeton, NJ, 1999), ix–xviii; Vogel, *To See a Promised Land*, 4–6, 98; Makdisi, "Reclaiming the Land," 688–89.

40. William M. Thomson, *The Land and the Book* (New York, 1908), 1: iv–v; Finnie, *Pioneers East*, 187; Kathleen Christison, *Perceptions of Palestine: Their Influence on U.S. Middle East Policy* (Berkeley, CA, 1999), 17, 20.

41. Thomson, *Land and the Book*, 3: 64–69; Muir quoted in Thomson, *Land and the Book*, 3: 427; Edward W. Said, *Orientalism* (New York, 1978), 151.

42. Mark Twain, *The Innocents Abroad, Or, The New Pilgrims' Progress* reprint (New York, 2003), 266.

CHAPTER 4
SAMUEL ZWEMER, WORLD WAR I, AND "THE EVANGELIZATION
OF THE MOSLEM WORLD IN THIS GENERATION"

1. Robert E. Speer, "How to Arouse the Church at Home to the Needs of Islam," in Samuel M. Zwemer, E. M. Wherry, and James L. Barton, eds., *The Mohammedan World of To-day* (New York, 1906), 270; Samuel M. Zwemer, "The Student Movement and Islam," in *Methods of Mission Work among Moslems* (New York, 1906), 231–32.

2. Albert H. Lybyer, "America's Missionary Record in Turkey," *Current History* 19, no. 5 (Feb. 1924): 808.

3. James H. Moorhead, "The Erosion of Postmillennialism in American Religious Thought, 1865–1925," *Church History* 53, no. 1 (Mar. 1984): 76–77. Andrew Porter has shown how premillennialism waned among British mission theorists during the period. Porter, "Evangelicalism, Islam, and Millennial Expectation in the Nineteenth Century," position paper no. 76, North Atlantic Missiology Project, 1998, 29–32.

4. James T. Addison, *The Christian Approach to the Moslem: A Historical Study* (New York, 1942), 196–97; J. Christy Wilson, *Apostle to Islam: A Biography of Samuel M. Zwemer* (Grand Rapids, MI, 1952), 28–33; Michael Parker, *The Kingdom of Character: The Student Volunteer Movement for Foreign Missions (1886–1926)* (Lanham, MD, 1998), 63–81; Dana L. Robert, *Occupy Until I Come: A. T. Pierson and the Evangelization of the World* (Grand Rapids, MI, 2003), 145–56; John Hubers, "Samuel Zwemer and the Challenge of Islam: From Polemic to a Hint of Dialogue," *International Bulletin of Missionary Research* 28, no. 3 (July 2004): 117–18; Michael B. Oren, *Power, Faith, and Fantasy: America in the Middle East, 1776 to the Present* (New York, 2007), 287–90.

5. Samuel M. Zwemer, *Arabia: The Cradle of Islam* 2d ed. (New York, 1900), 403.

6. Paul W. Harris, *Nothing but Christ: Rufus Anderson and the Ideology of Protestant Foreign Missions* (New York, 1999), 38–40; James Alan Patterson, "The Loss of a Protestant Missionary Consensus: Foreign Missions and the Fundamentalist-Modernist

Conflict," in Joel A. Carpenter and Wilbert R. Shenk, eds., *Earthen Vessels: American Evangelicals and Foreign Missions, 1880–1980* (Grand Rapids, MI, 1990), 76.

7. Porter, "Millennial Expectation," 26–29.

8. Henry Jessup, "Introductory Paper," in *Mohammedan World*, 19; E. M. Wherry, "Introduction," in *Methods of Mission Work among Moslems* (New York, 1906), 10–11; Stanley E. Brush, "Presbyterians and Islam in India," *Journal of Presbyterian History* 62, no. 3 (Fall 1984): 218–20; Brian Stanley, "Twentieth-Century World Christianity: A Perspective from the History of Missions," in Donald M. Lewis, ed., *Christianity Reborn: The Global Expansion of Evangelicalism in the Twentieth Century* (Grand Rapids, MI, 2004), 67.

9. E. M. Wherry, *Islam and Christianity in India and the Far East* (New York, 1907), 141, 147; Grant Wacker, "The Holy Spirit and the Spirit of the Age in American Protestantism, 1880–1910," in D. G. Hart, ed., *Reckoning with the Past: Historical Essays on American Evangelicalism from the Institute for the Study of American Evangelicals* (Grand Rapids, MI, 1995), 276.

10. James L. Barton, *The Unfinished Task of the Christian Church* (New York, 1908), 14, 50–56; James L. Barton, *Daybreak in Turkey* (Boston, 1908), 113–16.

11. Samuel M. Zwemer, *Islam, A Challenge to Faith* (New York, 1907), 210–13, 225; Wilson, *Apostle to Islam*, 173; Parker, *Student Volunteer Movement*, 117–18.

12. Zwemer, *Challenge to Faith*, 233–34, 256.

13. World Missionary Conference, 1910, *Report of Commission I: Carrying the Gospel to All the Non-Christian World* (New York, 1910), 1; Stanley, "Twentieth-Century World Christianity," 52–54.

14. World Missionary Conference, *Report of Commission I*, 6, 18, 20–21, 364.

15. Samuel M. Zwemer, "An Introductory Survey," in E. M. Wherry, S. M. Zwemer, and C. G. Mylrea, eds., *Islam and Missions: Being Papers Read at the Second Missionary Conference on Behalf of the Mohammedan World* (New York, 1911), 23, 36, 42; Wilson, *Apostle to Islam*, 173.

16. George F. Herrick, *Christian and Mohammedan: A Plea for Bridging the Chasm* (New York, 1912), 17–18, 212–15, 220; William R. Hutchison, *Errand to the World: American Protestant Thought and Foreign Missions* (Chicago, 1987), 138–45; Patterson, "Protestant Missionary Consensus," 84–85.

17. Samuel M. Zwemer, "Editorial," in the *Moslem World* I, no. 1 (Jan. 1911): 2–3.

18. Mrs. Howard Taylor, *Borden of Yale '09: "The Life that Counts"* (Philadelphia, 1930), 108–10. Thanks to Soren McMillan for drawing my attention to this book.

19. Taylor, *Borden of Yale*, 213–15.

20. Ibid., 252, 273–74.

21. William M. Miller, *A Christian's Response to Islam* (Philisburg, NJ, 1976), 7–9; Interview of William M. Miller by Robert Shuster on February 23, 1988, Collection 387, T1, Billy Graham Center Archives, http://www.wheaton.edu/bgc/archives/trans/387t01 .htm [accessed Aug. 29, 2006].

22. William M. Miller letters, Nov. 25, 1919, May 17, 1920, Nov. 5, 1957, in William M. Miller papers, Presbyterian Historical Society.

23. Editor's introduction to James L. Barton, "What the Defeat of Turkey May Mean

to American Missions," *Biblical World* 41, no. 1 (Jan. 1913): 3; Addison, *Christian Approach to the Moslem*, 100.

24. Frederick D. Greene, *Armenian Massacres, or, The Sword of Mohammed* (Philadelphia, 1896), xiv, 25–26.

25. Henry D. Davenport, *The Mohammedan Reign of Terror in Armenia*, appended to Greene, *Armenian Massacres*, 456–57, 467; Frances Willard, "Introduction," in Edwin M. Bliss, *Turkey and the Armenian Atrocities* (n.p., 1896), 2.

26. William M. Miller letter, Nov. 25, 1919, William M. Miller papers, Presbyterian Historical Society; H. C. Morrison, *The World War in Prophecy* (Louisville, KY, 1917), 45; Joseph L. Grabill, *Protestant Diplomacy and the Near East: Missionary Influence on American Policy, 1810–1927* (Minneapolis, MN, 1971), 64; Peter Balakian, *The Burning Tigris: The Armenian Genocide and America's Response* (New York, 2003), 176–80.

27. Clarence D. Ussher, *An American Physician in Turkey* (Boston, 1917), 244, 328–31; Balakian, *Burning Tigris*, 201–7.

28. Balakian, *Burning Tigris*, 279–80, 305–6; Suzanne E. Moranian, "The Armenian Genocide and American Missionary Relief Efforts," in Jay Winter, ed., *America and the Armenian Genocide of 1915* (New York, 2003), 192; also Moranian, "Bearing Witness: The Missionary Archives as Evidence of the Armenian Genocide," in Richard G. Hovannisian, *The Armenian Genocide: History, Politics, Ethics* (New York, 1992), 103–28.

29. James L. Barton, *The Story of Near East Relief, 1915–1930* (New York, 1930), 22, 29; "Mission Board Told of Turkish Horrors," *The New York Times*, Sept. 17, 1915; Moranian, "American Missionary Relief," 210.

30. Moranian, "Bearing Witness," 123.

31. Morrison, *World War in Prophecy*, 57; James L. Barton, "The Effect of the War on Protestant Missions," *Harvard Theological Review* 12, no. 1 (Jan. 1919), 17, 34.

32. Samuel M. Zwemer, *The Disintegration of Islam* (New York, 1916), 10, 64; Hubers, "Samuel Zwemer," 120.

33. Zwemer, *Disintegration*, 127, 186, 226. See also Samuel M. Zwemer, *Mohammed or Christ* (New York, 1916), 209.

34. Morrison, *World War in Prophecy*, 100; Timothy P. Weber, *Living in the Shadow of the Second Coming: American Premillennialism, 1875–1982*, enlarged ed. (Chicago, 1983), 105–15; Ernest R. Sandeen, *The Roots of Fundamentalism: British and American Millenarianism, 1800–1930* (Chicago, 1970), 233–35; Paul Boyer, *When Time Shall Be No More: Prophecy Belief in Modern American Culture* (Cambridge, MA, 1992), 100–102.

35. Scofield quoted in Charles G. Trumbull, *Prophecy's Light on Today* (New York, 1988, orig. 1937), 67; also Boyer, *When Time Shall Be No More*, 102; Simpson quoted in Dwight Wilson, *Armageddon Now! The Premillenarian Response to Russia and Israel Since 1917* (Tyler, TX, 1991, orig. 1977), 44; Timothy P. Weber, *On the Road to Armageddon: How Evangelicals Became Israel's Best Friend* (Grand Rapids, MI, 2004), 109–10.

36. A. E. Thompson, "The Capture of Jerusalem," in *Light on Prophecy* (New York, 1918), 144–46, 152, 154, 156, 162; Wilson, *Armageddon Now!*, 45; Weber, *On the Road to Armageddon*, 110–12.

37. *World Peace in the Light of Bible Prophecy* (Washington, D.C., 1919), 75–91.

38. J. Frank Norris, "Palestine Restored to the Jews," *Searchlight* 2, no. 49 (Oct. 21, 1920): 1–3; Barry Hankins, *God's Rascal: J. Frank Norris and the Beginnings of Southern Fundamentalism* (Lexington, KY, 1996), 80; Arno C. Gaebelein, "The Capture of Jerusalem and the Great Future of that City," in Arno C. Gaebelein, ed., *Christ and Glory* (New York, 1918), 155–56.

39. Keith L. Brooks, *The Jews and the Passion for Palestine in the Light of Prophecy* (Grand Rapids, MI, 1937), vii, 61–62; Wilson, *Armageddon Now!*, 60–62.

40. Charles R. Watson, *What Is This Moslem World?* (New York, 1937), 153.

CHAPTER 5
THE NEW MISSIONARY OVERTURE TO
MUSLIMS AND THE ARAB-ISRAELI CRISIS

1. R. C. Hutchison, "Christianity and Proselytism," *Atlantic Monthly* 140 (July-Dec. 1927), 621, 623; also Hutchison, "Islam and Christianity," *Atlantic Monthly* 138 (July-Dec. 1926), 706–10; William R. Hutchison, *Errand to the World: American Protestant Thought and Foreign Missions* (Chicago, 1987), 156–58; James Alan Patterson, "The Loss of a Protestant Missionary Consensus: Foreign Missions and the Fundamentalist-Modernist Conflict," in Joel A. Carpenter and Wilbert R. Shenk, eds., *Earthen Vessels: American Evangelicals and Foreign Missions, 1880–1980* (Grand Rapids, MI, 1990), 77.

2. John R. Mott, "Foreword," in John R. Mott, *The Moslem World of To-Day* (London, 1925), ix–x; Robert E. Speer, "The Issue Between Islam and Christianity," in ibid., 356; John R. Mott, "The Outlook in the Moslem World," in ibid., 373.

3. Hutchison, *Errand to the World*, 158–59; Patterson, "Loss of a Protestant Missionary Consensus," 86–90.

4. Robert E. Speer to William M. Miller, Jan. 10, 1933, in William M. Miller papers, Presbyterian Historical Society; Samuel M. Zwemer, *Thinking Missions with Christ* (Grand Rapids, MI, 1934), 23; Patterson, "Loss of a Protestant Missionary Consensus," 88–89.

5. Joel A. Carpenter, "Propagating the Faith Once Delivered: The Fundamentalist Missionary Enterprise, 1920–1945," in Carpenter and Shenk, *Earthen Vessels*, 131; Hutchison, *Errand to the World*, 176–77.

6. Ralph Fried, *Reaching Arabs for Christ* (Grand Rapids, MI, 1947), 124–25.

7. Barbara A. Cooper, *Evangelical Christians in the Muslim Sahel* (Bloomington, IN, 2006), 296–97; Burt Long, interview with Heather Conley, Nov. 26, 1986, Billy Graham Center Archives, at http://www.wheaton.edu/bgc/archives/trans/351t01.htm [accessed Oct. 25, 2006]; Rowland Bingham, *Seven Sevens of Years and a Jubilee* (New York, 1943), in Joel A. Carpenter, ed., *Missionary Innovation and Expansion* (New York, 1988), 15–16; Carpenter, "Propagating the Faith," 127.

8. Cooper, *Evangelical Christians in the Muslim Sahel*, 102–6, quote on 102.

9. Douglas Hursh to family, Aug. 3, 1942, and Laura and Douglas Hursh to family, Aug. 14, 1944, in M. Douglas Hursh papers, collection 186, box 1, Billy Graham Center Archives; Interviews with M. Douglas Hursh by Galen Wilson, Sept. 25, 1981, June 29, 1982,

transcripts, Billy Graham Center Archives, at http://www.wheaton.edu/bgc/archives /trans/186t01.htm, http://www.wheaton.edu/bgc/archives/trans/186t02.htm [accessed Oct. 25, 2006].

10. Robert H. Glover and J. Herbert Kane, *The Progress of World-Wide Missions* rev. ed. (New York, 1960), 278; Martha Wall, *Splinters from an African Log* (Chicago, 1960), 233–34, 248; Cooper, *Evangelical Christians*, 196.

11. Wall, *Splinters*, 265, 302, 317.

12. Eric G. Fisk, *The Prickly Pear: Mission Stories from Moslem Lands* (Chicago, 1951), 22, 36.

13. Finlay Graham letter fragment (missing page 1 of 3), n. d.; Finlay Graham to Mabel [Summers?], Feb. 19, 1954, Finlay and Julia Graham collection, Baylor University Library; Elwyn Lee Means, *World Within a World* (Nashville, TN, 1955), 105–7.

14. Pen Lile Pittard, *Clash of Swords* (Nashville, TN, 1952), xiii.

15. Means, *World Within a World*, 5–6, 115.

16. Finlay M. Graham, *Sons of Ishmael: How Shall They Hear?* (Nashville, TN, 1969), 13–14, 111; Baker James Cauthen and Frank K. Means, *Advance to Bold Mission Thrust: A History of Southern Baptist Foreign Missions, 1845–1980* (Nashville, TN, 1981), 401; "U.S. Aid Workers Killed in Yemen," at http://archives.cnn.com/2002/WORLD/meast/12/30 /yemen.doctors/ [accessed Aug. 25, 2006].

17. Thomas O'Shaughnessy, *Islamism, Its Rise and Decline* (New York, 1946), 8, 16, 31.

18. J. Christy Wilson, *Introducing Islam* (New York, 1954, orig. pub. 1950), 3, 18, 62.

19. Kenneth Cragg, *The Call of the Minaret* rev. and enlarged (Maryknoll, NY, 1985, orig. 1956), 209; Christopher Lamb, *The Call to Retrieval: Kenneth Cragg's Christian Vocation to Islam* (London, 1997), 170–71.

20. Cragg, *Call of the Minaret*, 313, 325.

21. "Energized" quote from J. Hoffman Cohn, "Disputed Passage," in John W. Bradbury, ed., *Light for the World's Darkness* (New York, 1944), 31–32; Samuel M. Zwemer, "The Return of Our Lord and World-Wide Evangelism," in ibid., 140; Timothy P. Weber, *On the Road to Armageddon: How Evangelicals Became Israel's Best Friend* (Grand Rapids, MI, 2004), 162–66, 172–73.

22. George T. B. Davis, *Rebuilding Palestine According to Prophecy* (Philadelphia, 1935), 98–99; Bingham and Carter quoted in Keith L. Brooks, *The Jews and the Passion for Palestine in the Light of Prophecy* (Grand Rapids, MI, 1937), 74–75; Charles S. Price, *The Battle of Armageddon* (Pasadena, Calif., 1938), 58; Dwight Wilson, *Armageddon Now! The Premillenarian Response to Russia and Israel Since 1917* (Tyler, TX, 1991, orig. 1977), 98–99.

23. Charles G. Trumbull, *Prophecy's Light on Today* (New York, 1937, reprint New York, 1988), 75, 169, 175; John F. Walvoord, "The Way of the Kings of the East: The Orient as a Factor in Prophecy," in Bradbury, *Light for the World's Darkness*, 172; Weber, *On the Road to Armageddon*, 168–69.

24. Dean C. Bedford, "Anti-Semitism: Its Origin, Development, and Final Doom," in Bradbury, *Light for the World's Darkness*, 182, 187; Weber, *On the Road to Armageddon*, 170; Wilson, *Armageddon Now!*, 71, 101–2, Brooks quoted on 102.

25. Paul Dean Votaw, interview with Robert Shuster, March 2, 1980, Billy Graham

Center archives, at http://www.wheaton.edu/bgc/archives/trans/105to2.htm [accessed Oct. 25, 2006]; J. Christy Wilson, *The Christian Message to Islam* (New York, 1950), 27–28, 38–39.

26. Henry Sloane Coffin, "A Heartening Church in a Disheartening World," *Christian Century* 64 (June 11, 1947), 739.

27. Reinhold Niebuhr, "Jews after the War," *The Nation* 154 (Feb. 28, 1942): 255; Reinhold Niebuhr, "The Relations of Christians and Jews in Western Civilization," in Robert McAfee Brown, *The Essential Reinhold Niebuhr: Selected Essays and Addresses* (New Haven, CT, 1986), 199–200; Richard W. Fox, *Reinhold Niebuhr: A Biography* rev. ed. (Ithaca, NY, 1996), 209–10; Paul Charles Merkley, *Christian Attitudes towards the State of Israel* (Montreal, 2001), 161–62.

28. M. R. DeHaan, *The Jew and Palestine in Prophecy* (Grand Rapids, MI, 1950), 61.

29. DeHaan, *The Jew and Palestine in Prophecy*, 64, 180; Weber, *On the Road to Armageddon*, 174; Wilson, *Armageddon Now!*, 162–63.

30. "International Crisis on the Sandy Wastes of Sinai," *Christianity Today* 1, no. 3 (Nov. 12, 1956), 24; Weber, *On the Road to Armageddon*, 177–78.

31. Oswald T. Allis, "Israel's Transgression in Palestine," *Christianity Today* 1, no. 6 (Dec. 24, 1956), 6, 9. See also Oswald T. Allis, *Prophecy and the Church* (Philadelphia, 1945).

32. Wilbur M. Smith, "Israel in Her Promised Land," *Christianity Today* 1, no. 6 (Dec. 24, 1956), 11.

33. William L. Hull, *Israel: Key to Prophecy* (Grand Rapids, MI, 1957), 39–40; Yaakov Ariel, *Evangelizing the Chosen People: Missions to the Jews in America, 1880–2000* (Chapel Hill, NC, 2000), 156–57; C. M. Ward, *Ishmael and Isaac: Two Brothers' Destiny* (Springfield, MO, 1955), 21; Charles E. Pont, *The World's Collision* (Boston, 1956), 215, 243; Wilson, *Armageddon Now!*, 173.

34. Hull, *Israel*, 49–53, 57.

35. Ibid., 82–86, 92.

36. L. Nelson Bell, "Unfolding Destiny," *Christianity Today* 11 (July 21, 1967), 29; Wilson, *Armageddon Now!*, 190; Weber, *On the Road to Armageddon*, 184–85.

37. William Culbertson, "Perspective on Arab-Israeli Tensions," *Christianity Today* 12 (June 7, 1968): 8.

38. James Kelso, "Perspective on Arab-Israeli Tensions," *Christianity Today* 12 (June 7, 1968), 9; Wilson, *Armageddon Now!*, 192–93; Merkley, *Christian Attitudes*, 42–43.

39. Wilbur M. Smith, *Israeli/Arab Conflict* (Glendale, CA, 1967), i, 7, 80, 106; Charles L. Feinberg, "Isaac and Ishmael," *King's Business* 58 (July 1968): 23; Wilson, *Armageddon Now!*, 199; Weber, *On the Road to Armageddon*, 186.

40. Frank H. Epp, *Whose Land Is Palestine? The Middle East Problem in Historical Perspective* (Grand Rapids, MI, 1970), 241; Charles C. Ryrie, "Perspective on Palestine," *Christianity Today* 13 (May 23, 1969), 8–9; Wilson, *Armageddon Now!*, 197–98.

41. Hal Lindsey, *The Late Great Planet Earth* (Grand Rapids, MI, 1970), 55; Weber, *On the Road to Armageddon*, 188–91.

42. Lindsey, *Late Great Planet Earth*, 56; Milton B. Lindberg, *The Jew and Modern Israel in the Light of Prophecy* rev. ed. (Chicago, 1969), 65, 71–73; Gershom Gorenberg, *The*

End of Days: Fundamentalism and the Struggle for the Temple Mount (New York, 2000), 121–23; Barbara R. Rossing, *The Rapture Exposed: The Message of Hope in the Book of Revelation* (Boulder, CO, 2004), 56–61.

43. Lindsey, *Late Great Planet Earth*, 72–73, 158.

CHAPTER 6
CHRISTIANS RESPOND TO MUSLIMS IN MODERN AMERICA

1. Muhammad Alexander Russell Webb, "The Spirit of Islam," in Michael A. Koszegi and J. Gordon Melton, eds., *Islam in North America: A Sourcebook* (New York, 1992), 37; Richard Brent Turner, *Islam in the African-American Experience* 2d ed. (Bloomington, IN, 2003), 62–65.

2. G. H. Bousquet, "Moslem Religious Influences in the United States," *Moslem World* 25 (1935): 44.

3. "Fall of Islam in America," *The New York Times* (Dec. 1, 1895): 21; Turner, *Islam*, 64–65; Jane I. Smith, *Islam in America* (New York, 1999), 190; Umar F. Abd-Allah, *A Muslim in Victorian America: The Life of Alexander Russell Webb* (New York, 2006), 3–6.

4. Turner, *Islam*, 5–6; Edward E. Curtis IV, *Islam in Black America: Identity, Liberation, and Difference in African-American Islamic Thought* (Albany, NY, 2002), 12–16.

5. Turner, *Islam*, 48–59; Curtis, *Islam in Black America*, 21–23; Hollis R. Lynch, *Edward Wilmot Blyden: Pan-Negro Patriot, 1832–1912* (New York, 1967), 4–6.

6. Edward Wilmot Blyden, *Christianity, Islam and the Negro Race* reprint (Edinburgh, 1967, orig. 1887), 10–12; Sherman A. Jackson, *Islam and the Blackamerican: Looking toward the Third Resurrection* (New York, 2005), 65–66; Lynch, *Edward Wilmot Blyden*, 67–74.

7. Blyden, *Christianity*, 26, 174–75, 241.

8. Ibid., 188; Turner, *Islam*, 55–58; Jackson, *Blackamerican*, 127; Edwin S. Redkey, *Black Exodus: Black Nationalist and Back-to-Africa Movements, 1890–1910* (New Haven, CT, 1969), 49–50.

9. Turner, *Islam*, 92, 96; Smith, *Islam in America*, 78–80.

10. Erdmann D. Beynon, "The Voodoo Cult among Negro Migrants in Detroit," *American Journal of Sociology* 43, no. 6 (May 1938), 894–96, 900–901; C. Eric Lincoln, *The Black Muslims in America* 3d ed. (Grand Rapids, MI, 1994), 12–14, 25–26; Claude Andrew Clegg, *An Original Man: The Life and Times of Elijah Muhammad* (New York, 1997), 27; Smith, *Islam in America*, 79.

11. Smith, *Islam in America*, 82–83; Lincoln, *Black Muslims in America*, 71–73; Curtis, *Islam in Black America*, 72–79; Karl Evanzz, *The Messenger: The Rise and Fall of Elijah Muhammad* (New York, 1999), 103–4, 117–18.

12. "Not So Sure," *Amsterdam News* Aug. 10, 1957, 6; Clegg, *Original Man*, 116.

13. George C. Violenes, "Christian World," *Amsterdam News* Dec. 21, 1957, 1, 24, and Dec. 28, 1957, 30; DeCaro, *Malcolm and the Cross*, 124–25.

14. Letters of William Holmes, J. M. Gervai, Willie Williams, *Pittsburgh Courier* Oct. 12, 1957, sec. 2: 7; DeCaro, *Malcolm and the Cross*, 109–10.

15. Letters of Joseph P. King, James Battle, Hattie Belle Perryman, Elaine Crane, and Eloise MC., *Pittsburgh Courier*, Oct. 19, 1957, sec. 2: 7.

16. Letters of Progressive Pentecostal Young People's Meeting, Arthur McGiffert, *Pittsburgh Courier* Oct. 25, 1958, sec. 2: 9; Letter of Rev. M. C. McKenney, *Pittsburgh Courier* Nov. 22, 1958, sec. 2: 6.

17. Martin Luther King, Jr., "Address at the Thirty-Fourth Annual Convention of the National Bar Association," Aug. 20, 1959, in Clayborne Carson, ed., *The Papers of Martin Luther King, Jr., vol. 5: Threshold of a New Decade, January 1959–December 1960* (Berkeley, CA, 2005), 269.

18. Charles S. Braden, "Islam in America," *International Review of Missions* 48 (July 1959): 316; "No Race Maintains a Monopoly on Hatred," *The Christian Century* 78 (Mar. 15, 1961): 318–19; E. Luther Copeland, *Christianity and World Religions* (Nashville, TN, 1963), 112; Beynon, "Voodoo Cult," 897; Sean McCloud, *Making the American Religious Fringe: Exotics, Subversives, and Journalists, 1955–1993* (Chapel Hill, NC, 2004), 59–60, 80; Philip Jenkins, *Mystics and Messiahs: Cults and New Religions in American History* (New York, 2000), 112, 168–69.

19. Malcolm X quoted in Louis A. DeCaro, Jr., *Malcolm and the Cross: The Nation of Islam, Malcolm X, and Christianity* (New York, 1998), 114.

20. Malcolm X with Alex Haley, *The Autobiography of Malcolm X* (New York, 1965), 163; DeCaro, *Malcolm and the Cross*, 113–14.

21. Albert B. Southwick, "Malcolm X: Charismatic Demagogue," *Christian Century* 80 (June 5, 1963): 741.

22. "Likens Malcolm X, Christ," *Chicago Defender* (Feb. 27–Mar. 5, 1965), 1–2; "Islamic Negro Nationalists," *Christianity Today* 9, no. 12 (March 1965): 644.

23. C. Eric Lincoln, "The Meaning of Malcolm X," *Christian Century* 82 (April 7, 1965), 431–33; James O'Gara, "After Malcolm X," *Commonweal* 82 (March 26, 1965), 8; McCloud, *American Religious Fringe*, 68.

24. Thomas Merton, "The Meaning of Malcolm X," *Continuum* 5 (Summer 1967): 433–35.

25. Kenneth E. Burke, *Black Muslim Encounter* (Atlanta, 1967), 6.

26. Walter R. Martin, *The Kingdom of the Cults* (Grand Rapids, MI, 1965), 11, 259–60, 274; Jenkins, *Mystics and Messiahs*, 51.

27. Walter Martin, *The Kingdom of the Cults* rev. ed. (Minneapolis, MN, 2003), 450–51, 454–55.

28. James L. Kidd, "'Yes Sir, Mr. Ali'-The Tale of a Talk," *Christian Century* 85 (Oct. 30, 1968): 1384–85.

29. James S. Tinney, "Black Muslims: Moving into Mainstream?" *Christianity Today* 17 (Aug. 10, 1973): 1168–69; James S. Tinney, "Bilalian Muslims," *Christianity Today* 20 (March 12, 1976): 631–32; James Emerson Whitehurst, "The Mainstreaming of the Black Muslims: Healing the Hate," *Christian Century* 97 (Feb. 27, 1980): 225–29.

30. Smith, *Islam in America*, 95; Mattias Gardell, *In the Name of Elijah Muhammad: Louis Farrakhan and the Nation of Islam* (Durham, NC, 1996), 251–52.

31. "Ben Chavis Joins the Nation of Islam," *Christian Century* 114, no. 9 (Mar. 12,

1997), 263–64; Gardell, *Louis Farrakhan,* 243; Elreta Dodds, *The Trouble with Farrakhan and the Nation of Islam: Another Message to the Black Man in America* (Detroit, MI, 1997), v, 201, 205–6.

32. Richard Abanes, *Cults, New Religious Movements, and Your Family: A Guide to Ten Non-Christian Groups Out to Convert Your Loved Ones* (Wheaton, IL, 1998), 132; 7.

33. Moody Adams, *Farrakhan, Islam, and the Religion that Is Raping America* (Baton Rouge, LA, 1996), 7, 90; http://www.pbs.org/wnet/religionandethics/week616/cover.html [accessed Sept. 26, 2006].

34. Andrés Tapia, "Churches Wary of Inner-City Islamic Inroads," *Christianity Today* 38, no. 1 (Jan. 10, 1994), 36–38.

35. Carl F. Ellis, Jr., *Free at Last? The Gospel in the African-American Experience* 2d ed. (Downers Grove, IL, 1996), 104–5, 126; "How Islam Is Winning Black America," *Christianity Today* 44, no. 4 (April 3, 2000), 52–53.

36. Haman Cross, Jr., and Donna E. Scott, *Have You Got Good Religion? The Real Fruit of Islam* (Chicago, 1993), 40–41, 61, 69; Haman Cross, Jr., and Donna E. Scott, *What's Up with Malcolm? The Real Failure of Islam* (Chicago, 1993), 11, 24, 49–50.

37. John L. Esposito, *Islam: The Straight Path* 3d ed. (New York, 1998), 208.

38. Smith, *Islam in America,* 51–52, 152; W. H. Lawrence, "President and Wife Doff Shoes at Rites Dedicating Mosque," *The New York Times* (June 29, 1957): 1, 9.

39. Joseph R. Estes, *A Baptist Look at Islam* (Atlanta, 1967), 2, 9; Kate Ellen Gruver, "Muslims on the American Scene," *Home Missions* 46 (March 1975), 38; R. Max Kershaw, "The Comparative Status of Christianity and Islam in the West," in McCurry, *Gospel and Islam,* 233.

40. Ray G. Register, Jr., *Dialogue and Interfaith Witness with Muslims: A Guide and Sample Ministry in the U.S.A.* (Fort Washington, PA, 1979), 8–9, 17, 68, 76.

41. R. Max Kershaw, *How to Share the Good News with Your Muslim Friend* (Colorado Springs, CO, 1978) 1, 4, 24; Edward J. Hoskins, *A Muslim's Heart: What Every Christian Needs to Know to Share Christ with Muslims* (Colorado Springs, CO, 2003), 29–30.

42. Roy Oksnevad and Dotsey Welliver, eds., *The Gospel for Islam: Reaching Muslims in North America* (Wheaton, IL, 2001), 15–17, 168, 207.

43. Oksnevad and Welliver, *Gospel for Islam,* 134–38.

44. Ibid., 160–62.

45. Shirin Taber, *Muslims Next Door: Uncovering Myths and Creating Friendships* (Grand Rapids, MI, 2004), 16–17, 63.

46. Bruce A. McDowell and Anees Zaka, *Muslims and Christians at the Table: Promoting Biblical Understanding among North American Muslims* (Philipsburg, NJ, 1999), xviii, 1, 217–19, 228.

47. Michael Youssef, *America, Oil, and the Islamic Mind* rev. ed. (Grand Rapids, MI, 1991), 129–31; Robert Morey, *The Islamic Invasion: Confronting the World's Fastest Growing Religion* (Eugene, OR, 1992), 17; Michael Fortner, *The Scarlet Beast: Islam and the Beast of Revelation* (Lawton, OK, 2006), 20; William Wagner, *How Islam Plans to Change the World* (Grand Rapids, MI, 2004), 14–15.

48. Wagner, *How Islam,* 17, 139–40, 144, 151–52, 217.

49. Charles Colson, "Terrorists Behind Bars," *First Things* 127 (Nov. 2002): 19–21; Charles Colson, "What's Hidden in the Shadows," *Breakpoint Commentaries* Sept. 26, 2006, http://www.breakpoint.org/listingarticle.asp?ID=5628 [accessed Oct. 3, 2006]; Colson cited Frank Cilluffo, et al., "Out of the Shadows: Getting ahead of Prisoner Radicalization," George Washington University Homeland Security Policy Institute and University of Virginia Critical Incident Analysis Group, September 19, 2006, at http://www.healthsystem.virginia.edu/internet/ciag/publications/out_of_the_shadows.pdf; Wagner, *How Islam*, 205.

CHAPTER 7
MATURING EVANGELICAL MISSIONS AND WAR IN THE MIDDLE EAST

1. J. Edwin Orr, *Evangelical Awakenings in the South Seas* (Minneapolis, MN, 1976), 178; Gainer Bryan, "Indonesia: Turmoil Amid Revival," *Christianity Today* 12 (Dec. 22, 1967): 40–41; "World Parish," *Christianity Today* 13 (May 23, 1969), 36; Kurt Koch, *The Revival in Indonesia* (Grand Rapids, MI, 1971), 21, 102, 194–95, 282–83; Orr, "The Call to Spiritual Renewal," in Don McCurry, ed., *The Gospel and Islam: A 1978 Compendium* (Monrovia, CA, 1979), 423–24.

2. "Documentation: Striving Together in Dialogue: A Muslim-Christian Call to Reflection and Action," *Islam and Christian-Muslim Relations* 12, no. 4 (2001): 487; Daniel R. Brewster, "Dialogue: Relevancy to Evangelism," in Don McCurry, ed., *The Gospel and Islam: A 1978 Compendium* (Monrovia, CA, 1979), 514–15; Warren Webster to Wade Coggins, Sept. 2, 1977, in the papers of the Evangelical Foreign Missions Association, collection 165, box 4, folder 7, Billy Graham Center Archives.

3. Anis A. Shorrosh, *Jesus, Prophecy, and the Middle East* (Nashville, TN, 1981), 2.

4. *Report of Conference of Missionaries to Islam* (Ridgefield Park, NJ, 1960), 1, 4.

5. J. D. Douglas, ed., *Let the Earth Hear His Voice: International Congress on World Evangelization, Lausanne, Switzerland* (Minneapolis, MN, 1975), 9, 26.

6. Douglas, *Let the Earth Hear*, 826–27; David W. Shenk, "Conversations Along the Way," in J. Dudley Woodberry, ed., *Muslims and Christians on the Emmaus Road* (Monrovia, CA, 1989), 5–7.

7. Don McCurry, "A Time for New Beginnings," in McCurry, *Gospel and Islam*, 13–14.

8. Ibid., 14, 16.

9. Arthur F. Glasser, "Conference Report," in McCurry, *Gospel and Islam*, 43, 51.

10. Charles R. Taber, "Contextualization: Indigenization and/or Transformation," in McCurry, *Gospel and Islam*, 149–51.

11. McCurry, "A Time for New Beginnings," 20; W. Stanley Mooneyham, "Keynote Address," in McCurry, *Gospel and Islam*, 23; "Report of the Islamics Task Force," (1980), 2, in papers of the Evangelical Foreign Missions Association, collection 165, box 39, folder 3, Billy Graham Center Archives; "The Zwemer Institute: A Story Waiting to Be Told," *Mission Frontiers* (July 1988), at www.missionfrontiers.org/1988/07/j884.htm [accessed Oct. 6, 2006].

12. Phil Parshall, *New Paths in Muslim Evangelism: Evangelical Approaches to Contextualization* (Grand Rapids, MI, 1980), 18–19, 25–26.

13. R. V. Davis, "Winnable but Not Yet Won," *Africa Now* (Sept.-Oct. 1970), 11; Raymond H. Joyce, "Deepening Insights into the Evangelization of Muslims," *Muslim World Pulse* 5, no. 2 (Aug. 1976); Greg Livingstone, "How We Can Reach Muslims by Working Together," *Evangelical Missions Quarterly* 22, no. 3 (July 1986): 246.

14. Lionel Gurney to Abe Thiessen, Oct. 6, 1969, in the Papers of the International Christian Broadcasters, collection 86, box 27, folder 3, Billy Graham Center Archives.

15. C. Richard Shumaker, ed., *Conference on Media in Islamic Culture Report: Marseilles, France, 1974* (Wheaton, IL, [1974]), 6, 41, 108–10, 112, 172.

16. Bilquis Sheikh with Richard Schneider, *I Dared to Call Him Father* (Waco, TX, 1978), 57.

17. Amina Rasul, "Do Muslims Believe in Jesus Christ and Mary?" (Dec. 24, 2006), at http://www.manilatimes.net/national/2006/dec/24/yehey/opinion/20061224opi5.html [accessed Sept. 7, 2007]; Carl W. Ernst, *Following Muhammad: Rethinking Islam in the Contemporary World* (Chapel Hill, NC, 2003), 15.

18. "The 10/40 Window: Getting to the Core of the Core," at www.ad2000.org /1040broc.htm [accessed Oct. 11, 2006].

19. George Otis, ed., *Strongholds of the 10/40 Window* (Seattle, WA, 1995), 109.

20. George Otis, Jr., *The Last of the Giants: Lifting the Veil on Islam and the End Times* (Tarrytown, NY, 1991), 58, 64–65, 121, 137.

21. Ibid., 144; Robert T. Coote, "'AD 2000' and the '10/40 Window': A Preliminary Assessment," *International Bulletin of Missionary Research* 24, no. 4 (Oct. 2000): 165, 166 n.30.

22. Robert Walker, "Introduction," in Carl F. H. Henry, ed., *Prophecy in the Making: Messages Prepared for Jerusalem Conference on Biblical Prophecy* (Carol Stream, IL, 1971), 12; Harold J. Ockenga, "Fulfilled and Unfulfilled Prophecy," in ibid., 309; Timothy P. Weber, *On the Road to Armageddon: How Evangelicals Became Israel's Best Friend* (Grand Rapids, MI, 2004), 213–14; Paul Boyer, *When Time Shall Be No More: Prophecy Belief in Modern American Culture* (Cambridge, MA, 1992), 188.

23. Marius Baar, *The Unholy War: Oil, Islam, and Armageddon* (Nashville, TN, 1980), 180; John F. Walvoord, *Armageddon, Oil, and the Middle East Crisis: What the Bible Says about the Future of the Middle East and the End of Western Civilization* (Grand Rapids, MI, 1974), 43.

24. Walvoord, *Armageddon, Oil, and the Middle East Crisis*, 102, 195, 202, 205.

25. Zola Levitt, *Israel in Agony: The Beginning of the End?* (Irvine, CA, 1975), 1, 24, 45, 74–75, 92–93; George Otis, *The Ghost of Hagar* (Van Nuys, CA, 1974), 87–88; Boyer, *When Time Shall Be No More*, 207–08; Robert C. Fuller, *Naming the Antichrist: The History of an American Obsession* (New York, 1995), 187.

26. Louis A. DeCaro, *Israel Today: Fulfillment of Prophecy?* (Philadelphia, 1974), 17, 19.

27. Bill Adler, ed., *The Wit and Wisdom of Jimmy Carter* (Secaucus, NJ, 1977), 139; Jimmy Carter, *The Blood of Abraham* (Boston, 1985), 4, 9; Carter also quoted in Michael B. Oren, *Power, Faith, and Fantasy: America in the Middle East, 1776 to the Present* (New York, 2007), 538–39, 552; Reagan quoted in Boyer, *When Time Shall Be No More*, 142.

28. G. Douglas Young, "Israel: The Unbroken Line," and Elisabeth Elliot, "Furnace of the Lord," in *Christianity Today* 23 (Oct. 6, 1978), 20, 22, 25–26. On Young, Paul Charles Merkley, *Christian Attitudes towards the State of Israel* (Montreal, 2001), 163–68.

29. Edgar C. James, *Arabs, Oil, and Energy* (Chicago, 1977), 13, 84, 104, 107, 127.

30. Paul Aaron, *Middle East in Bible Prophecy* (Dallas, TX, 1979), 38–40.

31. Lester Sumrall, *Jihad, The Holy War: The Destiny of the Moslem World* (Tulsa, OK, 1980), 89, 113, 129, 149, 156, 160.

32. Baar, *Unholy War*, 110, 152.

33. Ibid., 148, 171–72, 190.

34. Hal Lindsey, *The 1980s: Countdown to Armageddon* (New York, 1981), 44, 53–63.

35. Derek Prince, *The Last Word on the Middle East* (Lincoln, VA, 1982), 68–70; David Dolan, *Holy War for the Promised Land: Israel's Struggle to Survive* (Nashville, TN, 1991), 234–35; Dave Hunt, *Judgment Day! Islam, Israel and the Nations* (Bend, OR, 2005), 7.

36. Tim LaHaye, *The Coming Peace in the Middle East* (Grand Rapids, MI, 1984), 170; Charles H. Dyer, *What's Next? God, Israel, and the Future of Iraq* (Chicago, 2004), 85–86; Prince, *Last Word*, 139–40.

37. Mike Evans, *The Return* (Nashville, TN, 1986), 151–62, quotes on 151, 157–58.

38. Moishe Rosen, *Overture to Armageddon? Beyond the Gulf War* (San Bernardino, CA, 1991), 133; Boyer, *When Time Shall Be No More*, 280, 329–30.

39. Grant R. Jeffrey, *Armageddon: Appointment with Destiny* rev. ed. (Toronto, Ont., 1997); 269–70, 277–78; Charles H. Dyer, *The Rise of Babylon: Is Iraq at the Center of the Final Drama?* rev. ed. (Chicago, 2003, orig. pub. 1991); Mark Hitchcock, *The Second Coming of Babylon* (Sisters, OR, 2003), 132; Salem Kirban, *666* (Huntingdon Valley, PA, 1970), 156; Tim LaHaye and Jerry B. Jenkins, *Tribulation Force: The Continuing Drama of Those Left Behind* (Wheaton, IL, 1996), 277.

40. Elishua Davidson, *Islam, Israel, and the Last Days* (Eugene, OR, 1991), 26–27, 94, 102.

41. Harry Genet, "A Fresh Look at the Arabs Is Long Overdue," *Muslim World Pulse* 3, no. 1 (June 1974), 3, 5; Tim Matheny, *Reaching the Arabs: A Felt Need Approach* (Pasadena, CA, 1981), 72; Anthony Campolo, "Creating an Evangelistic Witness in the Middle East through a Commitment to Social Justice," in Wendy Ryan, ed., *Christianity and the Arab/Israeli Conflict* (St. Davids, PA, 1986), 58–59.

42. Samir Massouh, "Arabs: Second-Class Israeli Citizens," *Christianity Today*, 23 (Oct. 6, 1978), 29; Mark M. Hanna, "Israel Today: What Place in Prophecy?" and Jerry Falwell, "Jerry Falwell Objects," in *Christianity Today* 26 (Jan. 22, 1982), 15, 17; Joyce, "Deepening Insights," 3.

43. Louis Bahjat Hamada, *Understanding the Arab World* (Nashville, TN, 1990), 102–8, 174–75, 190–91.

44. Anis A. Shorrosh, *Jesus, Prophecy, and the Middle East* (Nashville, TN, 1981), 31, 56–57, 60; Anis A. Shorrosh, *Islam Revealed: A Christian Arab's View of Islam* (Nashville, TN, 1988), 286.

45. Donald E. Wagner, *Anxious for Armageddon: A Call to Partnership for Middle Eastern and Western Christians* (Scottdale, PA, 1995), 57–58, 181–83; Gary M. Burge, *Who*

Are God's People in the Middle East? What Christians Are Not Being Told about Israel and the Palestinians (Grand Rapids, MI, 1993), 180; Gary M. Burge, e-mail to author, 10/10/2006; Merkley, *Christian Attitudes*, 186–87, 193–94; Weber, *On the Road to Armageddon*, 248.

CHAPTER 8
AMERICAN CHRISTIANS AND ISLAM AFTER SEPTEMBER 11, 2001

1. Dayna Curry and Heather Mercer with Stacy Mattingly, *Prisoners of Hope: The Story of Our Captivity and Freedom in Afghanistan* (New York, 2002), 44.

2. http://www.patrobertson.com/PressReleases/bushresponse2.asp [accessed Nov. 14, 2005]; Harvey Cox, "Religion and the War against Evil," *The Nation* 273, no. 21 (2001): 29–31; "Riots, Condemnation, Fatwa, and Apology Follow Falwell's CBS Comments," at http://www.christianitytoday.com/ct/2002/140/41.0.html [accessed Nov. 14, 2005].

3. George W. Bush, speech of 9/17/01, at http://www.whitehouse.gov/news/releases/2001/09/20010917-11.html, speech of 9/20/01, at http://www.whitehouse.gov/news/releases/2001/09/20010920-8.html [accessed Oct. 26, 2006]; Randall Price, *Unholy War* (Eugene, OR, 2001), 222; Barry Hankins, "Civil Religion and America's Inclusive Faith," *Liberty* 99, no. 1 (Jan./Feb. 2004): 20–22.

4. Dave Hunt, *Judgment Day! Islam, Israel and the Nations* (Bend, OR, 2005), 121–22, 129, 135; "Bush Steps on Theological Toes," *Washington Post*, Nov. 29, 2003, at http://www.heraldnet.com/Stories/03/11/29/17790481.cfm [accessed Oct. 26, 2006]; see also J. C. Alexander, *The Kingdom of the Beast and the End of the World* (Ozark, AL, 2005), 318.

5. J. Dudley Woodberry, "Do Christians and Muslims Worship the Same God?" *Christian Century* 121, no. 10 (May 18, 2004): 37.

6. "Backgrounder: The President's Quotes on Islam," at http://www.whitehouse.gov/infocus/ramadan/islam.html [accessed Sept. 18, 2007]; Mark Silk, "Notes on the Judeo-Christian Tradition in America," *American Quarterly* 36, no. 1 (Spring 1984): 65.

7. Barbara Brown Taylor, "A Case of Mistaken Identity," *Christian Century* 118, no. 26 (Sept. 26, 2001), 32; U.S. Conference of Catholic Bishops, "Living with Faith and Hope after September 11," (Nov. 14, 2001), at http://www.usccb.org/sdwp/sept11.htm [accessed Nov. 30, 2006]; "War and the Common Good," *Commonweal* (Dec. 7, 2001), 6; Robert Spencer, *Islam Unveiled: Disturbing Questions about the World's Fastest-Growing Faith* (San Francisco, 2002), 22.

8. Alan Cooperman, "Anti-Muslim Remarks Stir Tempest," *Washington Post*, at http://www.washingtonpost.com/ac2/wp-dyn/A14499-2002Jun19?language=printer [accessed Oct. 26, 2006]; "Full Text of Missionaries' Letter on Islam," *The Baptist Standard*, Jan. 20, 2003, at http://www.baptiststandard.com/2003/1_20/pages/letter_fulltext.html [accessed Nov. 22, 2006].

9. Ergun M. Caner and Emir F. Caner, *Unveiling Islam: An Insider's Look at Muslim Life and Beliefs* (Grand Rapids, MI, 2002), 35–36.

10. Ibid., 41–45, 85.

11. Reza F. Safa, *Inside Islam: Exposing and Reaching the World of Islam* (Lake Mary, FL, 1996), 8, 145, 149.

12. Mark A. Gabriel, *Islam and Terrorism* (Lake Mary, FL, 2002), 28, 39, 217–28. On questions about Gabriel's identity, see http://www.markagabriel.org/index.php?option =com_content&task=view&id=33&Itemid=51 [accessed Oct. 27, 2006].

13. R. C. Sproul and Abdul Saleeb, *The Dark Side of Islam* (Wheaton, IL, 2003), 8, 84, 86, 91; Norman L. Geisler and Abdul Saleeb, *Answering Islam: The Crescent in Light of the Cross* rev. ed. (Grand Rapids, MI, 2002), 329.

14. John MacArthur, *Terrorism, Jihad, and the Bible: A Response to the Terrorist Attacks* (Nashville, TN, 2001), 29, 42–43, 59, 62, 122 n.21.

15. Hal Lindsey, *The Everlasting Hatred: The Roots of Jihad* (Murrieta, CA, 2002), 11, 127; Grant R. Jeffrey, *The Next World War: What Prophecy Reveals about Extreme Islam and the West* (Colorado Springs, CO, 2006), 14. On the jihadists' view of inexorable conflict, Mary Habeck, *Knowing the Enemy: Jihadist Ideology and the War on Terror* (New Haven, CT, 2006), 83–86.

16. Roy Rivenburg, "Christian Network, Author Lindsey Are Back on the Same Side," *Los Angeles Times*, Feb. 10, 2007, at http://www.latimes.com/technology/la-me-beliefs 10feb10,1,4476044.story?coll=la-headlines-technology [accessed Feb. 26, 2007]. Thanks to Barry Hankins for alerting me to this episode.

17. Robert A. Morey, *Winning the War against Radical Islam* (Orange, CA, 2002), 167–74.

18. James A. Beverly, "Is Islam a Religion of Peace?" *Christianity Today* 46, no. 1 (Jan. 7, 2002), 37.

19. Timothy George, *Is the Father of Jesus the God of Muhammad? Understanding the Differences between Christianity and Islam* (Grand Rapids, MI, 2002), 12–15, 35–37.

20. Ibid., 69–70, 97–99.

21. J. Dudley Woodberry, "Terrorism, Islam, and Mission: Reflections of a Guest in Muslim Lands," *International Bulletin of Missionary Research* 26, no. 1 (Jan. 2002): 4, 6–7.

22. Robert W. Sayer, in *Update: Arab World Ministries* no. 3 (2001): 1; David Lundy, in *Update: Arab World Ministries* no. 1 (2003): 1–2.

23. John Hagee, *Attack on America: New York, Jerusalem, and the Role of Terrorism in the Last Days* (Nashville, TN, 2001), 64–65.

24. Ibid., 67; Walvoord, *Armageddon, Oil, and the Middle East Crisis*, 132–33, 145; "The End is Nigh," *The Texas Observer*, 12/6/2002, at http://www.texasobserver.org/article .php?aid=1192 [accessed Nov. 14, 2006]; Timothy Weber, *On the Road to Armageddon: How Evangelicals Became Israel's Best Friend* (Grand Rapids, MI, 2004), 227.

25. Grant R. Jeffrey, *War on Terror: Unfolding Bible Prophecy* (Toronto, 2002), 7, 11, 13.

26. Mark Hitchcock, *Iran: The Coming Crisis* (Sisters, OR, 2006), 148; Jeffrey, *War on Terror*, 128, 133; Jeffrey, *Next World War*, 44, 62.

27. Michael D. Evans, *Beyond Iraq: The Next Move* (Lakeland, FL, 2003), 8, 27, 38–39, 48, 79.

28. Ibid., 88, 91–92, 104; Peter Steinfels, "Beliefs," *The New York Times*, Dec. 6, 2003, B6.

29. Charles H. Dyer, *What's Next? God, Israel and the Future of Iraq* (Chicago, 2004), 97–101, 103, 108.

30. Hitchcock, *Iran*, 67, 160–63; Mark Hitchcock, *The Coming Islamic Invasion of Israel* (Sisters, OR, 2002), 75–76; Jeffrey, *Next World War*, 136; Michael Rydelnik, *Under-*

standing the Arab-Israeli Conflict: What the Headlines Haven't Told You (Chicago, 2004), 178–83.

31. Rydelnik, *Understanding the Arab-Israeli Conflict*, 128, 185–91.

32. Glenn Miller with Roger Loomis, *The Prophetic Fall of the Islamic Regime* (Lake Mary, FL, 2004), 7, 60, 87, 100–101.

33. Ralph W. Stice, *From 9/11 to 666* (Ozark, AL, 2005), 9–21. On Muslims' belief in the Mahdi, see Timothy R. Furnish, *Holiest Wars: Islamic Mahdis, Their Jihads, and Osama Bin Ladin* (Westport, CT, 2005); Seyyed Hossein Nasr, *Islam: Religion, History, and Civilization* (New York, 2003), 73–74.

34. Stice, *From 9/11 to 666*, 73–75, 141, 169, 175, 188, 198.

35. Joel Richardson, *Antichrist: Islam's Awaited Messiah* (Enumclaw, WA, 2006), 32, 99; J. C. Alexander, *The Kingdom of the Beast and the End of the World* (Ozark, AL, 2005), 317–19.

36. Richardson, *Antichrist*, 100–101, 120–22, 126–27, 167, 207; Robert Livingston, *Christianity and Islam: The Final Clash* (Enumclaw, WA, 2004), 165–66.

37. Michael Fortner, *The Scarlet Beast: Islam and the Beast of Revelation* (Lawton, OK, 2006), 29–31.

38. Presbyterian Church (U.S.A.) General Assembly statement on Israel and Palestine, at http://www.pcusa.org/worldwide/israelpalestine/israelpalestineresolution.htm#1 [accessed Feb. 26, 2007]; C. Marvin Pate and J. Daniel Hays, *Iraq—Babylon of the End Times?* (Grand Rapids, MI, 2003), 76, 136.

39. Hitchcock, *Iran*, 189; Ralph Stice, "Mahdi Watch," at http://www.from911to666 .com/MahdiWatch.lsp [accessed Nov. 21, 2006].

40. http://pewforum.org/docs/index.php?DocID=54 [accessed Dec. 8, 2006].

41. Paul Boyer, *When Time Shall Be No More: Prophecy Belief in Modern American Culture* (Cambridge, MA, 1992), 142–46, quote on 146; James Inhofe, "Peace in the Middle East," March 4, 2002, at http://inhofe.senate.gov/pressapp/record.cfm?id=183110 [accessed Nov. 28, 2006]; Hunt, *Judgment Day*, 331–40; http://www.cbn.com/ CBNnews/news/020308c.aspx [accessed Nov. 30, 2006]; Jeremy D. Mayer, "Christian Fundamentalists and Public Opinion toward the Middle East: Israel's New Best Friends?" *Social Science Quarterly* 85, no. 3 (Sept. 2004): 699.

EPILOGUE

1. Ian Fisher, "Pope Calls West Divorced from Faith, Adding a Blunt Footnote on Jihad," *The New York Times*, Sept. 13, 2006, A6.

2. Philip Jenkins, *The Next Christendom: The Coming of Global Christianity* (New York, 2002).

3. James H. Huston, ed., *The Founders on Religion: A Book of Quotations* (Princeton, NJ, 2005), 221.

4. Virgil Goode, "Save Judeo-Christian Values," *USA Today*, Jan. 2, 2007, at http:// www.usatoday.com/printedition/news/20070102/oppose02.art.htm [accessed Jan. 22, 2007].

Index

Wahhabism, 54–55, 117, 118
Wall, Martha, 78–79
Wallace, Mike, 104
Walton, John, 13
Walvoord, John, 85, 130–32, 138, 154, 157
Ward, C.M., 89
Warren, Joseph, 46–47
Warren, Rick, 110
Watson, Charles, 74
Webb, Mohammed Alexander Russell, 96–98, 119
Wherry, E.M., 62–63
Whitefield, George, 13–14
Whitehurst, James, 109
Willard, Frances, 68–69
Williams, Roger, 10–11
Wilson, Sr., J. Christy, 82, 86, 95, 114
Wilson, Woodrow, 70
women, Muslim treatment of, 48–50, 80
Woodberry, Dudley, 146, 153, 164, 168
Woodsmall, Ruth Frances, 50

World Council of Churches, 12
World's Parliament of Religions (1893), 96
World War I, 70–71, 72–74

Yom Kippur War (1973), 130, 132
Young, G. Douglas, 134
Young Turks, 65, 69–70
Youssef, Michael, 117

Zaka, Anees, 116–17
Zionism: as barrier to missions, 81, 92, 124, 126, 140; Louis Farrakhan and, 109; opposition to, 133, 142; and Palestinians, 83; support for, 84, 87, 134
Zwemer, Samuel: and influence on views of Islam, 78, 80–82; and Kenneth Cragg, 83; and missions to Muslims, xv, xvi, xvii, 53, 58–68, 71–72, 74, 83, 95, 114, 120–21, 125, 168; and modernism, 76; and Mohammed Alexander Russell Webb, 98
Zwemer Institute, 124

Made in the USA
Coppell, TX
21 January 2021